The Legend of The Warsaw Mermaid

 There are many legends surrounding the Warsaw Mermaid, symbol of this historic city on the Vistula River. According to one legend, the security of the medieval city of Warsaw was defended by a manly and noble Griffin. Once when the Griffin sailed with Vistula River boatmen to the Baltic Sea, he met a beautiful Mermaid. They fell deeply in love and the Mermaid swam with them back to Warsaw. From then on, the Griffin and the Mermaid watched over the townspeople together. When the Swedes attacked Warsaw, the valiant Griffin was mortally wounded by the enemy and died. His companion, the brave Mermaid, seized sword and shield, and fought heroically in defense of the embattled city. The grateful Varsovians were so smitten with the courageous Mermaid that they placed her image on their city's coat of arms—a fitting companion to the city's mottoes: *Contemnit procellas* (It defies the storms) and *Semper invicta* (Always invincible).

The Mermaid and the Messerschmitt

War Through a Woman's Eyes
1939–1940

Second Edition

by *Rulka Langer*

AQUILA POLONICA (U.S.) LTD.
10850 Wilshire Boulevard, Suite 300, Los Angeles, California 90024, U.S.A.

AQUILA POLONICA LIMITED
1 Sybron Way, Crowborough, East Sussex, TN6 3DZ, Great Britain.

www.AquilaPolonica.com

First Edition © 1942 Roy Slavonic Publications
Second Edition © 2009 Aquila Polonica Limited
All rights reserved.
First Edition published 1942. Second Edition 2009.

ISBN (Second Edition, cloth): 978-1-60772-000-3

Printed in the U.S.A.
20 19 18 17 16 15 14 13 12 11 10 09   1 2 3 4 5 6 7 8 9 10

Library of Congress Control Number 2009904398

Acknowledgments:
Cover design and all maps in this Second Edition are by Stefan Mucha. Cover photographs are from the collection of Stefan Mucha. All Langer family photographs and illustrative material are from the collection of George O. Langer, and are reproduced with permission. Photographs credited as being from the respective collections of Sam Bryan; Stefan Mucha; National Library, Warsaw; Museum of the Polish Army, Warsaw; State Archive of the Capital City of Warsaw; and Zygmunt Walkowski are reproduced with permission. Photographs credited to USNARA are from the U.S. National Archives and Records Administration, and are in the public domain. Photographs credited to USHMM are from the U.S. Holocaust Memorial Museum, and are reproduced with permission. NOTE: The views or opinions expressed in this book, and the context in which the images are used, do not necessarily reflect the views or policy of, nor imply approval or endorsement by, the U.S. Holocaust Memorial Museum.

The publishers wish to extend special thanks to historical photo expert Zygmunt Walkowski of Warsaw, Poland, for his invaluable assistance in locating and identifying many of the historical photographs included in this Second Edition.

Translations from Polish to English provided for various illustrations and footnotes are by Jaroslaw Garlinski.

PRAISE FOR

THE MERMAID AND THE MESSERSCHMITT

FIRST EDITION 1942

Lewis Gannett, of the New York Herald Tribune:
"This book is one of the best pictures of war as civilians know war that has yet come out of the maelstrom. "

Renowned author Pearl S. Buck:
"A most interesting and touching work. "

The Saturday Review of Literature:
"More clearly than any account I have read she makes you see and feel what it is like to live day after day and night after night in a besieged and bombed city...It is difficult to be an impersonal critic of a narrative so moving as this."

New Canaan Advertiser:
"It is a warm and beautiful narrative of human beings under fire, a book to take to one's heart and remember with thoughts of the brotherhood of man."

Book-of-the-Month Club News:
"We may be thankful that Mrs. Langer escaped to write her straightly, well-told story. "

Cue magazine:
"One cannot read *The Mermaid and the Messerschmitt* without feeling profound admiration for the courage and resourcefulness of its author... and for the imperishable spirit of her nation."

New York Herald Tribune Books:
"It is hard to put the book away once you start reading it."

Contents

Contents

HISTORICAL HORIZON

Historical Horizon

INTRODUCTION

THE MERMAID and the Messerschmitt, Rulka Langer's extraordinary personal account of the opening chapter of World War II, covers the six-month period from August 1939 to February 1940—from the end of the last peacetime summer, through the Nazi invasion of Poland, the Siege of Warsaw and the first few months of the Nazi occupation.

Writing from intimate personal experience, Mrs. Langer gives us the civilian's war through a close-up lens. Her story begins against a backdrop of escalating aggression by Nazi Germany, outlined in the following section Prelude to War; the story's broader context is summarized briefly in the section which follows that one, entitled Blitzkrieg.

When *The Mermaid and the Messerschmitt* was first published in 1942, World War II was raging across the globe. Mrs. Langer had recently fled from occupied Poland to the United States with her two children. Memories of death raining from the sky, of hunger and fear, were sharp and clear in her mind as she wrote.

The major events chronicled by Mrs. Langer were current affairs for *The Mermaid's* original audience— reported on the radio, appearing as front-page copy in newspapers and featured in the newsreels that preceded movies in theaters.

Decades separate us from her original audience, World War II is fading into history, yet the human experience of modern warfare for those civilians caught in its terror remains as immediate and devastating as ever.

PRELUDE TO WAR

January 1933 ... Adolf Hitler becomes Chancellor of Germany. As leader of the increasingly powerful Nazi Party, Adolf Hitler is appointed Chancellor of Germany, a position similar to that of Prime Minister.

March 1933 ... Hitler consolidates power. The Nazi Party gathers enough support to pass the "Enabling Act," which gives legislative powers to the cabinet headed by Hitler.

August 1934 ... Der Führer. On the death of President Paul von Hindenburg, Hitler's cabinet passes a law making Hitler head of state and supreme commander of the military: *der Führer* (the Leader).

March 1935 ... Germany re-arms. In violation of the Treaty of Versailles which ended World War I, the German Third Reich under Hitler's leadership begins building up its military arsenal and imposes a national draft.

March 1936 ... German troops occupy the Rhineland. Under the Treaty of Versailles, the German Rhineland bordering France was to remain a demilitarized buffer zone. Re-militarizing the Rhineland is Hitler's first open challenge to Britain and France. They do nothing.

March 1938 ... The Anschluss: Germany takes over Austria. Without firing a shot, German troops occupy Austria, which is immediately incorporated into Germany. Britain and France do nothing.

September 1938 ... Germany seizes the Sudetenland: "Peace for our time." Germany occupies this northwest portion of Czechoslovakia. With the devastation of World War I still fresh in memory, Britain and France negotiate: the Munich Agreement permits Germany to keep the Sudetenland in exchange for Hitler's promise to go no

Hitler receives an ovation from the German Reichstag for the Austrian Anschluss, March 1938.

Synagogue in Hechingen, Germany, smashed during Kristallnacht. More than two hundred synagogues were destroyed, thousands of Jewish businesses and homes ransacked, approximately 25,000 to 30,000 Jews arrested and deported to concentration camps, and many Jews murdered.

further. British Prime Minister Neville Chamberlain returns to England, announcing "peace for our time."

November 1938 ... Kristallnacht. During one infamous night, the Nazis coordinate a sweeping attack on Jewish people and their property throughout Germany in early implementation of Hitler's anti-Semitic policy.

March 1939 ... Czechoslovakia and Memelland fall; Hitler demands the "free city" of Danzig. Supported by Germany, Slovakia declares its independence from Czechoslovakia and becomes a puppet of the Third Reich. German troops occupy the remainder of Czech lands. In the north, Germany annexes Memelland, the Lithuanian territory bordering East Prussia. Germany threatens to seize the Baltic port of Danzig (designated as a "free city" under the Treaty of Versailles), which would deprive Poland of its principal access to the sea. Britain and France pledge to support Poland in the event of German hostilities.

August 23, 1939 ... Molotov-Ribbentrop Pact. This surprise non-aggression treaty between Germany and Soviet Russia shocks the rest of Europe. Secret provisions provide for the division of Eastern Europe—shared occupation of Poland, Soviet occupation of the Baltic States and a part of eastern Romania.

BLITZKRIEG

Blitzkrieg—Adolf Hitler's "Lightning War"—was born on September 1, 1939, with the Nazi German invasion of Poland. On September 17, Stalin's Soviet armies smashed through Poland's eastern frontier to link up with Hitler's forces at the Bug River—Poland's fate was sealed.

Within a month, Poland fell. By June 1940, France, Denmark, Belgium, the Netherlands, Luxembourg and

Norway had all followed, and Great Britain was fighting for its life.

From the first day of invasion, Poland's capital Warsaw—modern, bustling, cosmopolitan, cultured, with a population of more than one million—was ruthlessly pounded and strafed by swarms of German bombers and Messerschmitt fighters. A week later, on September 8, the first German panzer tanks rolled into the southwest suburbs of the city. The Poles repulsed the initial attacks, but Warsaw was soon surrounded.

The brutal Siege of Warsaw lasted until September 27. The Polish *Armia Warszawa* (Warsaw Army) fought ferociously, but it fought against overwhelming odds. On September 25, infamous as "Black Monday," the Germans launched a massive, relentless artillery and air bombardment that finally shattered the city. The escalating civilian death toll and lack of food, water, ammunition and other necessities forced Polish General Juliusz Rommel to surrender.

When 140,000 Polish soldiers were herded out of the city as prisoners of war, the bodies of more than 40,000 dead civilians—men, women and children—lay decomposing in the streets... entombed under the rubble of collapsed buildings... buried in makeshift graves in gardens and town squares throughout the city.

On October 1, a triumphant German army marched into Poland's capital. Six years of Nazi terror had begun in the "City of the Mermaid"...

Aquila Polonica Publishing

Language

For most native English speakers, the Polish language—with its strings of consonants, diacritical marks and that strange "l" with a slash ("ł")—appears impenetrable. In *The Mermaid and the Messerschmitt,* Rulka Langer chose to anglicize the spelling of Polish words and names for the convenience of her English-speaking readers. In most cases, she simply omitted the diacritical marks and used the English "l" in place of the Polish "ł." In a couple of cases, she spelled a Polish word phonetically in English rather than keeping the Polish spelling. We have followed her practice in our new edition of her book.

The Second Edition

This Second Edition of *The Mermaid and the Messerschmitt* has been edited to update word usage, spelling and formatting, but carefully preserves Rulka Langer's engaging storytelling style. All footnotes, photographs, maps and other illustrations, and all supplemental material including chapter headings, the table of contents, Historical Horizon and other introductory material, the Afterword and Epilogue, have been added by the publishers for this new edition.

Aquila Polonica Publishing

THE MERMAID AND THE MESSERSCHMITT

To my mother

Rulka Langer, circa 1939

Author's Preface

ALL THE characters in this story are real, and so are the
episodes. I have changed the names of people and places
but I have tried to make them as true to life as I could. Even
conversations are reported almost verbatim.

I wrote this book because I was homesick.

I wrote it, also, to show my many American friends why
I was not happy to leave Poland in February 1940, even
though I was coming to the United States—the friendliest
and most hospitable country in the world—a country I love
so much. "Aren't you lucky to be out of that hell!" people
would exclaim when I first arrived. "I don't know. . . ,"
I would answer hesitatingly, and they looked at me with
surprise.

The fact was I didn't consider myself lucky. Perhaps it
was hell. But if so, it was my own kind of hell, a hell I loved
with all my heart. It was only for my children's sake that I
had left Warsaw.

Finally, I wrote this book to show my readers what it is
like for an average human being to live through the
Blitzkrieg. No war correspondent, however brilliant (and
American correspondents are the most brilliant the world
over), can ever do that. A war correspondent is always on
the spot wherever the most dreadful things happen. A
bombed hospital, an orphanage set in flames, he sees them
all. He talks to hundreds of destitute people. In fact, he sees
ten times more of the horrors of war than the average
person in the same city does.

And yet, a war correspondent, when he runs to that
gigantic fire, does not leave his own children behind in his

hotel room. When caught in an air raid, he doesn't tremble for the life of his own old mother. His brother has not vanished somewhere on the crowded roads threatened by strafing fighter planes. It isn't his own house, the house in which he was born and has lived for years, that has been set on fire by an incendiary. And if he himself goes through the agony of mortal fear, none of his readers will ever know about it. This is no part of his reporting job.

To the average person, I think, war horrors come pretty much like the pangs of childbirth. At first, in spite of apprehensions, life still goes on, almost normal, with all of its little trivialities. Then comes the pang: wild, screaming, inhuman. You think you'll never stand it—yet you do. It passes—once more you are yourself. Trivialities reappear. Another insane, unbearable pang... And yet another breathing spell with its tiny but insistent daily cares, its humor and its griefs...

And in that horrible process in which so many die, new human beings are born. For no one who has been through war will ever be quite the same person again.

R.L.

July 1942
NEW CANAAN, CONNECTICUT

THE WARSAW MERMAID (*SYRENKA WARSZAWSKA*)

CHAPTER 1

August 1939: The Last Peacetime Summer

IN FRONT of the house, under the big chestnut tree, Mother sat on a wooden bench talking to Uncle. Uncle, tall and gaunt, was leaning on his stick, while Ania, my towhead three-year-old daughter, tugged at his hand and made sweet eyes at him. She was a grand one with men, regardless of their age, Ania was. When she saw us approaching she let go of Uncle's hand and ran with outstretched arms to hug me.

"Who won?" Mother asked. We were just returning from a volleyball game. It was one of those riotous family affairs, in which the grown-ups joined the children and only children took seriously. But Mother was always immensely interested in all our games.

"They!" I said dramatically, while trying to free myself from Ania's embrace. "Let's go in for tea. I'm ravenous."

"Fresh croissants for tea today," Basia, our hostess, announced proudly.

"Hurray!" Warm, crunchy croissants, with butter which will melt and golden honey on top of that, dripping.

Before we entered the house I caught a glimpse of George's blue shirt and Tereska's red dress, flashing among the trees at the other end of the big, sloping lawn. Evidently another of the daily bike races between my eight-year-old son and his little cousin was in progress.

There was a mad scramble for the guest lavatory with its scented soap and embroidered towels for which we had no respect. We were all too worn out from our game to climb two flights of stairs to our respective bedrooms. We then filed into the big, cool, oak-paneled dining room. Basia had been right! The delightful scent of hot croissants, just from the oven, was hanging over the table.

Aunt Nina, mother of my five cousins, of whom Basia was the youngest, was already waiting for us. Aunt Nina has always been my idea of an empress—an empress, mind you, not a simple queen. She was tall, erect and stately. She always spoke with great precision in a slightly dogmatic tone. And wasn't she brilliant! When Aunt Nina was around there was no need for us to look up things in the *Petit Larousse Illustré*, our favorite reference book. She knew by heart all the kings, dates and battles in history; all the rivers and the mountains on the map; the names, dates and authors of all the masterpieces ever written, painted or composed. I shall never forget the time when the daughter of the Swedish Minister to Poland came to visit Wola.[1] The girl had lived in Poland for twelve years, spoke fluent Polish and had studied Polish history at the University of Warsaw. We felt rather badly when we discovered she knew more about it than we Poles did. But then Aunt Nina came out with her knowledge of Swedish history and, believe it or not, she knew more about it than did the Swedish girl!

It was one of Fate's little ironies that Aunt Nina, who was born to preside over an intellectual "salon," should have settled in the country, while Mother, who adored country life, married the editor of a newspaper and had lived in the city ever since.

We were fourteen at the tea table, all related to each other by blood or marriage. Only Aunt Nina, Uncle and Basia lived in Wola all year round. But to the rest of us

---

[1] Wola, the family estate, was located in southwest Poland near the town of Pilica.

2

the place was a sort of family Mecca, and we always managed to spend at least a few weeks there during the summer months. To anyone who belonged to the family clan, nothing on earth could replace that leisurely atmosphere of abstract discussions (led by Aunt Nina), family gossip and childhood memories that was Wola's own.

Aunt Nina had been listening to the afternoon radio news and was giving us now a precise résumé of it. News was bad as usual. This was August 21, 1939, and political tension was growing with every hour. However, radio news, no matter how bad, was only radio news to us and did not spoil our appetite for fresh croissants.

Nevertheless, Aunt Nina's report started once more the old argument as to whether we were headed for war or not. We had debated that problem over the tea table, or dinner table, a hundred times at least and opinions were still divided. Basia and I insisted that war was imminent; my cousin Hanka, the proud mother of three boys and an idealist if ever there was one, was convinced this whole war scare was all stuff and nonsense.

"Don't be silly! Do you think Hitler wants a war any more than we do? He is merely bluffing."

"But we are going to call his bluff. Then what?"

"He will back out."

This would go on for hours and neither side would be convinced by the other.

While the argument was still in progress, mail was brought in. Besides the usual pile of newspapers and circulars, there was a letter for Hanka addressed in Adam's handwriting. Adam was Hanka's husband. He was a member of the board of directors of one of the largest manufacturing firms in Warsaw and only occasionally was he able to run down to Wola for weekends.

Hanka read her letter, then calmly announced, "Adam has been mobilized."

"Adam? For Heaven's sake, why should they mobilize Adam? I should think he would be far more useful in some war industry department."

Adam had been a volunteer in the Polish-Bolshevik war of 1919.[2] He had been awarded a cross for bravery. He was a non-com at the time and had never bothered to obtain a commission afterwards, as this would require a special course at the military school and spending six weeks every other year at maneuvers. He could not be spared that long from his office. Besides, he was already forty-one.

"I don't know," said Hanka. "He is stationed in Warsaw, anyway. He says everybody is being mobilized. At the Tennis Club members are disappearing every day. Some are handed mobilization orders while on the court."

This quiet mobilization by individual orders had been going on ever since May. People were used to it by now. Half of the men I knew were already under arms, but Adam was the first member of our family to be drafted.

"I hope they will release him before it's time to go to the Carpathian Mountains," Hanka added as an afterthought.

---

[2] The Polish-Bolshevik war began in February 1919, immediately after the end of the First World War when Poland regained its independence after 123 years of partition among Austria, Prussia and Russia. The border between Poland and Russia had not been settled; Poland's leader, Jozef Pilsudski, wanted to incorporate as much as possible of historic Poland's eastern territory. Vladimir Lenin, leader of Bolshevik Russia, wanted to reincorporate Poland into Russia and spread the communist revolution to western Europe—for the Bolsheviks, the shortest route to Berlin and Paris lay through Warsaw. Over a two-year period, the newly independent Poland fought and defeated Bolshevik Russia. The turning point of the war came in August 1920 with the Battle of Warsaw, sometimes called "the Miracle on the Vistula," when in an unexpected and stunning victory, Pilsudski routed the Russian forces—a defeat that Josef Stalin, at the time a political commissar of Bolshevik Russia and in command of the Southwestern Front, would never forget or forgive.

Every September she and Adam would be off to shoot the big red deer in the Carpathian Mountains. For two glorious weeks they would forget children, business, politics and all. They would live in a small hut on the slope of a big mountain, lost in the woods, cut off from civilization. Climbing steep, slippery slopes they would trail the deer, guided by the magnificent roar of the courting buck. They would return to Warsaw full of wonderful hunter's tales, loaded with splendid trophies. The antlers of the Carpathian buck were known to be the best in Central Europe. Those two weeks in September were the climax of the year for Adam and Hanka. I looked at Hanka, but did not feel like resuming our old argument about war. Now that Adam was mobilized, what was the use of telling her that deer-shooting was over and man-shooting might start any day.

But Hanka's faith was unshaken. She would not let Adam's mobilization interfere with her vacation plans, so the next afternoon she, her three boys and I were off to visit Adam's sister and brother-in-law. It was a rather long trip and we would not be back for two days. The whole family gathered on the porch to bid us good-bye.

Thad and Andrew, the two older boys, were a pretty sight, both dressed alike in white shirts and fawn-colored breeches, on their splendid chestnut mounts. They sat well in their saddles, too. Hanka, a fine horsewoman herself, had seen to that. Andrew's fair hair gleamed in the sun.

Hanka's face was beaming with motherly pride as she gave them the last instructions:

"Remember to turn to your left as soon as you have passed the church at Zaba—and be careful of the bridge at Czarna; there is a hole in it. Andrew, don't hold her so tightly, you know she has a sensitive mouth."

The boys were to cut straight across the fields, while we were to follow the road. The fields from which the crops had already been gathered gave excellent opportunity for short gallops. Hanka had been on horseback all over the countryside and knew every path, every stone and tree, for miles around. This time, however, she had lent her mare to Andrew, who had no horse of his own yet, and was riding with little Paul and me in the horse carriage.

The boys were off, followed by the old groom, Francis.

We climbed into the *britchka*, an open, rather high vehicle with two comfortable seats, under which our suitcases were placed. Paul, who was to ride with the driver in the front seat, tried to sit with his back to the horses, facing his mother and me, but Hanka would have none of it.

"Don't you know, little fool, that the hind of a good horse is a far better sight than any human face?"

We all laughed. Hanka was a horsewoman all right.

"Have a good time!" Mother called from the porch, and we were off.

I love to ride in a horse carriage, it gives you such a wonderful sense of leisure. The world does not flash by as it does in an automobile. You have plenty of time to satisfy your idle curiosity, to observe scenes and scenery alike. You have time to find out whether the woman in the red kerchief, just stepping out of the cottage door, has come to fetch the wooden pail that stands near the doorway, or the big white featherbed airing on the fence. You can observe the brown earth sliding down the glittering knife of the plow. You can exchange a few friendly words with the little black dog that yaps at the horses and pretends he is going to scare you off. In fact, when you ride in a horse carriage you belong to the landscape—you are part of it. In an automobile you are always an outsider.

As we rode now, harvest time was over and the fields were, for the most part, deserted, save for large flocks of white and gray-saddled geese. Long fields, divided by narrow strips of grass on which cows and goats grazed, lay in the afternoon sun as if resting after the exhaustion of crop-bearing, and the pale melancholy of the late summer hung already in the air, even though the weather was glorious. Here and there, however, villagers were still reaping late spring oats and as we passed we would call to them the immemorial harvesters' greeting:

"God's blessings!"

Straightening their bent backs, they would call back:

"May the Lord give it."

The breeze brought to our nostrils whiffs of the sweet scent of yellow lupine, just in bloom.

We passed through villages built in a single file of houses, stretching for miles along the road. The walls of the cottages were exactly the color of the sky. Painted before every Whitsun with a mixture of whitewash and bluing, they would have, at first, the deep hue of June skies; then as the summer wore on and the sky grew paler, the walls would fade too. Little flower gardens in front of every house were overflowing with rosebushes, nasturtiums and sunflowers; tall honeysuckles reached the thatched, moss-covered roofs.

I had often wondered what it would be like to live one's whole life in one of those tiny cottages, so close to the soil. My own life had been so different. I was not even born in the country, and my real home was the spacious, old-fashioned apartment in Warsaw where my parents had moved right after their marriage and in which Mother had lived ever since.

My father was chief editor of the conservative daily *Slowo*,[3] and I was told that while he was alive, my parents' house was quite a center of Warsaw political, cultural and literary life, with Mother holding a "salon" on Monday and my father entertaining twelve of his political friends for lunch every Thursday.

I don't remember any of it however, for Father died when I was eighteen months old, and after his death the political lunches were discontinued. As for the Monday receptions, they slowly turned into gatherings of elderly, extremely respectable and well-bred ladies, with a sprinkle of Father's old friends and an occasional bishop or two. My brother and I loathed those Monday afternoons. I was invariably dressed for the occasion in a white woolen dress and Franek in a white woolen suit, with big lace collars, and we were severely reminded not to get dirty or ruffle our hair till we made our routine appearance in the drawing room. Thus dressed in state, we had to wait, sometimes two hours, till a polite guest would dutifully ask to "see the children." I used to stand on my head in the nursery for ten minutes after each such ordeal.

My next vivid recollections are those of the First World War. I was seven at the time and Franek eight. The outbreak of hostilities caught us at a summer resort in the Austrian part of Poland,[4] and ours was the last train which

---

3 *The Word.*

4 In the late 18th century, the entire country of Poland was divided up by Austria, Prussia and Russia (the Partitions of 1772, 1793 and 1795). What had been eastern Poland, including the Polish capital of Warsaw, was incorporated into Russia; southern Poland into Austria; and the north and west into Prussia. For 123 years, Poland literally disappeared from the map of Europe. The country was not reunited again as an independent nation until after the Armistice of November 1918 and the signing of the Treaty of Versailles in 1919, which officially ended the First World War.

crossed the Russo-Austrian frontier. It never got us to Warsaw, though. As soon as we were inside the Russian borders, all civilian passengers were told to leave the train, which was taken over by Russian troops, all of them drunk. It took us a week to reach Wola. We found it full of generals and high-ranking officers poring over big maps, drinking champagne at night. The Russian general staff had made its headquarters in the house. The place was simply buzzing with adjutants, liaison officers and whatnot, and among the general excitement we kids had the time of our lives.

There was the time, for instance, when the Cossack colonel, who was sweet on our French mademoiselle, let us have his field glasses and Basia, Franek and I stole to the roof of the house to observe the movement of troops. When my turn came, I had, at first, a hard time focusing the lenses, but at last I caught sight of three Cossacks riding along the distant road to Zarnowiec. They rode very fast and were about to disappear behind a cluster of trees, much to my regret, when suddenly three Magyars appeared in the focus of my lenses, right in front of the Cossacks.[5] I knew they were Magyars, for I could plainly see their red breeches and dark blue coats. Then the whole scene vanished in a cloud of dust. A column of dust had been trailing behind each group of riders and now the two columns met—I could not see anything. Suddenly a riderless horse shot out of the dust, running in a mad gallop towards Zarnowiec.

---

[5] In the First World War, the Allies (the British and Russian Empires, France, Italy and the United States) were pitted against the Central Powers (Germany, Austria-Hungary, the Ottoman Empire and Bulgaria). The Cossacks were Russian cavalry and the Magyars were the Hungarian forces. The Russians entered into a separate peace with the Central Powers in March 1918, after the Bolsheviks overthrew Tsar Nicholas II during the Russian Revolution of 1917.

I put down the field glasses, panting with excitement. At seven I had witnessed a real fight.

Then there was the day when Mother and Grandmother returned from a stroll in the park, crawling on all fours because machine gun bullets were whistling and cutting twigs all around them. We were not allowed to go out, so we spent our days at a top floor window watching golden stars, which were artillery shells, trace graceful arches over the horizon. A big battle was in progress and explosions shook the air. When we grew tired of watching, we tiptoed downstairs to peep through the drawing room door at the Russian generals bent over maps. Sometimes we were asked to come inside, and once Franek was even offered a drink of champagne.

Then one day the Russians had to retreat. The general warned the family that they would have to blow up the house because it stood on a high hill and could serve as an excellent vantage point for the advancing Austrians. We were therefore packed off in a hurry and sent to the home of another uncle further east. Only Basia's father remained behind to watch over the doomed house, which was never blown up after all.

Our trip east was most exciting. We met a large detachment of the retreating Russian army, plodding slowly along the sandy road in the intense August heat. Their columns stretched out for miles and slowed down our progress. We drove by the battlefields of yesterday, covered with trenches and barbed wire. The dead were already removed, but corpses of slain horses still lay by the roadside. Those dead horses produced a horrible impression on me. They were real, far more real than the fight in the colonel's field glasses. They showed their teeth in a mortal grin that seemed to mock me, the little girl with yellow pigtails who was driving by. . .

© 2009 Aquila Polonica Limited

Rulka and father, circa 1907.

Aunt Celinka, Aunt Nina and Rulka's mother.

Rulka, her mother and brother, circa 1923.

We did not return to Warsaw till a year and a half later, when it was occupied by the Germans. At first our life was pretty much the same as it had been before the war. We were sent to the best private schools, attended dancing classes, and had a German governess whom we hated. Mother still had her "at home" days on Monday, only now everybody talked politics and quarreled bitterly as to whether Poland should throw in her lot with Germany or with Russia. The choice was hard—both were age-long enemies—and the opinions were divided. "Of course the best solution," people used to say, "would be to have the last German soldier choke to death on the last Russian." And that was what actually happened, but seemed hardly possible at the time.

Meanwhile the issue was a vital one, for it meant either cooperation or lack of cooperation with the German authorities that occupied the country. Sentiments were running high and close friends would stop talking to one another if they belonged to opposite camps. Mother was a strong pro-Ally, and very soon her Monday teas were decimated—none of her pro-Central-Powers friends would call on her. My personal contribution to the Allies' cause was limited to sticking out my tongue at every German soldier and officer I met in the streets, a gesture doubly dangerous considering that I was always escorted by my German governess.

By 1916 we began to feel the real pinch of the war and conditions grew steadily worse. We were often hungry, and always cold. For three years I didn't have a new dress—nothing but Mother's old dresses made over for me. Considering that Mother had worn black ever since my father's death, from the age of ten to thirteen I wore black too. And the wooden-soled shoes, though wonderful for toe dancing, weren't so comfortable for walking. In the streets there were hunger riots.

The end of the First World War brought us the intoxication of independence—white bread made of American flour, greeted with loud cheers when, for the first time, it appeared on the dining room table, and American baked beans and rice served at school lunches.

It also brought a moratorium on mortgage debts. All the money left by my father was invested in mortgages.

Overnight we found ourselves penniless.

Mother had plenty of wealthy relatives to whom she could have turned for help, but she did nothing of the kind. She sublet four out of our six rooms, tightened the family budget as much as she could, and began to look for work teaching French. Even this was not easy to get at first. Mother used to lie in bed and wonder where the next meal was coming from. Yet the atmosphere of our home remained as cheerful as ever. At last she found a job as part-time French governess to a five-year-old boy of a nouveau riche family. It must have been pretty tough, but Mother never complained. Very soon she established a reputation as an excellent teacher and was flooded with pupils.

She wasn't doing it for the first time either. Thirty years before, when Mother was only sixteen, my grandfather, who belonged to the titled nobility, lost his estate. It seems rather amusing that it was Australian sheep which ruined my grandfather, but it is a fact. The vast estate which had been in the family for over three hundred years was principally used for raising sheep—the wool was exported to England and yielded good prices. Then one day in the 1880s, some troublesome inventor found a way to clean the fleece of innumerable Australian sheep of impurities which hitherto had made their wool useless, and in no time the English market was flooded with cheap, Australian wool. The Polish sheep raisers lost their market and my grandfather who, from what I could gather, was a gallant, dashing nobleman of the old school, with no more business sense than a newborn babe, found himself unable to cope with the situation. The big fortune went down with a crash. My grandfather could not stand it. Rather conveniently for himself he died of heart failure, leaving behind my grandmother, three daughters (the eldest of whom was barely eighteen), and innumerable debts.

The normal thing to do for the four bereaved women would have been to seek refuge in the house of some wealthy relative and from that time on lead the drab life of "poor relations." Instead, my grandmother and the three girls went to Warsaw and took a cheap apartment in a tenement house. My grandmother did the housework and the three girls ran from morning till night on their worn-out shoes giving French lessons at cut-rate fees, for they had no school diploma of any kind. In that way they managed not only to support themselves, but began to pay off my grandfather's debts. Word went around Warsaw Society (with a capital S) about the admirable pluck with which the beautiful Countess M. and her three handsome daughters were comporting themselves, and suddenly the four women found themselves the center of general attention and admiration. Shining horse carriages stood in line in front of the dilapidated tenement house and my grandmother, my mother and my aunts were flooded with invitations. According to Mother, for six years they never got enough sleep—they worked all day and danced most of the night. By and by the debts were paid off, Mother and Aunt Nina got married, and my other aunt Celinka became a nun.

Such was the family tradition I had been brought up in. To me it was also a challenge. I could not be outdone by my elders: at fourteen I began to tutor; at fifteen I was fully supporting myself, earning one-third of the family budget; at sixteen I graduated from school with full honors and secret dreams of a diplomatic career. These, however, were dashed to the ground by a young diplomat I met shortly after graduation:

"If you want to get into diplomatic life you must marry a diplomat. That's the only chance a woman has."

I almost asked him to marry me in that case, but I didn't quite have the nerve. He suggested that international commerce would be the next best thing and that it offered opportunities for women, and so next fall I entered the Warsaw School of Commerce. I was very much in love with the young diplomat that summer, I am afraid.

Silly as the reasons for my choice of a career were, I was never going to regret them, for during my third year at the School of Commerce, I was offered a scholarship to study in the United States. I was nineteen and going to America. America! The world belonged to me.

Those two years at Vassar (I had chosen Vassar because a Polish friend of mine went there and loved it) were wonderful.

True, at first I had a hard time because I didn't know the language. It's a terrific strain to listen for weeks, from morning till night, to a language which you cannot even break up into individual words. Each sentence sounds like one monstrously long word. In classes I would catch myself staring vacantly into space, the muscles of my face grown rigid with the effort of catching a familiar sound. It took me two months to understand what was said in class and a year before I could follow the general conversation at the dinner table.

During my senior year, I remember, I was taking Critical Writing. My professor, incidentally, was author

Hervey Allen. One day he made us write a critical essay on one of Poe's poems. Dictionary in hand, I tackled the assignment. After two lines, I had enough. I had to look up every word and the poem was a long one. I wrote across the page, "Sorry, all the English I know is what I picked up on the Vassar campus. Poe doesn't seem to use any of it. I don't understand a word," and handed the paper to Allen. He read it and looked up smiling. "Do you know," he said, "this is a pretty good criticism of Poe."

While still struggling with the language, I began to absorb America through every pore of my being. American life, American mentality, American attitudes and ideas. It was fun—I loved it. My friends told me later that it was a source of constant amusement to them to watch me change within a few months from a little Quaker girl with long hair and too-long skirts, into a regular American flapper. "When in Rome, do as the Romans do." I cut my hair and turned up the hem of my dresses. The only thing I was reticent about was makeup. Somehow, lipstick had always been associated in my mind with "bad women," and I could not bring myself to use it.

America is a wonderful country for making friends. It seems to be part of American hospitality always to give the stranger a chance. This chance, of course, is something in the nature of a test—if you fail, they drop you like a hot potato. What else can you expect? You had your opportunity, anyhow. But if you pass the test and are accepted as a friend, they will go to any length to make you happy.

During those two years at Vassar I failed many times, but on the whole I had invitations for every holiday, every available weekend. I went to football games, parties, theaters—I had the time of my life.

No wonder that when I stood on the deck of the east-bound *Aquitania* on an October night in 1928, I could not see the fairy-like sight that is New York seen from the sea at night, for the mist of tears which veiled my eyes. Would I ever see America again?

America, however, clung to me—or was it the other way around? At any rate, I soon found a job as copywriter at the Warsaw branch of the J. Walter Thompson Advertising Agency. It was lots of fun.

I also began to go into society. It was by no means my debut. I had gone to "grown-up" parties and dances before I went to Vassar, but at that time I was a washout.

Now, suddenly, I found myself fairly popular. If America had done one thing for me, it had improved my looks. I still was no raving beauty, but at least I was presentable; and my "exotic" (American) experience gave me an additional glamour in the eyes of young Poles, accustomed as they were to the prim and reserved society girls of those days.

"Of all your fiancés, Miss," Mother's cook told me one day, "I like the Swede best."

But it was not the Swede that I married. It was my boss at the J. Walter Thompson Agency—Olgierd Langer.

Olgierd and I had known each other for years. He had studied at Harvard while I was at Vassar, but we were no more than friends. It was really J. Walter Thompson which was responsible for our romance. I don't know why there should be anything romantic about the atmosphere of an advertising agency, but evidently there is. Perhaps the secret lies in the very advertising technique. For seven hours every day you have to whip up boundless enthusiasm for a brand of soap, car or breakfast cereal. It's all too easy to transfer the same enthusiasm to the girl at the next desk. Be this as it may, Olgierd

Olgierd Langer in Austrian army uniform, circa 1918.

OLGIERD LANGER (1896-1970) was born in Lwow, Poland, at that time a part of Austria. He graduated from the University of Lwow and the Harvard Business School (M.B.A., 1929) in the United States.

Mr. Langer is credited as the father of modern advertising in Poland—he taught the first university-level course in Poland on the science of advertising while Professor of Economics at the University of Lwow, and subsequently wrote the first Polish book on advertising theory while employed by the J. Walter Thompson Agency in Warsaw.

Over a long and varied career, Mr. Langer moved easily among academic, diplomatic and business circles. His service included posts as commercial attaché of the Polish Embassy in Washington, D.C., Trade Commissioner in Philadelphia for the Polish Ministry of Foreign Affairs, Polish Consul in Detroit, delegate of the Polish Red Cross to the American Red Cross, and work with the J. Walter Thompson Agency in New York.

OLGIERD I RÓŻA Z GODLEWSKICH

LANGEROWIE

MAJĄ ZASZCZYT ZAWIADOMIĆ, ŻE ŚLUB ICH ODBYŁ SIĘ

W WARSZAWIE W KOŚCIELE ŚW. KRZYŻA

DNIA 5 LUTEGO 1930 R.

WARSZAWA
LANGIEWICZA 20.

G. WATTSON, WARSZAWA

The Langers' wedding announcement: "Olgierd and Roza (nee Godlewska) Langer have the honor of announcing that their wedding took place in Warsaw in the Church of the Holy Cross on the 5th of February 1930."

On the back, a note from Rulka to the friend to whom this announcement was sent.

20

and I were first secretly engaged, then openly married—in fact, we eloped. We both thought it lots of fun, but Mother's friends shook their heads.

"You shouldn't have let her go to America," they said.

I was glad she did, though.

We were married in February 1930. For two years after that, I plunged into domesticity. Our first-born, George, was brought up strictly and scientifically according to American textbooks, thus bringing upon my head a host of criticism from the female members of both Olgierd's and my family.

After two years, however, the "career woman" reasserted herself. The depression had spread from the United States all over Europe, and Poland was hard hit too. Olgierd was making half the salary he used to earn when we were first married and, accustomed as I was to complete financial independence, I couldn't bring myself to ask him for money whenever any extras were needed. George, by that time, was already walking, putting his hands on anything he could get hold of, eating shoe polish on the sly and suchlike. American textbooks did not offer much help in the matter, so I entrusted George to the watchful eye of a nurse and got myself a job.

I was all wrapped up in my work with the Polish Radio when, quite unexpectedly, the Ministry of Foreign Affairs offered Olgierd the post of Commercial Attaché at the Polish Embassy in Washington. Thus, unexpectedly, my old dream of a diplomatic career became a reality. However, like most dreams that come true, this one proved to be a disappointment. At close range the life of a diplomat's wife bore little resemblance to the glorious adventure I had imagined it to be. After two weeks the glamour of big receptions and the excitement of meeting people one read about in newspapers wore out, and the never-ending social duties became a regular chore.

"Do you know if I have any stiff shirts left, or are they all at the laundry? We are going to the Peruvians tomorrow night."

"Oh, must we really? We were at the Egyptians only last night. I thought I could ask Mary and Red to come over to the house for a quiet chat."

But I knew there was no use protesting. The Ambassador had assigned us and the First Secretary of our Embassy to go to the Peruvian ball the next night and that was that.

During those eight months in Washington I used up nine hundred calling cards, drank probably several cases of champagne, exchanged platitudes with thousands of people, discovered that the men whose names make news are usually the dullest ones in a drawing room, and I was thoroughly relieved when it was all over. Olgierd was offered a better paying job in Poland and resigned from the service.

On my return to Warsaw I took a year off and had another baby. A girl this time—Ania. Later I went back to work.

In the spring of 1938, the Ministry of Foreign Affairs offered Olgierd, once more, a post in the United States. This time it was that of Trade Commissioner in Philadelphia. Now, if there is one thing Olgierd can't resist, it's America. He says he has been that way ever since he was four and an uncle brought him a box of American candy from the World Exposition in Paris (1900). The tin box was beautiful: it had the American flag on top; George Washington, Uncle Sam, the Statue of Liberty and the Flatiron Building decorated the four sides; and the candy was delicious. Olgierd decided then and there that a

Olgierd Langer, circa 1934.

Rulka Langer, circa 1939.

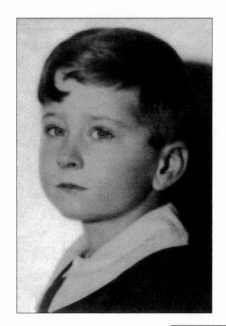

George Langer, circa 1939.

Ania Langer, circa 1939.

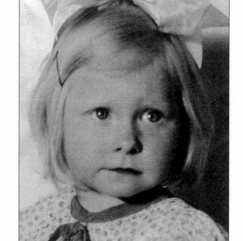

country which produces such marvels must be paradise on earth. It was not till twenty years later that, going through the attic, he stumbled upon the tin box again. He lifted it reverently. Suddenly an inscription in small type caught his eye—"Made in Austria" it said. By that time, however, Olgierd had visited the States and was more crazy about them than ever.

So when in 1938 another opportunity to go to America presented itself, he could not resist the temptation. Besides, the job itself was interesting and, this time, without diplomatic trimmings.

But the moment was awkward. Olgierd's family was just negotiating the sale of its land to the Polish government. It was a complicated transaction and to us it meant quite a bit of money. Someone should be on the spot to supervise the deal. At last it was decided that I should remain in charge, while Olgierd went to Philadelphia. As soon as the deal was put through I would join him in America, or else he would return to Poland.

After Olgierd left there did not seem to be any sense in keeping a six-room apartment for the children and myself. I put the furniture in storage and moved to Mother's. She was delighted to have both her children and her two grandchildren under the same roof with her.

With Hitler playing havoc all over Europe, Olgierd's and my plans did not work out the way we thought. We didn't expect a long separation—three, four months perhaps. However, the summer of 1939 came and still I was waiting. Waiting for the deal to go through, waiting for Olgierd to return . . . The Polish Government, faced with a threat of war, was in no hurry to invest money in real estate needed for peacetime ventures and the negotiations, despite all my efforts, dragged on interminably. And when in June Olgierd was due for a home leave, the

Ministry of Foreign Affairs cancelled all leaves due to the political tension.

"Wait another month," Olgierd's superior in the Ministry told me. "Perhaps by July the tension will relax, and your husband will be able to come."

But the tension did not relax—it grew worse. War was on everybody's lips. Suddenly I realized that if I wanted a vacation myself that year I had better take it right away. Therefore, at the beginning of August I asked for a leave at the Bank of Poland, where I was working at the time, packed two suitcases and went off to Wola. Mother and my two children had already been there since June.

I arrived at the tail end of the family reunion. Many members had already left. My brother Franek had gone to Zakopane;[6] but the big house was still full and the park resounded with the shouts and laughter of children.

Yet there was a strange poignancy about that last vacation.

A few months before, Olgierd had sent me *Gone with the Wind,* and the book made a tremendous impression on me. Somehow I considered it prophetic. I remember that just as I had finished reading it, it was time to put winter things away. As a rule I would pick out all my two-year-old dresses and suits and give them to the maid. Lord knows she didn't need them, she had more dresses than I ever had or hoped to have, but she always seemed to have plenty of needy relatives. This time, however, I suddenly remembered Scarlett O'Hara's best dress made of her mother's green plush curtains, and I decided not to follow the usual procedure.

"These may still be my best dresses in a year or two," I thought, putting the old things carefully away.

---

[6] Zakopane is a resort town in the Tatra Mountains, in southern Poland, well known for skiing in the winter and hiking in the summer.

Chapter 1

And many a time while watching a lively tennis game on the court shadowed by tall willow trees, or perhaps having coffee with the family on the big terrace, or riding, as I did now, in a horse carriage over the roads I had known since childhood, the thought would strike me suddenly, like a pang:

"Will all these be 'gone with the wind' next year...?"

CHAPTER 2

My Race with Hitler

IT'S A long drive from Wola to Rudnik, and the sun was already setting when we arrived. The house at Rudnik was a typical Polish manor, low, long and broad, with a high, tile-covered roof and a porch overgrown with vines. The whole family had gathered on the porch; they had sighted us coming down the hill. We climbed out of our britchka, rather stiff from the long drive.

In the long whitewashed hall there was the usual amount of face and hand-kissing,[1] and the usual shouts over and above each other's head:

"Did you have a good ride? What route did you take?" "Don't put that suitcase out there, it's mine." "My, the boy has grown, and he looks exactly like his father." "Auntie, see the new camera Daddy brought me from Cracow."

We were sitting now in the large, low-ceilinged dining room around the supper table. Sour milk[2] tasted delicious after the heat of the day and the dust we had swallowed on the road. Bits of family gossip were passed around as we ate.

"Did you hear Adam was mobilized?"

Yes, Tusia, our hostess, had a card from him.

"How is everybody at Klon?"

"Oh, fine, fine. The four youngest are just recovering from measles."

Klon, a large family estate, belonged to Tusia's oldest brother who was blessed with thirteen children. Infantile

---

[1] At that time (and even today among older Poles), it was traditional etiquette for a Polish gentleman to kiss a lady's hand on greeting and parting.

[2] Literal translation of *zsiadłe mleko,* a traditional Polish dish similar in consistency to yogurt.

28

diseases at Klon invariably took on the aspects of large-scale epidemics, and for that reason the four youngest children recovering from measles could hardly be considered news.

"Say, Tanio," Hanka turned to our host and a more interesting subject, "are you taking any horses to the army remount[3] this year? My brother Adzio is taking three next Friday to Kamien."

"As a matter of fact," Tusia answered for her husband with an embarrassed laugh, "Tanio has just given his two best remount horses to the National Defense Fund."

"The army would have taken them anyway, if war breaks out," Tanio said deprecatingly.

But we were impressed. A good remount horse was worth about two thousand zlotys,[4] and four thousand zlotys was a lot of money to give away as a patriotic gesture. Tanio and Tusia, we knew, were not very rich.

"How is the harvest?"

"We are almost through. The rest of the oats will be in tomorrow. The weather has been perfect."

"Well, well... It's the first time I hear a farmer who does not complain about the weather. I always thought it was impossible. I thought no weather could satisfy you. If the rain was good for the potatoes, it would ruin the hay and if sunshine was a matter of life and death for harvesting the wheat, it would burn out the clover and ruin the beets. In fact, I always thought you farmers would like the rain to fall and the sun to shine in little checkered patterns exactly fitting your fields, wouldn't you?"

"That's right. But it's the way we spread our risk, don't you see? You are right about the potatoes, though.

---

[3] The Army Remount Department was responsible for the procurement and training of horses for military use.

[4] At that time, about four hundred dollars.

They badly need rain. The wheat and rye crops, however, are exceptionally good this year. I've never seen anything like it."

"Exceptionally good crops mean war," one of the boys said sententiously.

"So they say."

Our host glanced at the big clock. "It's time for the evening radio news. Let's have it."

He turned on the old, battery-fed receiving set. For a moment we listened to the last bars of a military march —radio programs were full of them lately—and then the news came:

"The official German Agency announces tonight that a non-aggression pact between the Third Reich and the USSR was signed in Moscow on August twenty-third."

No further comment.

We sat there, horror-struck, silent. What had happened? Wasn't the British mission in Moscow discussing the terms of an identical pact? Wasn't Hitler the Soviet's most bitter foe? What *could* have happened? It was unbelievable, absurd, monstrous... Those two age-long enemies of Poland uniting again... Why, this meant ... this meant... But even in our thoughts we did not dare to formulate the full implication of the dreadful news. So we just sat silent, staring at each other.

When two days later we returned to Wola we found all the summer visitors, with the exception of Mother and my children, gone. Frantic telegrams from fathers, mothers and husbands had recalled them to their respective homes. Urgent telegrams took three days to get from Warsaw to Wola, evidently lines were overloaded with messages flashing in every direction.

Soviet Foreign Minister Molotov signs the German-Soviet Non-Aggression Pact in Moscow, August 23, 1939. Stalin (second from right) stands behind him.

© 2009 Aquila Polonica Limited

The partition of Poland as defined by the Molotov-Ribbentrop Pact.

Was there a telegram for me, too? No, there wasn't. I sighed with relief. Before leaving Warsaw I had arranged with one of my friends at the office to send me a wire when the situation grew really desperate. I did not want to be cut off from the capital.

That summer Herr Hitler and I had a little race of our own of which he, I am sure, was not aware. He wanted his war and I wanted my vacation. I had not had any in two years and I needed one badly. But would he let me finish it? I still had a week to go.

It was doubly lucky we did not have to travel right now, for those who came back from the station after seeing the guests off had awful tales to tell. Apparently the big rush of vacationers was already on. Many were recalled by telegram to their factories, offices and shops. Others were afraid to be caught by war away from home and were hurrying back now, before it was too late. While reserves tried to join their respective units, millions of civilians had only one idea: "Home. Let's go home!"

Trains were so crowded that passengers had to be pushed in and out of the cars through the windows and many a pane was smashed in the process. Some people climbed on the roofs, others hung on buffers or stood on running boards.

"You'll see that in a day or two trains will be running empty," Mother assured us. "Men are like sheep. They all have to do the same thing at the same time."

"I hope you're right." I couldn't imagine Mother, the two children and myself traveling on buffers. "Let's enjoy our vacation while we may."

Nevertheless, we felt restless. The big house, with so many visitors suddenly gone, seemed strangely quiet and deserted. Radio bulletins were full of frontier incidents and growing more ominous with every hour. The spell of the peaceful summer was broken.

I was relieved when Basia asked me to come with her to Kamien the next day, to assist at the remount sale. Why not? As long as Hitler let me...

Wind was sweeping the big enclosure in which the annual remount sale at Kamien was held. It was making the horses' manes stand on end and played havoc with women's skirts. Sales were already well in progress when we arrived in Adzio's car.

"They are taking a lot of them this year and paying good prices, too," one of the men informed Adzio as we walked towards the primitive wooden stall built along one of the sides of the large field. Along the other side stood open stables for the horses. Grooms were walking up and down leading the horses about to be presented to the Commission.

Motor cars and horse-drawn carriages were still arriving, pouring out families of the district gentry. The remount sale was to these people something of a social event. Most of the big estates in this part of the country had already been broken up and sold to peasants, and the remaining ones were few and far between. Their owners were too busy farming and fighting the ever-present shadow of the tax collector to do much visiting. The horse remount was one of the few occasions (besides funerals, weddings and shooting parties) at which they met, courted, discussed crops and quarreled over politics. It was also something of a contest: how many of their horses would be accepted and what prices would they fetch? This was important, too, for ever since depression times landowners were notoriously short of ready cash.

Sales were proceeding briskly today. One by one the horses were brought before the Commission: two elderly majors, and a handsome elderly civilian representing the local breeders. The beautiful three-year-olds, tail and mane floating in the wind, were first walked up and down in front of the stalls, then put through trot and gallop paces.

"Stop!"

Held close to the mouth by an excited groom, the horse would stand there, head high, eyes showing white, every muscle of the lovely body taut with suppressed excitement, while his teeth and legs were examined and measurements taken. After that the Commission would confer for a moment in low tones, while the owner of the horse stood by, his heart pounding, awaiting the verdict. The Commission was quick in reaching its decision: the horse was either led back to the stables, or handed over to a group of orderlies already waiting with army blankets to cover the new "recruit."

In the stalls, while eyes followed the horses, tongues were wagging fast. Local gossip, news, mostly war news.

"I don't see the Czapelski boys. Are they already mobilized?" The three Czapelski boys were the life of any social gathering.

"Yes. Old Edward, their father, tried to join too as a volunteer. But they wouldn't take him. He is already sixty-seven, you know."

"Kuba has promised me a new carpet for our drawing room out of his Berlin loot," a pretty girl with soft, brown hair said laughing. "You know the way Kuba talks." Kuba was the youngest Czapelski boy.

"Did you hear," someone was telling his neighbor right behind my back, "that those who live on the border have already received printed instruction what to do in case war breaks out? They have to clear out on the very first day. Burn the crops, take along as many cattle as they possibly can, slaughter and bury the rest and leave."

"What about us? We are only thirty miles from the frontier."

"I don't know, we will probably do the same."

"I wish you'd tell this gray mare of yours to stop kicking my bay," a tall man in riding breeches and a round green felt hat, called to Adzio. "He won't be fit to be presented to the Commission if she keeps drumming at him with her hooves."

Everybody laughed. The bay, about to be presented to the Commission, was already being walked up and down in front of the stalls. Every time he passed the group of horses awaiting their turn, Adzio's gray mare, who had a vicious temper, would rear and despite the groom's desperate efforts to keep her in place, send a furious volley of kicks at the bay's flank.

Adzio left his seat to straighten matters out. While he was gone a thin, dark-haired young man with a prominent nose appeared at the entrance to the stalls.

"Marek!" Basia called. Marek was an old beau of hers. He sighted us now and was worming his way through the thick throng of benches.

"I came to see the old crowd," he said as he kissed my hand and slipped into Adzio's seat at Basia's side, "but I should really have stayed home buried deep in my bed. I've been up all night."

"What has happened?" We noticed now that his face was drawn and his eyes red-rimmed with sleeplessness. Obviously he hadn't shaved that morning.

"The military commission arrived at Koziel at midnight to commandeer the horses. They dragged me out of bed

to show them around the village. God! It was awful!"
He shuddered. "They took the only horse of some of those
poor peasants. Of course they took all mine. All except two:
one is twenty-two and the other twenty-four. And the five
three-year-olds I sent here two days ago, I wish they would
be rejected but they probably won't. I wonder how they
expect me to carry on the fall plowing. Me and the rest of
the village. Oh well, it doesn't matter. Nothing matters now.
I hope they will draft me soon."

"Koziel is too near the frontier," Basia said. "The army
doesn't want to leave the horses to the Germans."

Adzio did not return to his seat. The turn of his horses
had come. We sat taut with excitement, watching first
the gray mare, then the two chestnuts performing before
the Commission. We couldn't hear the low whisper of
the horse experts, but very soon we saw the gray mare
and one of the chestnuts handed over to the orderlies,
while the other chestnut was led back to the stables.

"How much?" we asked Adzio as he returned to the
stalls, his face beaming.

"Two thousand for the mare, eighteen hundred for
the chestnut."

"Good for you, that's an excellent price. Why didn't
they take the other chestnut? He is the prettiest of the lot."

"Too low. He missed the mark by half a point. They
are very strict about that."

"Don't get too excited over the price," Marek put in. "All
you get now is scrip payable in September. You may never
see the money."

It was true. Adzio's face fell.

On our way home Adzio was slightly nervous. "I wonder
if there will be a mobilization order awaiting me at the
house," he said after a while. "I don't mind being drafted,
but the contract about the lease of the flour mill won't be

ready before next Monday. I should like to leave everything in order when I go."

For some time we drove in silence.

"What do you intend to do when war breaks out?" I asked Basia. "You can't stay at Wola, it's only forty-three miles from the frontier. You'll have Germans here on the second or third day. You know everybody says the front will be moving back and forth. You can't stay!"

"I will stay, though. What else can I do? Uncle is eighty and mother has a weak heart. How far do you suppose we can go in a horse-drawn carriage before the Germans overtake us?"

"It's alright for Uncle and Aunt Nina to stay behind. They are old, the Germans won't hurt them. But you are young and pretty. You'll be in danger."

"Well, I guess I'll have to take the risk," Basia smiled. "You don't suppose I'll run away and leave the old folks alone, do you? Besides, I don't want to leave Wola, I love the old place. It's where I belong, Germans or no Germans."

No mobilization order awaited Adzio on our return home, but there was a telegram for me. Even before I opened it, I knew what the contents would be. "Situation grave. Advise immediate return—Jan."

"When do we start?" asked Mother in a matter-of-fact tone. I opened the timetable. It was Friday night. The next express train for Warsaw would leave the nearest railway station the following noon. This would give us very little time for packing. One takes so many things along when traveling with children.

"Let's leave Sunday on the noon train. I'll be back at the office on Monday morning."

Damn it! Hitler had won the race.

CHAPTER 3

August 27: Back to Warsaw

MOTHER HAD been right about the trains. The railway carriage we entered on Sunday was almost empty; we had a compartment to ourselves. The children and I sat by the window watching the trains going in the opposite direction. They were full of soldiers, khaki uniforms in every window. The men had taken off their helmets, and we could see row upon row of close-cropped heads.

"Cannon fodder," I thought with a shiver.

We also passed long freight trains loaded with field artillery, machine guns, armored trucks and light tanks.

"This looks like war all right!" I said to Mother, turning away from the window. But Mother didn't answer. Her eyes were half-closed, her lips moved swiftly. She was praying. In her own way Mother, too, was getting ready for the war.

Even though Hitler had gypped me out of the last five days of my vacation, I was glad to get back to Warsaw. I always was. Warsaw was my town. I knew every land-mark, every store, almost every stone in the pavement.

With my own eyes I had seen the old place grow from a large but rather shabby provincial town under the Russian occupation before the First World War, to the lovely, big capital it was now. And I was proud of it, too. Proud of the Old Town Square with its narrow, gaily painted houses; of the Royal Castle and the lace-like Gothic Cathedral. Proud of the vast parks, and old palaces that had been trans-formed into ministerial buildings. Proud of the modern apartment houses, and restaurants, and cozy coffeehouses. Proud even of the big red buses that at every turn flopped a

39

big yellow arrow in a benevolent gesture of warning, as if saying: "Careful, children, I am about to turn to the right. I am big and heavy. Don't get in my way."

Why, even the streetcars of Warsaw were endowed in my eyes with a special dignity and stateliness no streetcar in any other city ever possessed. They were big, shiny and streamlined, and had the emblem of Warsaw—a mermaid—painted on the side. She was no soft hussy, this buxom mermaid of Warsaw. In her left hand she held a shield, while her right arm, raised high above the head, brandished a sword. Some girl!

And I was inordinately fond of the old *droshkies*, the one-horse carriages that went clop-clop along the streets and always jammed the traffic. I liked them far better than the tiny Fiat taxicabs which darted to and fro, and were so small that, as someone said, you had to use a shoehorn to get in and out of them.

As we stood now on this August 27, 1939, in front of the railway station waiting for a droshky to take home our luggage, I looked around to sense the mood of the city.

The excitement of pre-war days was already in the air. The newsboys shouted the latest extras, people walked faster, talked louder, a strange gleam in their eyes.

"People would never make wars if they didn't get so dreadfully bored with their drab, everyday life," I had told an American friend that summer. "They need war to get a kick out of life."

The people of Warsaw were getting their kick now. The whole street seemed slightly intoxicated.

At the house Cook was delighted to see us. The grocer on the street corner, her main source of political information, had told her that war would break out any minute now, and she had been afraid we would not come at all, and leave her to her fate. And the greengrocer had

From the collection of Stefan Mucha

Horse-drawn carriages known as droshkies.

From the collection of Stefan Mucha

A comprehensive network of streetcars runs throughout Warsaw.

With buildings dating from the 13th century, Old Town is the oldest district of Warsaw.

Napoleon Square, with the Prudential building, Warsaw's first skyscraper completed in 1933, visible on the left.

The Opera House, on Krolewska Street, was established in 1765 by King Stanislaus Augustus Poniatowski.

From the collection of Stefan Mucha

The 17th century Wilanow Palace in Warsaw—one of the most elegant examples of baroque architecture in Poland.

From the collection of Stefan Mucha

The Palace on the Water in Warsaw's Lazienki Park—considered one of Poland's finest examples of 18th century neoclassical architecture.

USNARA

Warsaw City Hall was located on Theater Square. In 1939 Mayor Stefan Starzynski led the civil defense of the city from here.

been even more emphatic. He said that the fighting had already begun, only the newspapers would not admit it. And she had washed the windows and waxed the floors; it would be a shame to have all that work go to waste.

Mother went at once into action, bursting with energy. She loved this apartment to which she had come first as a bride thirty-six years ago. At that time the house had been new, modern and quite swanky with its big marble staircase, huge mirrors at every landing, and plush-covered railings. Now it was old, a little shabby and quite obsolete: big porcelain stoves instead of central heating, coal-heated bathrooms and no maid's room. The six large rooms of our apartment were crowded with antiques and junk—Mother never threw anything away—but to us it was the most wonderful place in the world... it was home. And its very heart was the dining room clock.

"Wind the clock, please," were Mother's first words when we entered the apartment. No servant was ever allowed to touch it. I climbed on a chair and carefully inserted the old-fashioned key into the lock. You had to be careful with the old thing. If you pushed ever so little to the right the clock would be fast; if pressed to the left, it would be slow; and the whole household had always lived by the dining room clock.

While Mother busied herself with the summertime accounts (I am afraid I had made a mess of them during her absence), I went to the telephone. Cook and Leosia, the nurserymaid, were unpacking the trunks, and from the nursery I could hear the delighted shouts of George and Ania greeting their old toys.

I called Adam's apartment. I didn't expect to find him home, so I was quite surprised to hear his voice. He was very glad Mother and I were back but why didn't Hanka and the boys come? He had sent telegram upon telegram urging their return. Didn't she get them? No, she did not. Telegrams took a long time to reach their destination.

"But tell me," I asked him, "how does it happen I find you home? I thought you had been drafted?"

So he was. For two days he was kept in the barracks, but later on he was assigned to a military office and they let him stay home, except when on duty. What office? No—he could not tell me that (months later I found out it was the Bureau of Military Censorship).

"Don't you wear a uniform?"

"No."

"That's a pity. I know altogether too many officers and it has always been the dream of my life to go for a walk leaning on the arm of a swanky sergeant. I'll have to give it up, I suppose."

He laughed. "I have a military gas mask, though, with a long tube. It makes me look exactly like an elephant. Do you like that?"

"Not much, I'm afraid," I said with a sigh.

That night Mother and I held a war council.

"Mother," I said, "the children can't stay here when war breaks out. Warsaw will be the first place to be bombed. I have to stay with the Bank, and Franek will also have his duties. Couldn't you take the children and Leosia to Aunt Flika's place? She has always wanted you to come and stay with her; she will be glad to have you now. You'll be safe under those big trees, and it's so near that Franek and I will always be able to run up and see you all."

Aunt Flika was Mother's childhood friend. She had a big house with a beautiful old park and a few acres of land. The place was only ten miles outside of Warsaw, on the right bank of the Vistula River.

From the collection of the State Archive of the Capital City of Warsaw

Mokotowska 57, circa 1938—home to the Langer family.

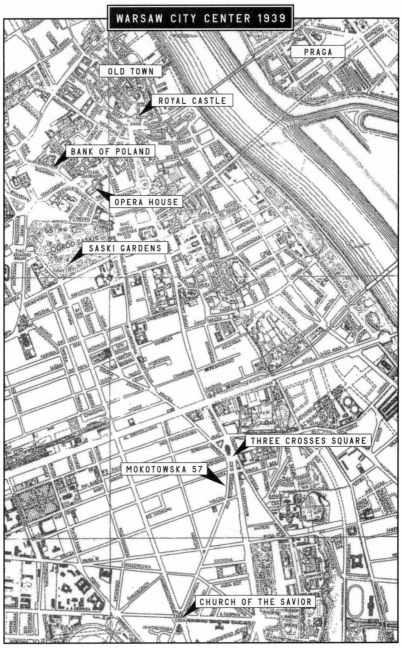

WARSAW CITY CENTER 1939

PRAGA

OLD TOWN

ROYAL CASTLE

BANK OF POLAND

OPERA HOUSE

SASKI GARDENS

THREE CROSSES SQUARE

MOKOTOWSKA 57

CHURCH OF THE SAVIOR

I could see Mother was loath to go away. She was not afraid of bombs, not Mother! And she would much rather have stayed and taken care of Franek, me and the apartment. But she loved the children, and she also saw my point.

So she only said, a little wistfully, "All right, I'll phone Flika. I am old now, I've had enough responsibility all my life. It's your turn to take the command, and the responsibility, too. Only don't make us go till war actually breaks out, will you?"

"No, of course not." I was touched, and a little scared to have Mother hand command over to me. Mother, who had always been such a wonderful leader!

The "children problem," as I called it, having been settled, we turned to the next matter on hand. This was war provisions. Cook was called in to participate in that part of the conference. Already in May, following the radio and press advice, Mother had bought and put aside large quantities of sugar, coffee, tea and canned goods. I had been strongly in favor of storing some flour, rice and oatmeal, too, but Mother had opposed my suggestion. "Don't you know you can't store flour except in a well-aired place? It will get musty, and we won't be able to use it anyway." So we had to get our wartime provision of flour now. But here Cook came out with unexpected bad news.

"Flour, Ma'am? Why you can't get flour in Warsaw for love nor money. People have bought it all up. I bought some myself, a week's supply perhaps. We are a large household, and I couldn't get more. No, there is no flour in Warsaw."

"What about rice?" No, no rice either. No rice, no oatmeal, no cream of wheat, no macaroni. We were late. The multitude of vacationists who had preceded us on the overcrowded trains had been buying, buying, buying for the last three days, and had completely cleared all the food stores like a cloud of locusts descending on a field. What were we going to do now?

"Well, I suppose we will have to wait a few days. New supplies will be coming to Warsaw soon," Mother decided.

Before going to bed I called up a friend at the American Embassy. Would he lend me his car and chauffeur to take Mother and the children out to the country when war broke out? Oh, yes, he would be glad to. Any time? Any time. On the first day of war then. I thanked him.

"On the first day of war," I thought, hanging up the receiver. "How far was that day?"

Sunshine was pouring through the open window as I entered my office the next morning. "Gosh!" I thought, "such perfect weather, and here I am back at work. Damn Hitler!"

The habitual pile of English and American papers lay on my desk, beside the green turtle, my office mascot. The good old *London Times*, the pugnacious *Financial News*, and the *Financial Times* printed on pale pink paper. Why a leading financial organ should use such girlish newsprint had always been a mystery to me. As I opened the ten-day-old *Wall Street Journal* the usual pungent smell of printer's ink, shipped still fresh across the ocean, caught my nostrils. Quickly I skimmed through the papers, pounded out the daily résumé of leading articles and news on the mimeograph plate, and called it a day. True, there still lay on my desk a whole pile of monthly bank reports waiting to be reviewed and digested. But I hoped our Board of Directors would not be interested on that morning of August 28, 1939, in the July reports of the English "Big Fives," or the

Chase National Bank of New York. At any rate, I wasn't. So I left them to the watchful eye of my green turtle and was off to greet the old office crowd.

I found them all in Jan's room, sprawled on chairs and desks, discussing the political situation. Apparently everybody felt about his or her work the same as I did about mine: careful money market analyses and surveys of farm prices had been shuffled into the topmost desk drawers, awaiting a more propitious moment. The midmorning tea was being served in tall glasses, the midmorning office tea that always tasted so good after the effort of the three first hours of work.

"No foreign newspapers tomorrow," someone called to me as I entered the room. "The Polish-German frontier was closed an hour ago."

"What shall we do for news, then?"

"A big radio set is being hooked up in the boss's office. We'll all take turns at taking notes."

I found the office crowd decimated. All men who were reserve officers had already joined their regiments. Only those remained who did not make the grade in the medical examination held before the military commission, and for that reason had never served in the army. My three best pals, however, Jan, Tomek and Roman, were among the latter.

"I am awfully sorry about that telegram," Jan apologized to me, "I didn't mean to spoil your vacation. But the situation is really very serious. War may start any minute now."

"Never mind my vacation. How is Rose, Roman?"

Roman and I had known each other ever since I could remember. Our mothers were close friends, and as it happened Roman and I were born within one week of each other. We used to play in the sand together. Later

51

we attended the same dancing classes, and had danced with each other, very solemn and stiff, at children's parties. As we grew up, for a while I lost track of Roman. I went to America and he to England. When I returned and got married, Roman was in Vienna working as a foreign correspondent for the official Polish News Agency. So I was delighted to find, when I first came to the Bank eighteen months before, that Roman and I were going to work in the same department, and that his office was just across the hall from mine. I was amused to discover that for all his brilliance Roman was not a bit ambitious.

"The dream of my life," he told me once, "is to become director of one of the branch offices of our Bank. We would live in some small provincial town, have a comfortable house, a garden and plenty of books. I like provincial towns. I've lived in London and Vienna and Warsaw, and I am pretty sick of them all by now."

"Wouldn't Rose mind?" I asked.

"I don't think so," he said smiling, "not when I am around."

He and Rose had been married for three years now, and they were terribly in love with each other. She was only eighteen when he married her, an adorable little thing, dark, pretty and full of fun. She and Roman were a constant butt of jokes, because they flirted with each other in public.

But Rose and Roman paid no heed. They went right on smiling into each other's eyes, and whispering little jokes into each other's ear.

When I asked him about his wife, Roman's face darkened. "Rose is coming back to town tomorrow. This war news upsets her terribly. You know the baby is due to arrive sometime next week."

"Of all times...," I thought to myself.

After a while I left Jan's office and went to the Bank's LOPP[1] headquarters to inquire about my war duties. The LOPP was the Polish counterpart of the British ARP,[2] an extremely active, nationwide organization which for the last five years or so had been preparing the general public to cope with any form of air attack. All Warsaw was divided into LOPP units; every block, every house, had its LOPP captain, fire brigade and first aid unit. Each house had been provided with a first aid kit and buckets filled with sand ready to be spilled over incendiary bombs. Every big organization had its LOPP unit, too. All quite ready for war.

As a matter of fact my war duties at the Bank had been assigned to me as early as May. After a thorough medical examination, I had been put on the Bank's fire brigade. I was thrilled at the prospect at that time. To be a fireman had been the dream of my life at eleven, and here quite unexpectedly it was to materialize. But it did not. The three-week intensive training of the volunteer firemen had been postponed till August, and I missed it when I went away for my vacation. It was a pity. How would the LOPP use me now?

The captain seemed at first at a loss to find me a war job. He scanned through a thick pile of papers, while I waited hopefully. Finally he looked up.

"Yes. Here is something for you. We seem to be short one stretcher-bearer. We will put you on that. You will get your outfit on the first day of general mobilization. You better report to Miss M. right away, you'll be under her direct command. Did you attend our first aid course?"

---

[1] *Liga Obrony Powietrznej i Przeciwgazowej*—League of Air and Anti-Gas Defense.

[2] ARP (Air Raid Precautions) was a British, mostly volunteer, organization dedicated to protecting civilians from the danger of air raids.

No, I had not. "You see, I was to be on the fire brigade," I tried to explain.

"Well, it's too bad. But it's too late, anyway. You'd better take this and study it carefully."

He handed me a thickish booklet. It was the LOPP first aid manual. I opened it at random, and glanced at a page.

"Iperit,"[3] I read, "one of the most virulent gases. The victim's face turns black, the body swells, death comes almost immediately, accompanied by strong convulsions."

"Fine," I told the captain while a shiver ran down my spine. "I certainly will."

---

[3] Mustard gas, one of the most feared agents of chemical warfare, first used by the Germans during World War I.

CHAPTER 4

August 29: Warsaw Prepares

"WHAT IS that?" I asked our messenger boy the next morning, as he staggered into my office carrying a large bundle of brand new spades. Spades were, to say the least, an unusual sight in the Economic Research Department of the Bank of Poland.

"The Bank supplies free spades to any employee who wants to volunteer for air raid shelter digging. Shall I leave one here for you?"

"Yes, certainly." I signed my name on the volunteers list. "Where do I apply for work?"

"At the District LOPP Office nearest your home."

That afternoon Jan, Roman and I left the office together, each brandishing a spade. I felt rather silly with my high heel shoes, a pert hat cocked over my right eye, and a spade on my shoulder. I was also at a loss how to handle my red handbag and gloves. As soon, however, as we got out in the street my embarrassment was gone. The sidewalks were crowded with figures as incongruous as myself. Elderly clerks with bulging briefcases, schoolboys, prosperous-looking, rotund businessmen, girls in fluffy silks, all carrying spades. All Warsaw was out to work at dugouts.

My two friends and I parted at the street corner. We had agreed to go home, change into more appropriate attire, and meet at four in the District LOPP Office.

I was the first one to arrive at our meeting place. The big room was packed tight with people of every age, sex and social strata.

As I stood waiting for my companions, I glanced around the walls. They were hung with big posters illustrating

Warsaw citizens, armed with spades, volunteer to dig air raid shelters.

for the most part first aid treatments. But right next to the door a horrible purple face, with eyes bulging, seemed to stare at me. "The victim's face turns purple... " I suddenly remembered my booklet, and I shuddered again. Chemical warfare was the thing I was really afraid of. Bombs, plain bombs, could not really be so bad.

Someone touched my elbow. My two friends were here. We pushed our way through the crowd towards the desk at which a pretty girl was taking down names and addresses.

"Have you your own spades?" she asked us.

"Yes."

"That's good. You won't have to wait then. All those people are waiting for spades, and we have only a limited supply of them."

She gave us the address of the place where we were supposed to dig. It was near the airfield. Rather far to go. Well, the big shots and famous people whose pictures, spade in hand, would appear in the next day's papers were digging in the squares and parks right in the center of the city, but we were the lesser fry. In order to save time we took a taxicab.

There was a large crowd at work when we arrived. The digging must have been going on since morning, for one air raid shelter was already dug out and was now being covered with boards, dirt and grass. The second was half done. The foreman, a tall sallow young man in the brown cap of the Technical School, directed us to the third one, scarcely begun. It was outlined with ropes, about four feet wide, a hundred and fifty feet long, running in zigzags. We were supposed to make it seven feet deep. We set to work at once.

At first it seemed easy; the ground was some kind of yellow, rather soft clay presenting not much resistance to our eager spades. But the deeper we went the harder it became. We ran into strong tree roots that had to be cut with a pickax; we hit upon big stones that simply refused to be moved; and by the time we got five or six feet deep, even lifting big shovelfuls of clay and throwing them outside the ditch nearly broke our backs. There were about forty of us working on that ditch, and probably not one had ever had any experience with a shovel and pickax. Well, not exactly...

Right in front of me there was a woman of about forty-five in a tweed skirt and heavy sport shoes. Her ruddy face shone with perspiration, but she certainly knew how to dig. It was a pleasure to watch her tackle the big roots or, with one easy swing of her broad shoulders, fling out enormous shovelfuls of earth.

"Why is it," I mused, while my spade rang again on hard rock, "that wherever there is work to be done you are sure to find an efficient female in tweeds who takes the lead?"

This one was magnificent. Not only did she work like five men, but at one point she jumped out of the ditch and disappeared only to return five minutes later with two pails of water and glasses for everybody to drink. The afternoon sun was still hot, and the drinks were most welcome.

The rest of us made up in enthusiasm whatever we lacked in skill. We got into each other's way, prodded the ribs of our neighbor with the spade handle, threw dirt into each other's shoes. But no one seemed to mind. The offender would just say "I am sorry," and the victim, with a pitiful smile, "It's perfectly all right," and both went on with their digging, working doggedly in silence. We all seemed to be in a terrible hurry. Every once in a while someone would glance at the sky, as if expecting enemy planes to appear.

But the sky was empty and blue, and the sun shone bright. Oh, why didn't it rain? Now that war was almost

USHMM, courtesy of Julien Bryan

USHMM, courtesy of Julien Bryan

The construction of air raid shelters is carried out by civilian volunteers from all walks of life...

USNARA

. . . and of all ages.

certain to start any day, why didn't the usual autumn rains come down, and change our famous dirt roads into bumpy pools of mud no motorized unit could ever attempt to pass? If it would only rain... This perfect weather could not go on forever. But the sky was blue, blue—not a cloud.

The sun had already set and we were still digging. I heard someone panting behind me. I looked around. It was Roman. He was leaning on his spade, and in the evening light his face looked almost green.

"What is the matter?" I asked him.

"Oh, nothing—it's just that silly heart of mine."

I had forgotten Roman had a weak heart.

"Why don't you go home and rest?" I suggested.

"How can we," Jan called to me from the other side of the ditch, "when you, the weaker sex, insist on keeping us here at work all night? It's up to you, you know, to give the signal to quit."

"Well, alright, let us all go home, then. The shelter is almost ready, and someone will finish it tomorrow while we are at the office. How long have we been working? Three hours? That should be enough for beginners."

Dragging our feet a little, but proudly carrying spades on our sore shoulders, we turned to look for the nearest streetcar stop.

I was very hot and very dirty when I rang the apartment doorbell that night. Franek opened the door for me. Franek—my brother—whom I had not seen for the last two months. He had just arrived from Zakopane. His suitcases and Alpine stick were still standing in the hall. We kissed and hugged, and he lifted me in the air as he always did, while Mother stood in the dining room door smiling. Now that all her little family was united under the old roof again Mother felt perfectly happy and confident. No war could upset her.

"I was so afraid," she said, when half an hour later we sat at the supper table, "that you would be cut off from us in case of war."

"Not me," Franek laughed, "I would have always found some way to reach you. I would have walked, if necessary. Probably I should have come earlier. But I simply could not drag myself away from the mountains. In this sunshine they are simply glorious. Everybody left five days ago—gee! what a panic that was—and after that I had the place all to myself. Not quite, though," he continued after a pause, and his face grew very serious, "a strange thing happened, you see. After everybody had left there were still seven people in my pensione—five men and two women. And they all spoke German."

"Probably German spies. Did you notify the police?"

"Yes, the police know about it. S. told them."

"What happened?"

"Nothing. The Germans were still there when I left last night."

We chatted for a while, but I was growing sleepy. This ditch digging had been quite a strain on my unaccustomed muscles.

"Mother," I said, "I think I'll go to bed right after supper. I feel terribly stiff, and my shoulder blades are quite sore."

The telephone rang and I went to answer it. It was Johnny. Johnny had been Franek's classmate and I had known him for ages. He was private secretary to one of the Vice-Ministers.

"Have you had your supper, Rulka?" he asked me now.

"Yes, I've just finished it. Why?"

"Well, I haven't had mine. I am still in the office in fact, and I thought it would be nice if you and I drove to one of those suburban restaurants and had a bite. My car is waiting right in front of the building. Please, do come."

"But I am tired tonight. I've been digging all afternoon, and I will be dreadfully dull."

"So am I. I've been in this stuffy office for the last thirteen hours, and if I don't get a breath of fresh air, my head will burst. Come on, be a good sport. I'll come and get you in ten minutes, may I?"

"Alright. I'll come."

As I returned to the dining room Mother was laughing.

"It's just like you," she said, "to be dead tired at one moment, and off to a party next. Whom are you going out with?"

"Johnny."

"Well, have a good time. And don't forget the keys. You'll probably be out late, and Franek and I have not been digging, but we are going to bed just the same. Goodnight."

"I am going to take you to a new restaurant in Mlociny," Johnny said as I squeezed into his tiny car ten minutes later. "Do you know Mlociny?"

I knew that Mlociny was a large village on the highway leading to the fortress of Modlin, about ten miles out of Warsaw, and that it was a favorite spot with Warsaw picnic goers, but I had never been there before.

We drove in silence. We were both really tired, and I could see black circles under Johnny's eyes. As we reached the outskirts of the city our car was stopped by a policeman, who took the car's number and looked inside to see how many passengers were in it.

"They are checking every car coming into or leaving Warsaw," Johnny informed me as the policeman waved us on. "There is a lot of dirty spy work going on."

The place to which Johnny took me was really lovely. It must have been built in the 18th century by some Francophile Polish nobleman, for it rather looked like a French chateau. The lines of the main building and the two wings were exquisite in their simplicity. The house stood in a park of very old trees—I could not see in the dark how large it was—and a wide lawn sloped gently from the terrace to the bank of the Vistula.

"It is a shame," I thought, "that such a lovely private residence should be turned into a restaurant." But then times were hard, taxes high, and it must have cost a lot of money to keep up such a sumptuous house.

A large and rather noisy party was dining on the terrace, so we descended the few steps leading to the lawn, and sat at a little table under the old elms. Johnny ordered a big meal for himself and a whiskey and soda for me, and we just sat there, relaxing. It was not till he had eaten that we started to talk.

"It's good to be out in the fresh air again," Johnny said. "I have hardly been out of the office for the last five days. We are getting ready for the M-day, you know. Want me to tell you something?"

I nodded.

"You must promise you will tell no one. Upon your word? Alright. The general mobilization was to be proclaimed tomorrow. The posters are ready, date and all. It was all settled at the Cabinet meeting today at noon. And then they had a long conversation with London over the phone, and decided to postpone it till the day after tomorrow. There won't be any new posters printed, though, no time for that. They will have to use those that are all ready, only the date August 30 will be blotted out, and August 31 stamped over it. Wait till Thursday. You will see them all over the place."

"I suppose this means we shall have war before the end of the week?"

"Oh, certainly."

He seemed very cool about it. I was not. It was Tuesday night. Only four more days to go, four days at the most.

Well, we had to face it. Perhaps it was better to have the thing come and get it over with. The suspense at some moments was almost unbearable. In a week we may all be dead—but who cares?

We had finished our drinks and decided to walk down to the river. The night was dark and warm save for a slight breeze coming from the water. Behind us the house shone with lights and the merry party on the terrace had broken out in song. In front of us was the river, broad and calm. The moon had not risen yet but the water was the color of dull silver. On the distant bank opposite us, we could see tiny lights blinking in cottage windows and tall black trees silhouetted against the dark sky. But for the revelers on the terrace the night was incredibly still, not a leaf, not a twig stirred. There was something ominous in this stillness, something unnatural, ghostly... War was brewing in the dark.

A light appeared down the river and slowly moved toward us. It was a river boat.

"It is coming," I said almost in a whisper.

"What's coming?" Johnny's voice was low, too. But I didn't answer. I didn't know myself what I meant. What was coming? Was it the boat? Was it war?

We watched the boat silently slide by. The deck was lighted, but there didn't seem to be a soul on board. A ghost ship. As it passed us tiny waves began to lap the bank at our feet. Suddenly a feeling of immense, hopeless weariness overcame me.

"Let's go home, Johnny," I pleaded. "I think I've had enough for today."

CHAPTER 5

August 31: On the Edge

IT WAS August 31, and the general mobilization posters were out. I could see their big white sheets with heavy, black lettering on every street corner. I glanced at the date. Yes, Johnny had been right. August 30 had been blotted out, and August 31 stamped in purple ink above it.

Little groups of men and women stood in front of the posters reading, nodding their heads in mute acknowledgment. Everybody knew what this meant; the general mobilization had been postponed as long as there was the last little flicker of hope to maintain peace. The flicker had gone out now. War was about to begin. I noticed that practically everybody in the streets was carrying a gas mask flung over the shoulder.

Other posters had appeared too. They represented a greedy hand reaching out for the the map of Poland and a Polish soldier, rifle in hand, ready to strike the rapacious fingers. As I looked at it, I suddenly wished that the artist had not made the hand quite so big, or else had added an inch or two to the stature of the Polish defender. As it was, the whole picture looked too much like an illustration to *Gulliver's Travels*.

In the office that morning everything was topsy-turvy. Half of the staff of our department was transferred to the Issue Department to count out big piles of banknotes that for years had been waiting in the Bank's vaults, ready for M-day. They were packed now in big sacks and shipped off to different localities for army use. Those of us who still remained in the Economic Research Department had a terrible time following the news that

Patriotic posters and official notices begin appearing across Warsaw, pasted even on the Opera House walls.

From the collection of Zygmunt Walkowski, courtesy of the National Library, Warsaw

"I suddenly wished that the artist had not made the hand quite so big."

kept pouring over the radio from London, Paris and Berlin. We sent news bulletin after news bulletin to the Bank authorities, who were probably too busy to give them so much as a glance.

I was called to the LOPP headquarters to get my uniform. It was the regular army air defense uniform, complete with boots, gloves, broad belt and steel helmet. The uniform was made of heavy, khaki-colored linen impregnated with some kind of stuff that made it gasproof. It was air-proof, too, and terribly hot; almost as soon as I tried it on my whole body was moist with perspiration. The boots were simply enormous, probably size 12, just right for the regular trooper, but certainly not for a woman's feet. Well, I would see how I could manage in them. I tried a few dancing steps and nearly tumbled over.

"Those boots are meant for rescue work, and not for dancing," the captain of our brigade reprimanded me sharply.

Alright, alright, I knew that. I just wanted to find out whether they were comfortable. We certainly looked funny, we, the sixteen girls of the first aid squad, in those military uniforms that were much too big for us and those gigantic boots. We looked at each other and laughed. Safety pins were brought out, and the ample folds readjusted to our respective sizes. We decided to discard the belts; why, one belt could have easily held two of us. The fitting over, we neatly stacked our outfits in the main air shelter of the Bank, inspected our first aid kits to see that nothing was missing, and were told to report at once at the first air raid alarm. And to be sure from now on to carry our gas masks wherever we went.

As I returned to my office I saw men at work in the largest room of our department. They were attaching a big loudspeaker to the central wall. "To be used for air raid alarms," I was told.

A fresh pile of radio news awaited me on my desk. I was hard at work on them when Roman came to say good-bye.

"You don't mean to say you are mobilized?" I asked him incredulously, remembering his weak heart.

"Not exactly," he explained, "but you know that the Knights of Malta have fitted out and opened a big hospital in the Blue Palace. Well, I am one of them, and I've been told to report at once. I will work with an ambulance. Oh, how I hate this war," he added bitterly.

I could understand that.

"What about Rose?" I asked.

"She will stay with my mother. I won't be home, you see, I have to live at the hospital. You can imagine what a state of nerves she is in."

Poor little Rose!

I didn't dig that afternoon. Air raid shelters were practically finished all over Warsaw, and there was plenty to be done at home. As I left the office I noticed that the streets had acquired a new aspect that was military and businesslike at the same time. There were no strollers, everybody walked briskly, intent upon some important errand. Gas masks everywhere; my own was also dangling at my hip. Almost everybody I met wore some kind of badge, either the Red Cross or the green and yellow badge of the LOPP. Volunteer nurses hurried along the sidewalks smiling brightly, a little self-conscious in their new, very white, and very starched uniforms. Yet there did not seem to be many army men around, apparently they had all joined their regiments somewhere at the frontier.

Even the houses looked strangely unfamiliar, for every pane, every shop window was decorated with a checker pattern of white paper stickers. Those stickers were supposed to protect the glass from air vibrations caused by nearby explosions. But they looked like some fantastic, modernistic decoration. Warsaw, the defiant City of the Mermaid, had put on her war makeup. She was ready now, waiting in the afternoon sun.

As I neared the house, I saw that the windows of our apartment were covered with paper stickers. Franek, Cook and Leosia must have been working on them while I was at the office. I saw Leosia now, leaning out of my window, fixing a large sheet of black paper on the inside of the pane. Blinders for the blackout.

I helped Franek and Leosia with the blinds, and then we turned to the next problem, namely, which room should be turned into a gas-proof shelter? Every household was supposed to have one, and detailed instructions for making it gas-proof had been given over the radio and in the newspapers. After long deliberation we settled on the nursery. It had only one large window, and a little, dark passage led directly from it to the bathroom. We decided to include the bathroom in the gas-proof area. It would be convenient for more reasons than one. The children were going to leave for the country on the first day of war anyway, and the provisions, our precious war provisions, would then be moved into the nursery.

The children were delighted. To have a gas-proof nursery seemed the height of comfort to them. While Franek started to work on the window with cotton, glue and Vaseline, and I on the door (narrow strips of felt and nails), George and Ania would simply not leave our side. Ania felt it was exactly the right time to give her favorite doll Stas a nice carriage ride, and any time we moved about we were sure to step into the darned thing. George leaned over my elbow putting his nose right in the way of the hammer. We tried to send them away to the kitchen, but Cook was busy with the kitchen window and would not have them around, smart woman, so they were back within the next two minutes. Mother was out on a last and unsuccessful attempt to obtain some flour and rice, Leosia was helping me and Franek, so there was really no way to get rid of the children. And we were in a hurry, for the radio had announced that Warsaw was going to have its first blackout that night, and we had to finish our work before it got dark.

At last, Franek with a deep sigh of relief turned away from the window.

"Look at that. Doesn't it look gas-proof?"

"Perfect. Does it close?"

It did not. Franek pushed and pulled and struggled with the window, but it simply refused to close. He had stuffed too much cotton in the hinges, and had to do it all over again. I was not more successful. After I had used up my whole supply of nails, and most of the felt strips, I turned off the electric switch in the nursery to see if any light would filter through the door from my room. It did. The door was old, and the joints loose; they could absorb any amount of felt strips.

Finally our work was done. We could not swear to the fact that the room was absolutely gas-proof but we had done our best to make it so. And there was no felt left anyway.

"You feel safe, now, I hope," Franek said.

"Well, I don't know. What if a bomb drops somewhere near and the whole window pane drops out?"

"Don't you remember the old saying, 'The goat dies but once'?"

That was true. The goat dies but once, and so do we. Who cares?

While we were removing ladder, hammer, Vaseline and cotton, the whole mess of our gas-proofing activity, the doorbell rang and the postman handed me a cable.

It was from Olgierd.

"If war breaks out," I read, "ask Dan (Dan was our friend in the American Embassy) to arrange transportation for you and children to the States."

"If"... There was no longer any "If." War had become a certainty.

But even so I would not go to America. I could not. The children would be perfectly safe in the country. Who would ever think of dropping bombs on a country house? It was the cities that were bombed, and I had my job in Warsaw. I could not leave it now. I would not be a quitter. Who leaves his family, his friends, his country, in moments of distress? I certainly would not be a deserter to everything I loved. Olgierd could not leave his post to come and join us, why should I leave mine?

And deep underneath all these legitimate and high-sounding reasons, there was another one, just as strong, although I hardly liked to admit it to myself: the curtain was about to be raised, and I could not miss the Big Show...

So I set out for the post office to send a cable to Olgierd, telling him about the war plans we had devised.

It was a strange street I plunged into immediately upon leaving the house. Gone were the brightly lit store windows, and the gay blue and red neon signs. Gone the cozy cafés on street corners where by the windows elderly gentlemen used to sit, and over watery demitasse discuss and settle the fate of Europe. "If I were Mussolini...," they used to say or even, "If I were the

British Government..." Gone were the red buses, the droshkies, the tiny ubiquitous taxicabs...

The streets were black. Black and rustling with suppressed excitement.

There seemed to be a lot of people about, but I could not see anyone, and no one spoke aloud. Whispers. Whispers everywhere, the warm, velvety night seemed to be full of them. Here and there a cigarette flickered in the dark, and I could hear muffled sounds of footsteps. Silent automobiles crept along the drive, invisible but for the blue or purple glow of their blinded headlights. I was afraid I might tumble off the sidewalk, or run into a lamppost, so I kept close to the walls. But apparently I was not the only one who had devised this clever scheme, for constantly I ran into other people.

When at last I reached the Post Office I found the inside of the building half-dark and crowded. Foreign correspondents—or were they businessmen—were nervously writing out long dispatches. I had to wait in line for over an hour before I was able to hand my own cable to the clerk, who looked pale and worn in the light of a heavily shaded lamp.

CHAPTER 6

September 1: WAR!

WHY DIDN'T my red bus come?

I was standing on the street corner, waiting for the bus to take me to the Bank. It was almost eight o'clock, and if the bus did not come within the next two minutes I would be late at the office. We started work at 8:15. Nervously I glanced up and down the street—no sign of a bus anywhere. A man passed in a droshky; he looked at me and laughed. Why was he laughing at me? Suddenly I realized what was the matter. The buses did not run any longer—they had been commandeered for the army.

"Probably they will get a regular military uniform," I mused as I hurried to the nearest streetcar stop, "a coat of khaki-color paint. You could not expect red buses to run back and forth to the front. Too visible. Thank God Warsaw could not be deprived of her streetcars for military purposes. What would we do without them?" Warsaw was a big city.

I was late to the office. As noiselessly as I could, I sneaked through the hall and tiptoed to my room. It was empty. So were all the adjoining rooms. A strange silence hung over the office. Yet, I could see through a door left ajar that there were people in the boss's room. Curiosity getting the better of my embarrassment at being late, I walked in.

All that was left of the Economic Research Department sat there in a wide circle, still and silent. All eyes turned towards me as I entered, but no one smiled. All faces had a solemn, strained look.

And the head of the department said in a level voice:

"The German army has crossed our frontiers at almost every point early this morning."

So it had come. War was on. I was conscious of a strange feeling in the pit of my stomach. Something like a contraction.

"What is the date, today?" I heard Jan say. "September first? Well September seems to be Hitler's favorite month. He could not waste a day of it."

And then I remembered the children. They and Mother were to leave Warsaw on the first day of war.

"Can I use the telephone?" I asked the boss. "I have to send my mother and my children out to the country." For the last three days we had been asked to refrain from personal telephone calls. The lines were overloaded with official and business calls. But this was different. It was important, terribly important.

"Certainly, go ahead," the boss replied amiably.

I first called the American Embassy. While waiting for the connection I looked out of the window. Our office was on the fifth floor, and from where I stood I could not see the narrow street. But the sky was blue, so blue. (Oh, Lord, why didn't it rain?) In the window of the house across the street I could see white and red geraniums swinging gently in a slight breeze. "Warsaw in flowers," I suddenly remembered Mayor Starzynski's slogan.

I got my connection. Yes, Dan would send me his car and chauffeur exactly at twelve. Thanks. I rang off. We did not mention the war, we did not discuss anything, every moment seemed strangely precious and could not be wasted on idle talk. Same with Mother. The war has broken out. Could she and the children be ready at noon? Yes. I would come home and see them off. Mother, be sure the children don't take too many toys.

From the collection of the National Library, Warsaw

SEPTEMBER 1, 1939

"GERMANY HAS TREACHEROUSLY ATTACKED POLAND"

From the collection of the Museum of the Polish Army, Warsaw

From the collection of Stefan Mucha

German air raids begin over Warsaw.

78

We will have to travel light. Alright. That was all.

As I put down the receiver sirens began to wail. And at the same moment we heard a very loud voice calling from the next room:

"I announce an air raid alarm for the city of Warsaw. I announce an air raid alarm for the city of Warsaw." And then, "It has passed DX point nine. It has passed DX point nine."

It was the newly installed air raid alarm loudspeaker that spoke for the first time. It was a quarter to nine.

"The Germans certainly don't waste time," Jan remarked as we all ran to our respective rooms. We closed the windows, grabbed our gas masks, put them on as we had always been told to, and flocked into the staircase. We were straining our ears for the sound of airplanes or anti-aircraft guns but we could not hear anything. Unhurriedly we descended the stairs while air alarm wardens counted us out to make sure that nobody was missing.

Outwardly everybody was calm. But again I was conscious of this strange feeling in the pit of my stomach. Not that I was not used to air raid alarms. We had had plenty of them, just for practice, and everybody knew exactly what he or she was supposed to do. But this was real. Terribly real. When would the bombs begin to crash?

As soon as we were in the shelter—a big basement room—we of the first aid brigade struggled into our uniforms and boots, grabbed our first aid kits and stretchers, and stood waiting. "Waiting for the first casualties," I thought. Nothing happened. The loudspeaker in the shelter kept repeating monotonously, "The alarm is on. The alarm is on. The alarm is on." And then again, "It has passed DQ point three. DQ point three. The alarm is on."

The DQ point three and the DX point nine must be code symbols for anti-aircraft observation points, I thought with one half of my brain, while the other half desperately tried to remember the instructions I had read in my first aid manual. In vain, my memory was a blank. I could only listen and wait...wait...wait...

At last the all-clear signal was sounded. With a sigh of relief we rushed upstairs. We did not take off our uniforms. Our captain had decided that it took us too long to put them on, and that we might just as well be ready for the next alarm. She was right. We had barely time to open our windows and look out in the crowded street, when the sirens wailed again.

"I announce an air raid alarm for the city of Warsaw. I announce an air raid alarm for the city of Warsaw," the loudspeaker was calling from the next room.

The excitement of the first alarm had worn off, and we took this second one as a personal insult. "Wouldn't the Germans let us work at all this morning?" we asked each other. Running up and down five flights of steps was not fun, not in those big, heavy boots. And we were already terribly hot in our uniforms. As I put on the gas mask, I discovered that my curls which used to cling so nicely around my head were now becoming a dreadful nuisance. They got into my eyes under the mask and blinded me. One wisp of hair got even further and was tickling my nose. "I'll have them all cut off this very afternoon," I decided then and there.

We had three air raid alarms that morning before I was able to leave the office at 11:30. But not a sound of airplanes, bombs crashing or anti-aircraft guns. Even so I felt pretty tense; I was afraid things would begin to happen before I had time to get Mother and the children out to the country.

"You don't have to come back this afternoon," the boss told me as I was leaving the office. "I see that you are on first aid duty tomorrow afternoon. You can listen to the radio communiqués then, and take notes for the bulletin. I don't think the Germans will let us do much work this afternoon anyway."

That was fine. I could drive with Mother and the children to Aunt Flika's place, and return in Dan's car afterwards.

I found the car waiting in front of the house, and the hall of the apartment littered with suitcases. The children were ready, too, terribly excited and pleased with themselves, their tiny gas masks flung over their shoulders. Ania as usual was pressing Stas to her heart—she would not leave him behind.

"That's an awful lot of luggage for wartime, it seems to me," I said viewing critically the pile of suitcases. "Couldn't you do with less, Mother?"

"Well, I don't know. Here is my suitcase and my traveling bag,"—they were certainly small—"and here are the two children's suitcases,"—I knew them. The children could not do with less.

"What about those two," I pointed to the two biggest suitcases.

"Those are Leosia's."

"Leosia, for Heaven's sake," I turned to the nurse, "what are you taking with you?"

"Oh, nothing, Madam, just my dresses."

"You don't mean to tell me you are taking all your dresses?"

"Why, yes, Madam. I thought we may stay for a long time in the country."

"Look here, Leosia," I told her impatiently, "this is war, and not a house party. You unpack this, take four dresses besides the one you have on, and leave the rest. And hurry. There is no time to waste."

While Leosia was reluctantly unpacking her belongings, Mother took me and the children to her bedroom and we all knelt before the image of the Virgin. It was a very old picture, painted in the Byzantine manner. Against a background of gold, a dark-faced Madonna stiffly held a tiny and very upright Holy Child. The picture had been in the family for over two hundred years, and for some reason was considered miraculous. We all held it in great respect. As we said a short prayer now, I could see from the corner of my eye that Ania was trying to make Stas kneel, too. But the stiff legs of the doll would not bend.

As soon as the prayer was said, Mother got up from her knees and with a wide sweeping gesture traced a sign of the Cross in the air, as if blessing the whole apartment. Then, without as much as a glance back, she walked out of the house.

"Don't forget to wind the clock on Monday," she reminded me as we reached the last step of the staircase.

Not until the car reached the outskirts of Warsaw did I relax. As long as we were within the city I sat silent and tense, holding Ania in my lap. What if the German planes chose to raid Warsaw now? We would be caught, children, suitcases and all, right in the middle of the street. Obviously we would all run for the nearest shelter, but what about the suitcases and the car? No, the prospect was not a pleasant one. Fortunately, no German plane appeared, no siren wailed. We were on the highway now, and Mother and the children were safe. Or so I thought. I heaved a sigh of relief.

I was surprised to find the highway almost empty. We passed a few army trucks, and a small detachment of soldiers. That was all. On both sides of the road flat fields stretched peacefully in the glow of the noon sun. It seemed almost impossible to believe that war had already broken out.

We did not have to go far. Pretty soon our car left the highway, and turning to the left began to bump along a sandy dirt road, shaded on both sides by tall poplar trees. At the far end of the half-mile drive we could already catch a glimpse of the large stucco mansion lost in a dark maze of trees that was Aunt Flika's country place. But the wheels of our automobile were grinding sand now, the chauffeur had to shift the gear, and it took us fully ten minutes before we swerved around the big green lawn and came to a stop in front of the house.

"I don't suppose any motorized unit will ever get us here," Mother laughed as we climbed out of the car and began to pull out suitcases and bags.

Aunt Flika was running down the front porch steps to greet her childhood friend. Aunt Flika was always running. She was tiny, dark, and must have been awfully pretty when she was young. In fact it was darkly hinted in the family that when she was twenty Aunt Flika had actually gone on the stage ("Opera, of course. Oh yes, she had really a beautiful voice. But, my dear, you can imagine what a terrible blow for the whole family that was. She was an orphan, you see. That explains it. Still, it's better not to mention this long-forgotten past, now that Flika has settled down.")

Well, if that was what the family called "settling down"... I've never seen anyone as active as Aunt Flika. She attended every social occasion in town, was on every committee, every charity, managed the big fortune her husband had left her, helped and ran the lives of half a dozen needy relatives, three neighboring villages and the local parish. No wonder she was always in a hurry.

I declined Aunt Flika's offer to stay for a while and see the family take up their new abode. I did not want to detain Dan's car and chauffeur. So I just kissed Mother and the children good-bye and was off.

Back in Warsaw I did not return home immediately. The memory of all the trouble my curls had caused me that morning was still fresh in my mind, and I decided to get rid of my stylish coiffure first.

"Please cut off all these silly curls," I told my old friend Mr. Felix as he tucked a pink gown under my chin.

"Why, Madam, it's a shame—we've been working on them for the last two years now, and they are most becoming, I assure you. And still very much the style."

"Never mind that," I told him, "I am setting a new wartime fashion. Something that goes well with the gas mask, you know. Times are changing, and so will the styles. How is business, by the way?"

"Good, very good indeed," Mr. Felix surveyed the shape of my head critically as he began to click his scissors in preliminary tuning. "In fact, this place was simply crowded this morning. Permanents, shampoos, marcels. Miss Helenka and I didn't know how we would be able to manage everything. All our clients seem to want to have their hair set for the war."

"Good for them. That's the right spirit. And good for you, too."

"Yes, only I doubt if it will last. You can't expect a beauty parlor to flourish in wartime, can you?"

No, certainly, I had to admit that hairdressing was no war industry. My curls lay on the floor now, and as soon as Felix's job was done I tried on my gas mask. It slipped on quite easily, and was as comfortable as a gas mask can be. I was pleased, even though I did not at all like my reflection in the mirror.

As I was leaving the beauty parlor sirens began to wail. I had only a few yards to go, as Felix's establishment was next door to our apartment house, so I did not hurry. But all about me people were running for cover, disappearing into doorways and stores. No one looked scared, and there certainly was no panic, but people were given only five minutes to clear the streets, and orders were strictly observed. When I reached the apartment, Cook was hurrying from room to room, closing the windows with a bang. Cook did look scared. Her face was ash gray, and her lips pale. "Those horrible Germans will kill us all," she moaned as she brushed past me.

"Oh no, they won't either," I tried to comfort her. "Even if one person in every ten is killed in this war—and that will be a lot—we still have more chance to be among the nine that will survive."

But my statistical arguments were completely lost on Cook. In fact, I don't think Cook wanted to be comforted. As time went on I even began to suspect that she enjoyed being scared. She was proud of it, talked about it constantly, but somehow those famous terrors of hers never seemed to interfere with anything she was doing at the time.

It was a relief not to have to go to the shelter—there was no shelter in our apartment house. Instead I went to the window and looked out into the street. It was completely empty.

Suddenly I heard the bark of anti-aircraft guns. It started somewhere far off but with terrific speed drew nearer and nearer, louder and louder. In no time it was here, right over the roof of the house, filling the blue sky with deafening noise and shaking our window panes. And then through the hurried, uneven staccato of anti-aircraft fire I heard the deep roar of airplane engines. Again I was conscious of the strange feeling in the pit of my stomach.

"Here they come," Cook called to me from the nursery window.

Yes, I could see them too. They flew in triangle formations, seven or nine planes to each triangle, very, very high. It was strange that their roar should be so loud and distinct, coming as it was through the noise of artillery fire. I tried to count them: seven, sixteen, twenty-five... Here was a triangle of only three, and there another group of nine planes. Or did I count them before? Suddenly I saw that the whole sky was filled with airplanes. Fascinated, I watched.

"Strange," I thought, "some of them do not seem to move at all." The din of the anti-aircraft fire seemed to grow fainter, and I no longer heard the roar of the engines, yet the planes remained in the sky, motionless. But now they turned white, grew larger and dimmer. Only then did I realize my mistake. What I had taken at first for motionless planes was the smoke of anti-aircraft shells, which for some reason took on the form of planes, and now were dissolving into the air.

Again I heard the crescendo of the anti-aircraft bark returning our way, and the real planes reappeared in the sky over our street. I could see that there were scores and scores of them, but by that time I had given up counting, they were too fast for me. Besides, I was absorbed now in watching the anti-aircraft shells (I no longer had any difficulty in recognizing them) rise into the sky to meet the planes. Would they score a hit? Would I see an enemy craft plunge and spin, trailing a cloud of smoke the way

I had seen so many times in the movies? No, the planes were flying too high. Moreover, our street was narrow, and my field of observation rather limited.

The huge wave of planes disappeared, and only two or three were still moving slowly across the sky. In the house across the street I could see in every window faces pressed to the panes; everybody was watching the raid. Back and forth it rolled over the sky, the appearance of planes always preceded by a rising wave of anti-aircraft fire.

For twenty minutes I stood at the window following the fascinating sight, every muscle of my body tense with excitement. And then a strange feeling of drowsiness began to steal over me. I could hardly keep my eyes open. I turned away from the window, and although anti-aircraft guns were banging away harder than ever, and the drone of airplanes was plainly audible right over our heads, I lay down on the couch and fell instantly asleep.

When I opened my eyes Franek was standing at the foot of the couch, looking at me and smiling.

"Congratulations," he said, "you certainly can sleep through anything. Here we have one hundred and fifty German planes roaring over Warsaw for almost two hours, and the anti-aircraft guns raising the worst racket I've ever heard, and I find you sleeping as peacefully as an innocent babe. Didn't you hear anything?"

"Oh, yes. I watched the battle for twenty minutes perhaps. It was fascinating, only for some reason it made me sleepy. I don't know why this whole war makes me so drowsy. I swear if someone told me now that the war has been called off I would go to bed for twenty-four hours and just sleep. But how do you know there were a hundred and fifty planes?"

"That's what everybody is saying; we will find out in the evening papers."

"Did they drop any bombs?"

"Not in the center of the city. Perhaps in the outskirts. They dropped some before noon, you know, destroyed several buildings and killed scores of people."

"That's strange. I didn't hear anything this morning, no bombs, not even anti-aircraft fire."

"Well, Warsaw is a big place, you can't expect to hear everything that's going on. You were probably in the shelter, too."

"Yes, I was. But what about you? Where were you? I didn't see you here when Mother and the children were leaving."

"I went to the recruiting office. Wanted to volunteer. But," Franek's voice grew bitter, "they flatly turned me down."

"What else could you expect? They don't take D class men, not on the first day of war, anyway."

Ten years before, when doing his military service, Franek had caught rheumatic fever, which had kept him in the hospital for three months and let him out of the army with a D mark in health classification and a ruined heart. For years afterwards he was almost an invalid, and even now he was not allowed to ski, row, play tennis or exert himself in any way.

"I still can shoot a rifle, and as long as I have to die some day anyway, I may just as well die now fighting the Germans."

"Come on, now. There are plenty of other things you can do. Why not join the air defense service? As far as I can remember you had some special LOPP training, didn't you?"

"Yes, I had. And that's exactly what I decided to do. As soon as I left the recruiting office I went to the LOPP captain of this block, and got an assignment. I am assistant warden for this house, if you please, and you'd better obey my orders."

"Alright, only don't make them too harsh, will you? When do you start your duties?"

"Tonight. I have to keep watch from nine to eleven, go over all the attics to see there is no fire, check on the blackout, and look out for bombs, of course. Tomorrow my watch comes at eleven PM, and the next night at one AM. What are your plans for tonight?"

"I guess I better study some more of my first aid manual. The knowledge may come in handy tomorrow, or even tonight."

For two solid hours I plunged into detailed descriptions of fractured skulls, broken limbs, wounds, poison gas, burns, hemorrhages, asphyxiations and whatnot, and the first aid to be applied in each case. There certainly was an amazing number of ways people could get injured in wartime, and they did not make pleasant reading, particularly not on the first day of war when somehow you imagined them all happening to your beloved ones. After two hours my head was buzzing with horrors: I could see myself carrying Mother on a stretcher (remember *not* to walk in pace with your teammate—or you will jolt the victim on the stretcher), reviving Franek with artificial respiration (one two three, one two three—don't give up—it takes sometimes three or four hours to get any results), bandaging George's head... Stop it! This was really getting too morbid. I put down the book, and went to the kitchen.

Supper was served in my room. We did not have enough black paper for the big dining room window that took up almost half of the wall. This was really too bad, because the radio set was there. Still, one could listen in the dark.

After supper while Franek was getting ready to take up his warden's duties, I went to see Adam. I needed his cheerful company and his matter-of-fact attitude towards life. I was missing Mother.

Quite unexpectedly I found Hanka, too. Four days before she and the boys had returned from Wola—oh, very reluctantly, indeed—why should one give up such glorious weather out in the country just for another war scare. Why, we had had war scares twice a year, as regular as a clock—and what had come of them? Nothing. Still, as soon as his family arrived in Warsaw Adam, notwithstanding Hanka's protests, dispatched them to Hanka's sister who lived in the country near Warsaw. Adam had no illusions as to the present war scare. This morning Hanka had come to Warsaw just for the day, to get some extra blankets for the boys—the small house at Cisowa was overflowing with guests—and had discovered to her utter dismay that the war had actually broken out. She was completely dazed.

"I can't believe it, I simply can't believe it," she kept repeating. "It's perfectly awful."

"Won't you have a highball?" Adam asked me.

"Yes, I will. I really think I need one. I got pretty sick of skull fractures, and the victim turning black, and all that, you know?"

"What are you talking about?" Hanka asked nervously.

"Nothing. I've been studying my first aid manual this afternoon, that's all."

But Hanka shook her head. She did not like the flippant way in which Adam and I talked about the war.

We discussed the first war communiqués. The Germans were certainly not wasting time. They had bombed Warsaw,

Cracow, Posen, Lodz. They had completely destroyed a small, innocent village near Czestochowa. Forty-seven of their planes had been downed during the day, according to the official communiqué—that was good. And only two of our own planes were missing. This really seemed too good to be true. And our planes had been over Berlin. Still, the German motorized units were advancing pretty fast, they had almost reached Czestochowa. Of course, we knew the front would be moving back and forth, but was it not letting the Germans go a little too far inside the country? Well, the military authorities knew best where to stop them, we had supreme confidence in our army. Too bad the roads were so dry, and did not hinder the invader's progress. Fortunately rains were due any day now.

One question puzzled and worried us. Why did German fliers drop bombs on Anin, Wawer, Konstancin? Those were residential suburbs of Warsaw, and certainly could not be considered military objectives. Would the country around Warsaw be just as unsafe as the city itself? Were our children running the risk of being bombed too?

A German bomb had destroyed a house next to Ambassador Biddle's villa in Konstancin, and another fell right into the Ambassador's garden. We gloated over this incident. Not on account of Ambassador Biddle, of course. Ambassador Biddle was a true friend of Poland, and the most popular foreign diplomat in Warsaw. Everybody was glad he had escaped injury. But this German bomb planted in the garden of the American Ambassador was the typical German gaffe; it would do more harm to Germany's reputation abroad than it did to the Ambassador's garden, and that on the very first day of the war.

Newspapers were already full of spy stories, and Adam made fun of them.

"Did you read the story of the boy and the canary in the evening papers? Didn't you? A boy who lives near Inowroclaw had a canary. The bird escaped from the cage this morning and flew out of the room. The boy went after him, but the canary kept evading him. Finally he saw the bird perched on the highest branch of a tree in the cemetery. He began to climb the tree, and suddenly looking down he saw far below something moving inside a newly dug grave. He climbed down and went to report to the police. And the police found out that it was a German spy who was giving light signals to airplanes. A lovely little piece of fiction. I read it fifteen years ago in a volume of short stories, only at that time the boy was a little Belgian, and the thing had presumably happened in 1914. Those newspapermen will dig up any old story, and pretend it has just happened."

"Still there must be a lot of spy work going on now."

"Oh, surely, but not as crude as all that. Still, people will believe anything, and the newspapers know it."

I bade Hanka and Adam goodnight and plunged into the darkness of the blackout. The streets were almost completely deserted—no one wanted to be caught in an unfamiliar spot where he would have to grope his way to the nearest shelter in case of an air raid alarm. I walked as fast as the darkness would permit me, my steps echoing through the empty streets. My heart was beating fast as I strained my ears for the first sound of sirens. But no sirens wailed.

Warsaw had no more air raid alarms that night.

CHAPTER 7

September 2: Our First Refugees

"A LA guerre comme Langer!" chanted Jan as I appeared in the office the next morning. "I see you are inaugurating a new fashion in hair dress."

"Yes, it's a war fashion. Do you like it?"

"I would not call it particularly becoming, but it must be most comfortable."

It was the second day of the war, a glorious, sunny day, and in spite of the fact that from the military point of view the beautiful weather was disastrous, it made us feel cheerful. After all no one could tell how long this war was going to last and we might just as well settle to a nice, everyday war routine with air raid alarms and bombs taken all in the day's stride. I put on my uniform and sat at the radio to take down foreign communiqués for our news bulletin. But my good resolution to take war in a perfectly matter-of-fact way was not to last long.

"Do you remember the messenger from the credit department?" asked Lila, our secretary, entering the boss's room.

"Which one do you mean, the tall, lean one or the short, bald-headed one?" I knew them both.

"The bald-headed one. He lost his home, his wife and two children in yesterday's bombing. He lives in Grochow"—Grochow was one of the city's outskirts that had been heavily bombed the previous day— "and when he returned from the Bank last night, he found his little house in ruins, his wife dying in the hospital with an arm and a leg torn off, and two children dead.

The third child was not hurt, and the neighbors are taking care of it."

It was only the second day of war, and already victims among people I knew. How many stories of this kind would I hear during the days that would follow?

We went to the credit department to shake hands with the poor man. We found him standing in the middle of a group of Bank officials, his bald head bent low, a tear slowly dripping along one side of his protruding nose. I've seldom seen men cry, and I was deeply moved.

In a low, colorless voice he kept repeating over and over again his pathetic little story:

"Everything was gone. Just a heap of ruins. And my wife won't live, the doctors said so. Perhaps it's better for her to die: no arm, no leg, how would she manage? I have not seen the bodies of the children, they were taken away before I returned. The little one is alright—she was in the neighbor's house when it happened. Yes, everything is gone."

Without a word we shook his hand—what was there to say?—and ran upstairs, back to work. But the Germans would not let us work. We had three air raids that morning, and four in the afternoon. Back and forth to the air raid shelter, up and down the five flights of stairs, while the loudspeakers boomed through the big Bank halls and office rooms, "I announce an air raid alarm for the city of Warsaw. I announce an air raid alarm for the city of Warsaw. Attention. It has passed T point four."

We could hear, as we descended the stairs, the distant barking of anti-aircraft fire, but still no sound of bombs crashing. Yet we knew bombs were being dropped, for every radio communiqué brought some fresh news of destruction and death in the suburbs. When would the German bombers attack the center of Warsaw? We snatched every free minute in the intervals between air raids to work on our foreign news bulletins, but most of the morning was spent in the shelter. There we sat in a big circle, on chairs and tables, listening to the dispassionate voice of the radio announcer repeating the air raid warning over and over again at regular intervals. It was dreadfully monotonous. I remembered now what Adam had told me once ages ago—or was it only at the beginning of this week? "War in reality consists mostly of waiting." Yes, that was true. We were waiting, waiting ... What were we waiting for? The all-clear signal or the first bomb to crash on the Bank?

As the day dragged on, the strange mixture of tensity and drowsiness I had experienced the day before assailed me again. I would have given anything to lie down in some corner and take a nap.

Funny how war affects people in different ways. There was a girl on our first aid squad, a tall, broad, placid-looking girl, who was constantly eating. She said the excitement made her hungry. Every time the alarm was sounded and we all trooped into the shelter she would appear with a new supply of sandwiches carried in a brown paper bag, and as soon as she found a seat she would start nibbling at one. I looked at her with admiration and a faint feeling of disgust. Even now, on the second day of war, I had not overcome the slight contraction in the pit of my stomach every time I heard the sirens wail, and eating was the last thing I felt like doing. In fact, I had completely lost my appetite, and could hardly swallow anything at mealtimes.

Around noon while we were having one of our short respites from the raiders, Roman appeared in the Economic Research Department. He had come to collect the private papers he had left in his office desk. Roman was a meticulous person, and wanted to leave everything in order; just in case, you know...

We were all delighted to see him. Where was he? What was he doing? Had he many casualties to attend?

He was in charge of a first aid point in Mokotow, on the southern outskirts of Warsaw. No, they did not have many casualties, the German planes had not started bombing Mokotow yet. They concentrated their efforts on the northern part of the city, and on Praga, the part of Warsaw that lay on the right bank of the Vistula. There were a few casualties, however, mostly people who had not waited for the all-clear signals and were injured by the falling fragments of our own anti-aircraft shells. Those splinters would fall sometimes ten minutes after the firing had ceased, and coming as they did from great height, they caused serious head injuries.

"Well, I guess that from now on I'd better wear an opera hat whenever I go out in the streets," Jan remarked. "It seems to me an opera hat should be good protection from those missiles. It would probably just close with a snap and send the splinter right into the air again."

I asked Roman about Rose. But he had nothing to report. The baby had not yet arrived.

If the morning of that second day of war was hectic and tiresome, the afternoon was even worse. It was Saturday, and everybody in the Economic Research Department left at one. Everybody but me. I was on duty. The Issue Department was working overtime, and there were many officials living on the Bank's premises, so that there always had to be at least two girls from the first aid squad on the lookout for possible casualties.

My teammate was working in the Issue Department, and was kept pretty busy all afternoon. I didn't see her except during air raid alarms. In the intervals I was left completely alone in the big south wing of the Bank building, of which the Economic Research Department occupied the top floor. Every time I moved I could hear the heavy footsteps of my seven-league boots echoing through innumerable empty corridors and office rooms. The solitude made me uncomfortable—at times of stress you crave human company.

I tried to fiddle with the big radio set in the boss's room; I had promised the boss to listen for any important news coming from London or Paris and telephone him what I'd heard. He was attending a conference—bank authorities were constantly in conference those days—and would not be able to follow the foreign news himself that afternoon. But try hard as I would, I was unable to catch any of the BBC and French programs. Every time I tried to tune in, the loudspeaker would start howling, and after a while I would hear the guttural voice of a German speaker or a German military march. The German broadcasting stations were purposely interfering with the reception of French and British programs—what else could we expect? The airwave war in the ether was an old and favorite trick with all Continental stations, even in peacetime.

After several futile attempts, I gave up and tuned in the Warsaw station. But even with the radio going full blast, I felt uncomfortable and lonely. It was almost with a sigh of relief that I greeted the wail of sirens, announcing another raid of German bombers. At last I could go to the shelter, back to the comforting atmosphere of human comradeship.

The all-clear signal after the eighth alarm of the day had just been sounded, and leaving the shelter I went out into the Bank's courtyard for a cigarette. Dusk was already falling, and everything seemed very calm. As I stood there, inhaling deeply and with relish (we were not allowed to smoke in the shelter, and the alarm had lasted almost an hour), the big gate of the Bank swung open and a truck drove in. It stopped in front of the garage, at the farther end of the courtyard, and in the gathering dusk I could see dark silhouettes climbing out of the truck, men and women each carrying a suitcase. They stood in a little cluster around the car, and our LOPP captain went out to meet them. For a minute they conferred in low voices, and then the whole group, eight men and three women, still carrying their suitcases, advanced towards the entrance to the air raid shelter, where about a dozen of us had gathered and stood waiting for them with speechless curiosity.

"These are our colleagues from the branch office at Warka," the LOPP captain said in introduction. "Warka was severely bombed early this morning, and was later occupied by the Germans. They have escaped with nothing but the Bank files and the suitcases they have here."

So they were war refugees! And our colleagues, too! With the Bank's policy of shifting its employees around from the main office in Warsaw to the branch offices in provincial towns, and vice versa, how easily any one of us might have found himself or herself in those people's shoes. Our hearts went out to those poor, tired figures we could hardly distinguish in the dark. We shook their hands, grabbed their suitcases and ran for chairs and benches. While supper was being prepared in the Bank's cafeteria, the LOPP captain went to the telephone in order to reserve hotel rooms for our road-weary guests. The Bank would foot the bill, of course.

While he was gone the refugees told us what had happened. They had been roused from sleep at half-past five that morning by the sounds of a none too distant battle. Guns were banging away, and they could hear the incessant tac-tac-tac-tac-tac of machine gun fire.

Then the roar of planes swept over the quiet little town, and the air shook with bomb explosions. At eight the Polish military authorities advised the head of the Bank that they were going to withdraw and surrender Warka to the enemy. The Bank had to evacuate, and evacuate at once. The German tanks were expected to enter the town within the next twenty minutes. It was fortunate that practically all the employees of the Bank lived on the premises. The Bank files were already packed and waiting to be removed. The men and women grabbed their suitcases, they all crammed into the Bank's truck, and within fifteen minutes they were off, leaving their belongings behind. As the truck rushed at full speed along the highway they saw clouds of smoke rising over Warka; the town apparently had been set on fire.

The story was told in low, colorless voices, without a trace of feeling. Those people, it was obvious, were dog-tired and completely bewildered. As we took them to the dimly lit cafeteria I saw their faces—they all wore that blank expression, the "refugee look" I was to see on so many faces in the days that followed.

"At last I've found rooms for you," the LOPP captain emerged from the darkness outside. "But what a time I had finding them! I had to telephone eleven hotels before I found anything. Everything was already taken, wherever I called. Apparently you are not the first refugees who've struck this town."

Quarter to nine. In fifteen minutes I would be allowed to take off my uniform and go home. Martial law was announced in Warsaw, and the curfew was sounded at eight. I would have to wear a LOPP badge, otherwise I could not go out in the streets. The LOPP captain had provided me with one and I was fastening it to my summer coat while I listened to the radio in the Bank's air raid shelter. There were very few of us left in the shelter now: the captain, four firemen, the other girl from the first aid squad and I. We were tired and the glow of the electric bulb made us blink—it was so dark outside when we went out for a cigarette!

"Warsaw has just been bombed for the ninth time today," the radio was saying. "Yes, that was right," I thought, we had just had our ninth alarm, and alarms meant bombs, I knew it now. Still, I was in Warsaw, in the very heart of Warsaw for that matter, and I had not heard a single bomb crash. How different war must seem to those who listen to radio reports from what it is to us!

And suddenly I thought of Olgierd. Somewhere in Philadelphia he was sure to listen to the radio news, even now, and if he heard that Warsaw had its ninth bombing— he probably thinks we are dead. Poor old Olg, how terribly worried he must be. I could almost see his face contorted with anguish hearing the radio commentators tell about these nine bombings. They would not spare him any grim details of the damage and casualties caused by the raids. Even the Polish radio was full of them right now. And what was Poland to American listeners: a distant, outlandish country. Both the press and the radio would be sure to play the Warsaw bombing horrors for all they were worth, but most probably would omit the names of the streets.

I could see Olgierd getting up from the chair and pacing the room, up and down, up and down, as he always did when something upset him. Every once in a while he would stop, and rumple his hair—another favorite gesture of his. Poor Olgy! I must send a cable telling him that we are all safe. I must send it at once.

I glanced at the clock—ten minutes to nine. Slowly, very slowly the arms of the clock crept on while I worried over

Olgierd worrying about us. At last I heard footsteps in the staircase. The two girls who were taking over our duties for the night had arrived. I slipped off my uniform, got into my civilian attire, and rushed to the nearest telegraph office.

"I will not be able to keep up this reassuring game for long," I mused as I handed to the girl in the telegraph office the required amount of cash. "If I send him a cable every day I'll be broke by the end of next week."

The next day was Sunday, and I was off duty at the Bank. So I went to see Mother and the children at Aunt Flika's country place. On my return to Warsaw that afternoon I learned from the extra editions of the newspapers that England and France had declared war on Germany.

"You should have been here," Franek told me, his big blue eyes shining with excitement as he opened the apartment door for me. "You've never seen such boundless enthusiasm. Thousands and thousands gathered around the British Embassy. I was there, too. People went simply wild with joy, we yelled and whooped and cried, and almost kissed our neighbors. We sang 'Jeszcze Polska'[1] and 'God Save the King.' Of course no one knew how to sing that, but we all tried our best. Then we all went to the French Embassy and sang the 'Marseillaise' and yelled 'Vive la France!' till our voices were hoarse."

"Hurray!" I cried and gave Franek a hug.

Now that Britain and France had joined the war, Hitler was sure to be beaten. Germany could never stand a war on two fronts. If we could only hold out for some time our Western allies would launch a big offensive, and then the pressure on our front would be relieved. Then our army, too, would start an offensive and we would chase the

---

[1] Popular name for the Polish national anthem, "Mazurek Dabrowskiego" (Dabrowski's Mazurka), taken from the first words: *Jeszcze Polska nie zginela* (Poland has not yet perished).

Germans as far as Berlin. Yes, Berlin. The big brutes needed a lesson. They would get it. Now that Britain and France had decided to fulfill their pledge to come to Poland's rescue whenever she was attacked by Germany, we no longer had to worry about the outcome of this war. No matter what hardships and sacrifices lay ahead of us, the final victory was assured.

And at the bottom of our hearts we had to admit that we needed reassurance. For ever since the second day of the war, there was, for some reason, a strange apprehension in everybody's mind.

The war communiqués put out by the Polish high command were reassuring enough in their impersonal matter-of-factness, yet we felt we were not being told the whole truth. Rumors were rampant. Rumors of communication lines cut off at the most vital points, of false or conflicting orders issued to various army detachments, rumors of treason in high quarters.

And spies. Spies everywhere. Thousands of spy stories, some quite fantastic, cropped up every day, and became the favorite topic of conversation everywhere. People were becoming suspicious of strangers, and anyone with a German name became automatically if not actually a traitor, at least a prospective one. We were warned over the radio not to move without a passport or an identification card, ready to be presented to any authority whenever required. The whole atmosphere was sticky with suspicion.

No, there could not be any doubt about it, this war was turning out to be something quite different from what we had expected.

We had feared that Hitler's planes would drop poison gas bombs, instead they dropped parachutists. Parachutists who shot at peasant children, and escaped into the woods to cut telephone lines and play havoc with our army's liaison lines. We knew that Warsaw, Cracow and other big cities were going to be bombed, but we did not expect villages, small towns and quiet residential suburbs to fall first victims to the aerial warfare. We had expected the enemy planes to drop bombs, but not to swoop down almost to the level of treetops and strafe laborers in the fields with machine gun fire. We knew that the population along the borders would be evacuated, but we were not prepared to see thousands of refugees in the streets of Warsaw on the third day of the war.

And above all, although we knew that the front would be a swiftly shifting one, we could not help a feeling of apprehension at the lightning pace at which German motorized units advanced towards Warsaw. As day followed day, the picture of the war became more unfamiliar, more bewildering.

So far there had been only one bright spot in the gloomy, swiftly unrolling film of war events—Westerplatte. There was something so strangely familiar, so very Polish about those three hundred men and two officers, the garrison of the tiny triangle of Polish territory in the port of Danzig, who had refused to surrender, and for the third day now were holding out against an overwhelming enemy force. Day and night they were shelled by shore artillery and by the big guns of German battleships. Their doom was sealed, no rescue could reach them now. And they knew it, too.

Yet they went on fighting, repulsing constant day and night attacks, determined to die to the last man rather than surrender a piece of Polish land that had been entrusted to them. From the very first day, the rest of the country followed their desperate struggle in breathless suspense. Westerplatte was on everybody's lips. Overnight it had become the symbol of national spirit, the spirit of defiance. Fight to the last man... don't surrender...

But now that Great Britain and France had declared war on Germany, Poland no longer ran the risk of becoming a huge Westerplatte herself. Rescue, powerful rescue, was coming. For the first time in the last three days Warsaw relaxed a little.

But not so the German bombers. The blackout of the capital was not complete that night. Incendiary bombs had started big fires in the industrial districts and a huge red glow hung over the city.

CHAPTER 8

September 5: The Bank Evacuates

"GOOD MORNING, Mr. K."

No answer. Like a charging bull the boss rushed through the office, his forehead lowered, his rather protruding eyes almost falling out of their sockets, his face a deep purple hue. As he brushed past my desk I heard him muttering something to himself, something which sounded like: "Gone to pieces, gone to pieces." I could not make head or tail of what he meant by that, and as I followed him with wondering eyes he plunged into his office, and slammed the door behind him.

What on earth had happened to the boss? Had he gone mad? He had been absent from the office the day before, presumably the Board of Directors had sent him on some confidential mission out of town. He must have returned just now, his suit was rumpled as if he had slept in it. My curiosity was pricked and I went to Jan's room to investigate the matter. Jan, after all, was the boss's assistant, and he, of all people, would certainly know what had happened.

I found Jan at his desk, sorting papers. He was as cool as ever.

"Have you any idea what has happened to the boss?" I asked him. "He seems completely beside himself."

"Yes, I know, he just left my office a minute ago. Pretty ghastly experience he has been through, only this morning. He was returning from Piotrkow where he had taken a large amount of cash—fifteen million, I think it was—for the army. Midway between Piotrkow and Warsaw his train was bombed. Two people in the compartment next to his were killed, and several wounded. One of the carriages was completely wrecked. And as the terrified passengers left the train and hid themselves in the ditches, the enemy plane returned once more and strafed them with machine gun fire. Enough to unnerve anybody, I should think, don't you?"

I knew the boss was no coward. He had earned his commission in the Polish-Bolshevik war of 1919, and would have joined the army long ago if it were not for our Board of Directors who had claimed him from the military authorities as "a man whose services were indispensable to the Bank." Yet I could not help feeling rather shocked at the way in which the bombing had upset him. Was bombing and strafing really such a horrible experience, I wondered, or were the boss's nerves simply frayed with overwork and worry?

I meant to ask Jan whether he knew what Mr. K.'s cryptic utterance "gone to pieces" referred to. But before I had time to do so the telephone on the desk began to ring.

I watched Jan out of the corner of my eye while he answered the phone, trying to tell by the expression on his face who was calling him. It must be one of the big sticks downstairs, I decided, for Jan's mobile features had assumed a formal, extremely businesslike expression.

It was a brief conversation.

"I'll be right down, sir," was all I heard, and Jan replaced the receiver.

"I'm afraid I'll have to leave you now," he turned to me with his usual politeness. "The general manager wants to see me at once."

He was gone, and I returned to my room and my mystery story. For I had brought a crime book to the office that morning. It was Tuesday, the fifth day of the war, and I had already learned that there was no use pretending that we were doing any work at the Economic Research Department. It had become increasingly difficult to listen to British and French radio news on account of German interference, and besides, our listening-in was constantly interrupted by air raid alerts. As for the pile of July bank reports which still littered my desk, I could not even bring myself to lift a cover, they seemed so futile. What my office day, seven long hours, really amounted to was waiting for alarms. I decided that reading a good thriller might help to pass the time, and take my mind off the war. Nothing like a good murder to quiet overwrought nerves!

It did not take me long, however, to discover that I was unable to concentrate even on a crime book. Although the book I had brought with me that morning belonged to that type of criminal fiction in which the author considers a page wasted unless a good, bloody murder is committed on it, the story failed to captivate my attention. I felt restless, every nerve of my body itched for action. If only I could have walked for miles, lifted heavy objects—oh, I don't know—done something that would require tremendous physical effort...

But there was nothing of that kind to be done at the Bank, and I could not leave the office so, fretfully, I read on.

Before I got to the fifth murder (page seventeen), the door burst open, and Jan stood in front of me. The moment I saw him I knew that he was the bearer of some momentous tidings. His face was terribly serious, and his gestures jerky with suppressed excitement.

"Mrs. Langer, this is official," he said in a stiff, formal voice that was in strange contrast to the usual, bantering tone of our conversations. "The Bank is going to evacuate this afternoon...and if you wish to leave Warsaw, I can reserve a seat in one of the cars for you. Only one seat;

unfortunately we have not room enough for our staff's families. You would leave by nightfall. Only one suitcase per person is allowed. Could you tell me right away whether you intend to go or stay?"

"Look here," I looked straight into his eyes and grinned—I was not going to play up to his melodramatic manner. "You don't expect me to go and leave my mother and my children behind, do you? Why, the idea... Of course, I'll stay!"

Jan's hitherto tense face lit up suddenly with a broad smile. Once more he was his old self.

"Right," he said. "As a matter of fact I never expected any other answer from you. But I had to ask you the question just the same. Official inquiry. I have to make up the list of those who want to leave with the Bank. So I have to give everybody their choice."

"And what about yourself?" I asked. "Are you staying or leaving? And what about your wife and your little girl?"

"Oh, I was not given any choice, simply ordered to go. I'm leaving at three thirty this afternoon. My family is still out in the country, near Rowne, and I hope I'll be able to join them somehow."

He went into the next room. As he left the door slightly ajar I could not help overhearing my neighbor's answer to the proposal of leaving, and it made me smile.

"Leave today?" he said in his usual, drawling voice. "No, I could not think of it. Why, I have just paid three months' rent for my apartment, and I cannot let all that money go to waste. I'll stay."

I lit a cigarette, and considered the situation. So that was how things stood. The Bank of Poland, and most probably all government institutions, were being evacuated. I understood now what the boss had meant by "gone to pieces." He must have known about the evacuation of the Bank before any one of us did, and this knowledge, rather than the bombing, had so completely unnerved him.

For the evacuation meant that something had gone wrong, terribly wrong, at the front, and that Warsaw was going to be surrendered. Hitler's soldiers in Warsaw! The prospect was appalling. Still, even the Germans could do nothing to the civilian population, and women and children, in particular, would be absolutely safe. Besides, this was only temporary, the war was not over, and our army was sure to recapture Warsaw sooner or later, I was certain of that.

I would have to bring Mother and the children back to Warsaw, however. Aunt Flika's place was on the right bank of the Vistula, while Warsaw was on the left. What if the Polish army chose to hold the Vistula line? They had already done it once during the Bolshevik war in 1920. I could not run the risk of being cut off from my family. Perhaps Dan could lend me his car again? I phoned the Embassy, then Dan's house, and learned that he had left Warsaw an hour ago. So the Embassies had already left . . . Well, things being what they were, Mother and the children would have to wait till tomorrow. I could not possibly go and get them this afternoon, I was on night duty at the Bank.

Having thus decided my personal problems, I went downstairs to see what was going on. The fact is I could not keep still.

The inside of the main building looked funereal. The long, broad corridors and huge halls were dotted with small groups of people, talking in low tones, their faces mournful and set. Messengers dragged big wooden crates and steel filing cabinets. Every once in a while the secretary of some member of the board rushed by, carrying a sheaf of papers and looking terribly important. Somehow those young, smartly dressed men always managed to convey the impression that the fate of the Bank itself depended on them.

I glanced through a window and saw that the usually empty courtyard was now packed with cars, small and large passenger cars, trucks, and two of my buses, the red street buses I had missed so much in the last few days. So that was the task they had been put to, the evacuation of Warsaw! And I had thought them at the front, moving transports of soldiers. Well, this evacuation was not much safer; they ran a pretty heavy risk of being riddled with machine gun bullets. I recognized the buses only by their make, for they were not red any longer, but covered with a fresh coat of field gray paint. I also noticed that the covered trucks were decorated with green twigs, as if returning from a happy picnic in May. There was something pathetic in this war camouflage, so strongly reminiscent of the old, carefree days.

As I wandered idly from group to group along the corridor, everybody I knew asked me whether I was staying or leaving. This, apparently, was the chief topic of conversation. I also learned that we were going to be paid three months' salary that afternoon. This, of course, was tantamount to the cancellation of our respective contracts with the Bank, but it would keep us in funds for some time, and who could tell today what would happen three months hence?

In a corner I saw Jan talking to Tomek Malachowski. Indecision was written all over Tomek's juvenile face. Tomek was twenty-five and a Ph.D., but for all his brilliant mind he looked like a schoolboy. It was obvious that he was unable to make up his mind whether to go or to stay.

As I approached them, Jan was saying, not very helpfully, I thought, "...but whatever you decide you may be practically sure to regret it afterwards. That's what always happens in wartime. Those who stay always say later on, 'If I had only left...' and those who leave, 'If I had remained this or that would not have happened.' That's war."

"I just can't make up my mind whether to leave or to stay," Tomek turned to me, his black eyes full of anguish. "It looks as if every man of my age is escaping from Warsaw. Still, I hate to leave my wife and sister alone. I don't mind so much about my wife, she is as self-reliant as I am, she can manage any situation. In fact, I trust her more than I trust myself. But my sister is all in. Her husband has joined his regiment, and she was left alone with an eighteen-month-old baby. She was seriously ill this spring, and has never been very strong since. The poor girl seems to take this war pretty badly; she cries and doesn't sleep nights. It seems a shame to leave her in that state. What shall I do?"

He looked from me to Jan, as if asking our advice. But we did not dare to give any. One is only too ready to give advice where no responsibility is involved, but here too much was at stake. The poor boy would have to reach the decision by himself, and Jan quite bluntly told him so.

"By the way, Tomek," he added, "if you decide to stay, will you do me a favor? I am leaving my apartment completely unprotected, my wife has taken the maid along with her. Our most precious belongings, my wife's jewelry and suchlike, are already in a safe place. But I had no time to dispose of the silver. Would you take care of it? It's locked in the bedroom wardrobe, and the key is in the second right drawer of the little antique desk in the living room. There are some other things in the wardrobe, too. My wife has collected a lot of war provisions. I know there are a lot of candles, soap and chocolate on one of the shelves. I don't remember what else. But you can have it all."

I don't think I paid much attention to what he was saying. The whole thing seemed so trivial, yet somehow all the details of that conversation registered in my brain, to come back later, much later.

At that point an air raid alarm sent us all to the shelter. Although to the people living on the outskirts of Warsaw every air raid meant destruction and death, to those of us who lived and worked in the center of the city alerts had become a sort of routine nuisance. Not a single bomb had crashed so far on any of the central districts, and the sensation of imminent danger had worn off. But we still obeyed with docility the LOPP instructions and trooped into the shelter whenever sirens shrieked.

The big basement room was today more crowded than ever. Besides the familiar faces (the girl with an appetite was eating pears this time, I noticed), there were many people I had never seen before. I soon learned that they were evacuees from our western branch offices, who had sought refuge in Warsaw. Not for long, poor things, they would move east tonight with the rest of the Bank.

I was used to refugees by now, the streets of Warsaw were full of them. You could spot them at once by the way they were dressed, always slightly provincial, by their subdued manners, and above all by this bewildered, refugee look in their eyes. But, for that matter, all faces which surrounded me now bore that peculiar, lost expression. Even before leaving Warsaw my colleagues had "refugee" stamped all over their countenances.

I noticed in particular an elderly couple sitting almost in the middle of the room. I had never seen them before. The woman held a small traveling bag pressed closely to her breast. They did not talk to each other or to anyone else, just sat there, staring straight ahead, passive and resigned. I felt sorry for them, and as I passed them I sent them the brightest, most comforting smile I could muster. They responded at once. Both faces became suddenly alive.

"You don't seem much worried," the woman said, looking at me with a pale ghost of a smile. "Are you staying or leaving?"

"I am staying. I have two children, you see," I replied with a tinge of pride, as if having two children at such times was quite an accomplishment. I did not look very maternal, though, in my khaki uniform and with that new boyish bob of mine. "What about yourself?"

"We are leaving in an hour," the man answered.

"Don't worry. You'll be back here soon. This is a shifting war, our army is sure to recapture Warsaw soon."

"This is a shifting war" had become a sort of slogan with me that day. I kept repeating it to everybody, right and left, and I believed it, too.

The man did not say anything. He just smiled.

A minute later I saw one of the high officials of the Bank approach my new acquaintance and address him as "Mr. President." It was my turn to stare. So this was Mr. Byrka, the president of the Bank of Poland, the brilliant parliamentarian, the great power behind the stage of the country's finances, the man of whom everybody at the Bank spoke with awe...

I withdrew into a far corner and did not speak to Mr. Byrka again, but as the all-clear signal was sounded and we all left the shelter, I saw that both he and his wife were looking in my direction and smiling.

I helped Jan pack the office files. From now on he would be in charge of the Economic Research Department in exile, so he was taking the most important documents and a typewriter along. In no time our usually immaculate floors were all littered up with discarded papers and excelsior from the crates brought in by hurried messengers. The bang of the hammer resounded through empty office rooms, and the whole place became at once unfamiliar and desolate. As soon as the last lid was put on and nailed, the crates were whisked away, and Jan escorted them downstairs. I leaned through a window, and saw that some of the cars were already moving out of the courtyard, while other empty ones entered the Bank's gate. The evacuation had begun.

Half an hour later Jan returned to bid me good-bye. It was a brief farewell, and we both tried to be casual about it. But there was a catch in Jan's voice when he wished me good luck, and I felt a big lump in my throat when I told him that I wished him the best of luck, too. Whereupon he kissed my hand and was gone.

Now that Jan had departed there were only two of us left in the Economic Research Department: Lila, the secretary, and myself. Lila was busy with the payroll, while I answered the phone. For now, all at once, all the telephones in the Economic Research Department began to ring. People who once upon a time used to work at the Department wanted to know whether a seat could be found for them on the Bank's buses, others asked if the boss and Jan had already left, still others where so-and-so could be found. I answered all inquiries as best I could, running from room to room, from desk to desk, stumbling over discarded files. Pretty soon Lila called to me from her room.

"Will you do me a favor?" she asked. "I had an urgent phone call from Mother and I would like to go home for an hour. Could you take this over while I am away?" She pointed to the payroll and large stacks of banknotes lying on her desk.

"You are not leaving Warsaw, are you?" I eyed her suspiciously.

"Heavens, no, I'll be back within an hour. And you and I are on duty tonight, remember."

"Don't worry, I shan't forget it. Only don't be long now. It's already long past office hours, and I should like to see something of my own home before I return here for the night."

Twenty minutes later Lila called to tell me that she was not coming back to the Bank. With her mother and uncle she was leaving Warsaw in less than fifteen minutes. Could I manage alone?

"What about tonight?" I asked.

"Oh, you'll always find someone to help you in case of emergency. I really can't stay."

Thus I was left alone in charge of the empty shell of the Economic Research Department. Telephones continued to ring and people kept dropping in to get their three months' pay. In the courtyard below, the roar of departing motors had become almost continuous.

I had telephoned Roman's house that money was waiting for him, and he put in a short appearance to collect it. His ambulance (for he was driving an ambulance now) was waiting at the door. Roman, of course, was not going to leave Warsaw, but he looked tired and sad. Rose's baby had not arrived yet, and Roman hardly ever saw his young wife—he slept at the hospital and was on duty all day long. I promised to look Rose up and was rewarded with a grateful but rather pale smile. There was something so dejected in Roman's attitude that again I felt a lump rising in my throat. And as he bent over my hand to say good-bye, I was moved by a sudden impulse and kissed the smoothly combed top of his head.

Was I growing sentimental over this war business?

After the departure of Roman the office suddenly became very quiet. The telephones lapsed into silence, and as I checked the payroll I saw that there were only two more salaries to be paid. Both payees were at the front, but the wife of one of them lived in Warsaw and was sure to come for it, while the other was a bachelor and his family was in Posen. Posen was already occupied by the Germans; I would have to turn back his money to the cashier's office tomorrow morning. I wondered how long my colleague's wife would keep me in the deserted office waiting for her?

Outside, the sun was already setting, and a big patch of light on the whitewashed wall opposite my desk grew a deeper red every minute.

I fell into a sort of reverie but was soon roused from it by quick steps in the hall. It was my brother. Franek's face bore the same bewildered expression I had seen on so many faces that day.

"Listen, Sis," he began hurriedly, "I came here to ask your advice. Should I stay or go? All my friends are leaving, and the military radio spokesman, Colonel Umiastowski, you know, has apparently requested all men of military age to leave Warsaw at once. What shall I do?"

He paused and looked at me with his terribly earnest blue eyes, as if awaiting my verdict. But how on earth could I decide for him? I would not, dared not, take the responsibility. Still, he had come here to get my advice, and I could not let him down. I must help him to make up his own mind. If only Mother were here...

"To be frank, dear," I said after a moment's hesitation, "I really don't know what to tell you. I've been cloistered in this place all day long, and I have no idea what's going on outside. All I know is that everybody at the Bank is leaving. But at such moments, I think, the best thing to do is to trust one's own instinct. What is your hunch: do you feel like staying or leaving?"

"Leaving, I think."

"Well, go then. What route will you take?"

Apparently he must have given the idea of leaving quite a bit of thought before coming to the Bank, for he had his plans carefully laid out. One of our uncles had a place east of Warsaw, and Franek would try to reach it, walking if necessary. The trains that left the city, he told me, were more crowded today than those that had arrived in Warsaw in the latter part of August, and he had but a slender chance to get on one. Once at Biala, Uncle Marian would certainly supply him with some means of transportation to continue his eastward progress.

"I'll go as far as the marshes of Pinsk, if necessary. No motorized army will ever get there, and I have always wanted to see that part of the country," he added with a smile. "Tell Mother good-bye for me, will you?" He looked more serene now that I had helped him toss the coin. He embraced me, kissed me on both cheeks, and hurried away.

"Don't forget to take your warm sweater and woolen socks," I called after him. Why is it that in times of emergency women's minds automatically turn to heavy sweaters and socks for their men?

Franek's visit left me a little dazed. Things were happening too fast for me that day. Mentally and emotionally I was unable to keep abreast of them.

My last customer for the day, the girl whose husband was in the army, arrived finally. She was in a state of complete panic.

"I can't...I can't remain in Warsaw," she told me between sobs. "The Bank must find some way to get me out of here. My husband is a reserve officer, and if the Germans find out, they will surely kill me and my child." (The child was two months old.) "If the Bank authorities have any conscience at all they must take me along. Oh, please, tell them...They must..."

I tried to argue with her, to dispel her fears, but in vain. She would not listen. The Germans would kill her and her baby if she stayed, and that was that. At last, in despair, I gave her the money and made her count it. The effect was surprising. There must be something soothing in counting money, for by the time she finished it and stuffed the money in her bag, she had regained her composure, although she still insisted on leaving the city.

I promised to talk to the Bank authorities about it, and let her know the next morning. After she left, I locked up the office for the night and went downstairs.

In the courtyard men and women, dressed in coats and hats, stood in small silent groups, awaiting the departure of the buses and cars. Suitcases were piled high on both sides of the gate. Dusk was already falling.

I looked around for people I knew, and sighted the boss and his family standing by a car loaded with luggage. I walked up to bid him good-bye, and was asked by the boss to call his mother as soon as they departed and tell her that they were safely on their way. "The poor old lady is terribly upset," the boss told me.

He was right. The voice which answered, when half an hour later I dialed the number Mr. K. had given me, was old and shaky and broken by low sobs.

"Oh Lord," she kept repeating, "what will happen to them? What will happen to us, oh Lord?"

I told her all the comforting things I could think of. The evacuation was only temporary, her family would be back soon, this was a shifting war, and so on. The gratefulness with which she accepted my words was almost pathetic. She thanked me and blessed my soul at least a dozen times. But she was still crying when I hung up the receiver.

In the air raid shelter where I went to report for my night duties I found an argument in progress. With the Bank authorities gone, and morale badly shaken, the usual discipline had also disappeared. Nobody was going to take anybody else's orders. Sharp words and bitter remarks were exchanged. People's nerves were on edge today.

Disgusted, I withdrew into a far corner and plunged again into my crime story. I was sick of the whole mess. Sick of crying women, and of men with that lost expression on their faces, sick of smiling and telling people that this was a shifting war. A nice, bloodcurdling murder (the fifth victim of my book was strangled with barbed wire) was so much more cheerful than an evacuation!

A belated air raid alarm made me realize suddenly that in case of emergency I was the only girl of the first aid squad left at the Bank.

"Oh well," I thought philosophically, "I'll manage. After all, one is not the mother of two little rascals without learning how to attend slight wounds. And if anything serious happens we will have to telephone the doctor anyway."

But I could not carry the stretchers alone. So I asked one of the men who, blinking, had just come in from the darkness outside, to help me with them if need be. He looked a little scared, but promised his assistance. Fortunately, there was no need for it. I sat up until eleven, reading my book and listening to the rumble of cars departing under the cover of darkness.

Then I was told that there were army cots in the Foreign Exchange Department, and that I could go there and lie down. The big loudspeaker was certain to wake me in case of alarm.

I had a hard time locating the cots in the immense room; the windows were not blinded, and I could not switch on the lights. And when after a ten-minute struggle to unfold the cot (I could not find the fastener that kept it folded) I finally slipped off my boots and lay down, I became unpleasantly conscious of the fact that the room was two stories high, and surmounted with a glass roof. Imagine a bomb crashing through that roof... My capacity for sleep seems to be unlimited, however, so I soon fell into a heavy slumber.

The next morning I was up at six. In the courtyard the cars that were there the previous night had already departed, and a fresh line of empty cars awaited further transports. Very few people were as yet in sight.

At seven breakfast was served in the Bank's cafeteria, a defeatist breakfast consisting of dry bread and unsweetened tea. After that I wasted two hours waiting for the man in charge of payrolls; I had to return the salary of the man whose family was in Posen. The Bank was a dreadful mess that morning. Nobody seemed to know who was in charge of anything. And everybody was cross.

It was nearly ten o'clock when at last I returned to the Economic Research Department to change into my civilian garb and go home. I had not taken off my uniform for twenty-six hours. It was a relief to slip back again into my cool dress, silk stockings and light shoes. Yet, strangely enough, now that I was free to go home, I felt sorry to leave the office.

"You watch over this place," I told the green turtle on my desk. "I'll be coming back soon."

But I never did. The bomb that ten days later crashed through the hall in front of the boss's room made the passage to my room inaccessible. For all I know the green turtle is still there on my desk, waiting for me, watching over unreviewed bank reports of July 1939.

Chapter 9

September 6: Mortal Fear

THE BRIGHT noon sun made me blink as I emerged from the dark, stuffy little station into the open of the railway platform. The train that was to take me to Mother and the children was late, and the station crowded.

Harassed-looking housewives accompanied by large broods of unruly children, pale-faced clerks, schoolboys in their uniform caps, peasant women wearing shawls thrown over their heads and carrying enormous baskets and milk cans, thronged the narrow platform—the usual humble crowd of a small suburban line that ran parallel to the river, from Otwock, twelve miles south of Warsaw, to this little wooden station called "The Bridges" (for it was located directly under the oldest Warsaw bridge over the Vistula). From here the line continued to Jablonna, twelve miles north. The trains that ran on the narrow tracks were brave survivors of the era of horse-drawn streetcars, a line of miniature wooden cars pulled with a great show of puffing and rattling by a funny little engine which long ago should have found its way into a museum, and was commonly and fondly referred to as "the Little Samovar."

The day was unusually hot for September, and the deep blue sky absolutely cloudless. No, it wouldn't rain, it would never rain again. I felt depressed and weary; the tension of the preceding twenty-four hours was beginning to tell. Idly I gazed at the bridge, almost overhead.

At long last the train from Otwock puffed and rattled its way into the station, and immediately began to spill its contents onto the platform—an unbelievable stream of humanity, mostly Jewish (for Otwock was predominantly a Jewish resort), trunks, huge bundles of bedding, baby carriages, tubs, wicker baskets filled with kitchen utensils. Evidently the population of Otwock, which for the last three days had been a favorite target of German bombers, was running for safety to Warsaw. This was strange, considering how many thousands of people were only too eager to leave the capital and at this very hour were probably thronging the east-bound trains.

In no time the narrow platform, already crowded with those who like myself waited to depart in the direction of Jablonna, was swamped with the new arrivals. A heavy wicker basket nearly knocked me off my feet, and as I struggled to recover my balance, a wooden box came in painful contact with my shins and made me swear under my breath.

Suddenly I saw a sight that instantly made me forget the indignity of a crowded railway platform. Out of the nearest car a little yellow stretcher was carried, and on it lay the small motionless figure of a child, all covered with bandages. It might have been Ania's age, four years at the most. I could not see the face, only tiny bloodless lips and a small, pointed chin showed from under the bandages. This was the first war victim I had seen and it would have to be a child. Ania's age, too...

As my eyes followed the little yellow stretcher quickly disappearing in the crowd, the stationmaster yelled "All aboard." A bottleneck had formed at the wicket gate, and he apparently wanted to get rid of at least the departing crowd, for once we climbed into the carriages the train did not show the slightest intention of proceeding on its way.

I found a seat near the window. Opposite me sat a pale, slender girl, dressed in a purple blouse and a navy blue skirt. The combination of colors was hideous, but there was something strangely appealing in the girl's black, moist and slightly slanting eyes, reminding me somewhat of a deer. We quickly exchanged smiles, in manner of introduction, and plunged into conversation. The war had abolished any barrier between strangers.

I soon learned that the girl had been working in a munitions factory at Grochow. She was married, but her husband was in the army. Her factory had been evacuated, like my bank, and she was leaving Warsaw to stay with an older sister who had a large family and a small house just outside the city limits.

"I am not coming back to town. Not if I can help it. Warsaw has become a hellish place. Day before yesterday we were all talking and laughing at the office, not paying much attention to the air raid alarm. You know how it is, one gets used to it. Suddenly a bomb struck the building across the street. We all fell off our chairs, it just threw us on the floor. And afterwards... You see, the bomb hit the elevator shaft, and people were just riding down to the shelter. Fourteen killed. I've seen them..." She shuddered. "No, I am not coming back!"

She was terribly concerned about the political situation, too. It was the end, the end of everything. In five days the war had been lost.

"Not at all," I told her and proceeded to develop my shifting front theory. She drank my words with avidity.

"I am terribly glad I met you," she told me afterwards. "I hope you are right, in fact I believe you are right. If only everybody believed it, perhaps things would not be so bad."

"That's just the point. That's why I think that it is my duty, and your duty, and everybody else's duty to tell

From the collection of Stefan Mucha

The Little Samovar.

Dive-bombing German Stuka.

people we meet that everything is not over, that the war will continue, and we will win it!"

(Well! I suddenly reflected with an inward smile, doesn't this sound like good old, typical propaganda!)

But propaganda or no propaganda this train had no business to stand here as if it were never going to start. What were we waiting for anyway? If the train had started at the usual time I would already be with Mother and the children.

Suddenly sirens began to wail. This meant another half hour of delay. The train could not depart while an alert was in progress.

I was so sick of waiting that I had forgotten that an air raid may mean something more than mere waste of time.

Even before the sirens had ceased shrieking, anti-aircraft guns began to bang away somewhere quite near us, and planes appeared high in the sky. The girl and I leaned out of the window to count them. Ten, twelve, fourteen. Yes, fourteen. Little clouds of white smoke began to rise in their direction, and suddenly one of the planes plunged into a mad dive.

"It's a hit! It's a hit!"

In wild joy we rose from our seats and clapped our hands. The plane was rapidly growing larger as it approached the earth. Where would it fall? Suddenly I saw a small shining point detach itself from the falling craft and at the same time the plane suddenly turned its nose upward. Holding my breath in terrible suspense I watched the bomb fall. A geyser of dust, smoke and debris rose high into the sky, and a fraction of a second later we heard the deafening sound of the explosion.

"They are bombing!" someone yelled in the back of the car. "They are bombing the bridges!"

Good Lord! We were right under the bridge.

"Let us pray," my companion said with such compelling authority that everybody in the car obeyed her command. Kneeling on the floor, we started in very loud voices to drown the noise of the motors:

"We fly to your patronage, O holy Mother of God..." (The planes were diving directly over our heads now, and their terrific noise shook the wooden carriage. I felt my cheeks grow cold, my eyes dilate.) *"... despise Thou not our petitions in our necessities..."* (My heart was racing, and pounding, pounding.) *"... but deliver us from all dangers..."* (Through the open window I saw another plane dive and drop its bomb. Crash! My heart was surely going to burst!) *"O kind, O sweet, O holy Virgin Mary..."* (Across the aisle I could see an old peasant woman crying. Tears were streaming down her ash gray face, and her tightly clasped hands were shaking. Oh, my heart!) *"Have mercy upon us..."* The deafening roar of the planes was drowning the words of our prayer. I could not stand it any longer! Oh God! Let him drop it and get it over with—

Crash! Crash!

We had stopped praying. In mortal terror we waited for the third crash that would put an end to this agony... But it did not come. Instead the noise began to recede, the roar fell to a drone... Somewhere in the distance the antiaircraft guns were still barking, and then their sound too trailed off into silence. The raid was over. Half a minute later the broken wail of sirens proclaimed the all-clear signal.

A little shakily we got up from our knees and resumed our seats.

"It was my first one," I said somewhat apologetically to my companion.

"Yes, I know," she nodded sympathetically. "Isn't it horrible?"

It was. I had never experienced mortal fear before, and I had not dreamed it could be that bad. My heart was still pounding.

We did not feel much like talking now. Just sat there, waiting for the train to depart. I was growing terribly sick of the sight of the wooden station building, the narrow platform, the bridge almost overhead... Let's start, let's start! What were we waiting for, anyway?

And then once more the sirens began to shriek. Oh God, no! Not again...!

We crouched in our seats.

"You damn fools! What are you waiting in those wooden boxes for?" the stationmaster, hurrying along the platform, his red cap all askew, yelled at us. "Get off the train and go to the shelter!"

"Where is the shelter?" I called back.

"There," he pointed. "Hurry, hurry!"

Precipitately we climbed out of the carriage. The sirens continued to wail, but there were no planes in sight—yet. A little further down the platform a small wire gate led into a sort of garden in which an air raid shelter had been dug out, the same kind of zigzagging trench as the ones at which I had been working only a week before. Apparently there had not been time enough to finish it, for the dugout was uncovered.

The ground on this side of the river was sandy, and as we descended the few steps that led to the shelter our feet sank into fine sand. Little cascades of sand kept falling from the walls every time anyone moved. "If a bomb falls anywhere near, we will all be buried alive," I reflected gloomily. The open blue sky above our heads worried me, too. That's where the bombs would come from. In the train at least you could not see the bombers diving right over your head, you just heard them. Here you would see death coming...

The narrow dugout was already crowded, and people still kept arriving. "Move on, move on," a man's voice called somewhere behind me. "Let those in the front advance as far as they can." I tried to press a little further but it was no use trying; we were packed as tight as sardines in a can.

"Look here, Madam," the same man's voice continued, "you cannot take suitcases into the shelter. There isn't room enough even for people. Give it to me, I'll put it outside."

"No, no," a shrill woman's voice protested. "I can't part with it. All my valuables are in there. Let me keep it here."

"Human life is more precious than your valuables," the man's voice was stern. Despite the protests of the owner the small suitcase was hoisted out of the dugout.

I had lost sight of my train companion, and felt strangely lonely among those unfamiliar faces. In front of me a broad, middle-aged woman wiggled constantly, while at my back a twelve-year-old boy kept poking with his finger at the sandy wall, sending down at every stroke little rivulets of sand.

"Stop destroying this shelter," I admonished him crossly over my shoulder. Sand was getting into my left shoe.

The noon sun beat hard upon our heads as we waited. The bombers were slow in coming this time.

At last we heard the ominous drone of the motors, the quick staccato of the anti-aircraft fire, and a moment later the fearful roar of the raiders was upon us. We ducked, almost lying on each other's back.

Vrrrrrrrrrr...!

Terror, mad terror, once more clutched at my heart. I felt I was dying, dying of fear...

But the agony lasted only a few seconds. Then, quite suddenly, something inside me went numb, my mind turned completely blank. I didn't care whether I lived or died.

I had forgotten the bombs. All I was conscious of was the wild throbbing of my heart, and the terrific roar overhead. Those two sensations filled my whole being, nothing else existed. I tried to concentrate on the roar, for my heartbeats were becoming more painful with every second.

Almost unconsciously I lifted my head, saw a column of dust and smoke rise on my left, heard the muffled sound of an explosion and ducked again. Two more explosions followed.

Vrrrrrrrrrr...!

I put a hand to my side and pressed it hard. But it didn't help. My heart continued its wild gallop.

What was that? My strained ears became suddenly conscious of the decreasing volume of the noise overhead. It was fading, fading rapidly.

Silence, the blessed, sun-drenched silence of the noon hour was settling once more upon the world. But we could not believe it. We just couldn't. Nobody in the shelter dared to stir, although we suddenly became aware of the discomfort of our precarious positions.

Not till the all-clear signal pierced the air, in what seemed to me a triumphant fanfare, did we scramble to our feet, straightening our bent backs and brushing our sand-covered clothes.

Did I say that the day was hot? I found myself shivering with cold as I followed the crowd back to the railway platform. My knees felt so weak that they hardly seemed able to carry the weight of my body.

I found the girl in the purple blouse standing in front of our railway carriage, waiting for me. I was terribly glad to see her again, by now we had become old friends.

"Does my face look very green?" I asked her with a feeble attempt at a smile. For a second she eyed me critically.

"No," she said. "You look exactly as you did before. I think you are very brave."

"Heavens, no!" I protested vehemently. "I feel a terrible coward."

I did. The experience I had just been through was not only horrible, it was ignominious, humiliating. No decent human being had any right to be as scared as I had been only ten minutes before. "A fine hero I would make if circumstances required it," I thought bitterly. "Weak knees, a thumping heart and a mind that goes blank. Pooh!"

We returned to our seats. A miracle evidently had happened, for no sooner did we reach them than a whistle was blown and the train began to move. No more waiting this time.

We advanced so slowly, it seemed as though the Little Samovar was cautiously feeling its way, afraid that the narrow rails might suddenly fail its wheels. The first crater gaped only three yards from the tracks, as soon as we passed under the bridge. A half-overturned telegraph pole hung perilously over our heads, but the tiny train managed to sneak under it. A little further a bomb had destroyed part of the Zoo enclosure. How, I wondered, did the wild beasts take the bombing? We passed two more craters in an empty field; not much damage here. But as we neared the railway bridge we saw small groups of khaki-clad figures hurriedly working with spades on the steep slope that led to the bridgehead.

"Look to your right," called the girl. "A bomb has hit the army barracks."

So it had. One of the wooden buildings that stretched in a long row on the right of the tracks was but a sad mess of sharp splinters wildly pointing skywards. Two soldiers were running in the direction of the ruin, carrying empty stretchers.

Now that we had passed the railway bridge the train began to gather speed. Both the girl and I heaved a sigh of relief and settled back in our seats.

"I am certainly glad we are at last out of it," she said.

"Same here. The only thing that worries me is that I'll have to come back on this line tonight. I hate it."

"You are not coming back, are you?" she looked at me with such a horrified expression that I could not keep from smiling.

"Oh yes, I am." I explained about Mother and the children, and my plan to bring them back to Warsaw now that the capital was going to be surrendered.

"But you can't do it. You can't," she insisted. "You have no right to bring your children into this inferno. Please, please, promise me you won't return to Warsaw." She had grabbed my hand and her moist deer-like eyes looked into mine with such deep concern that I simply could not resist their plea, and promised to think it over.

And when a minute later the train stopped at a small wooden shack marked "City Limits" and the girl left the train, I suddenly felt I was losing a friend. She waved to me from the platform.

"Don't go back, remember," she called as the train moved slowly on.

I didn't know her name. I was probably never going to see her again. But we were friends. Real friends. Or rather... what do you call it?

Oh yes—front comrades.

CHAPTER 10

At Aunt Flika's

ANIA, WHO was playing on the wide lawn in front of the house, was the first to greet me, when weary and dust-covered I arrived from the station.

"Mommy!"

She ran across the grass, which was beginning to turn yellow, as fast as her short, fat legs would permit and threw herself into my arms.

It was good to hold that energetic, warm, small body tightly in my arms, feel the velvety cheek against my own. The picture of the yellow stretcher with the tiny motionless figure was still haunting me.

But Ania, her effusiveness satisfied with one big hug and half a dozen kisses planted indiscriminately upon my dusty face, came right down to business. She wriggled herself out of my arms and grabbed my hand.

"Come and see the kittens," she ordered.

"Wait a minute, wait a minute, Ania."

For now George had emerged from under the chestnut trees, and he too was galloping across the lawn in our direction.

"Mommy!" he called with a note of triumph in his voice. "We have an air raid shelter here. A real dugout, like the one you and I were working on in Warsaw." (I had taken George once to help with the digging, and he was very proud of it.) "Only it's much more comfortable. Come quick. I'll show you."

"I will, darling, but let me first say hello to Grandma."

Down the path that led to the nearby church I saw Mother's tall black figure, leaning on a stick, advance rapidly toward us.

"What a nice surprise," she called gaily. "We did not expect you till Saturday." I ran to her, and kissed both her hands.

"Oh Mother, Mother dear! It's good to see you all again. I came here to take you and the children back to Warsaw, but I got into an air raid and — "

But Mother did not let me finish the sentence. Her face beamed.

"I am so glad you decided to take us back to Warsaw. Perhaps I am getting senile," she smiled, "but I miss my home dreadfully here, even though Flika is simply wonderful to us. And here she is," she added hastily as Aunt Flika, evidently attracted by the noise of our greetings, appeared on the porch. "Let's go to her."

We all sat on the long white bench which faced the lawn. I was terribly glad to see them all again, yet somehow I felt a little out of tune, a little lost and bewildered, as one does when returning home after a long absence. Yet it was only three days since I was here last.

No one except George seemed in the least impressed with my bombing experience. After all it was wartime, and everybody was expected to go through it sooner or later. The essential was that I had escaped without a scratch. As for George, he wanted to know all about it—what did the bombs look like, did the bombers shut the motor off when they dived, at what distance from the ground did they release the bombs?

Ania had completely lost interest in our grown-up conversation and was playing with the two kittens that had followed Aunt Flika out of the house.

"Tell us the news," Aunt Flika asked with eager curiosity. "What is going on? We are completely cut off from the world here. No mail, no newspapers in the last two days. And the old radio set broke down. It would, precisely at such a time. How is the war situation?"

I told them all I knew. Aunt Flika was terribly upset by what she termed "the complete collapse," but Mother was chiefly concerned with Franek's flight.

"Why did he do it? Did he really have to leave the city? Why didn't you tell him to come here first, we would have talked the matter over?" Mother's voice sounded grieved.

"Oh Mother, everybody was in such a hurry to leave Warsaw yesterday. And this place seems sort of out of the way for anyone who tries to evade the Germans. Franek wanted to be on his way as soon as possible." I tried to explain, for I felt that Mother held me to some extent responsible for my brother's rash departure.

But all she said was: "Well, what's done is done. No use discussing what might have happened. All we can do now is to pray to God that no harm befalls him."

This, with Mother, was not a figure of speech. Mother, whose faith was as simple as it was deep, prayed for people, as she mended their socks—with the same feeling of doing something for them. And when she promised, "I'll pray that you should succeed in this," you actually felt that she was helping things to go right for you.

"Do you know," she turned to Aunt Flika, dismissing the subject of Franek's flight, "that Rulka came here to take me and the children back home?"

"Nonsense," Aunt Flika answered with her usual vivacity. "It's much safer here. Why don't you all stay till this thing blows over? You know how I love to have you here. The only thing that bothers me is the fact that I can't give you the hospitality I'd like to. Every day quartermasters come here to commandeer foodstuffs, and I haven't stored many provisions anyway."

"You see, you see," Mother broke in, "and we have provisions in Warsaw. Why should we eat yours?"

"You and your provisions!" Aunt Flika laughed scornfully. "A dozen cans and twenty pounds of sugar! You better stay here, I tell you."

"It's for Rulka to decide."

But I did not feel equal to any important decision that afternoon.

"Thanks, Auntie," I said. "I left Warsaw with my mind all made up to take the family back to town. But this bombing gave me a bad shock. I really don't know whether we should stay or go. So, if you two don't mind, I'll spend the night here, and tomorrow we will decide one way or another."

But the next morning, even before I had time to make up my mind, Aunt Flika's manservant who had been sent to the station in search of newspapers returned with the news that trains no longer ran from Jablonna to Warsaw. A bomb had destroyed the narrow tracks late on the previous afternoon.

"That settles it," I said, almost with relief, "we can't go back."

But Mother would not accept defeat.

"Why don't we hire horses in the village?" she suggested.

"If you wish," I answered dubiously.

Both Leosia and the manservant were sent to the village, but their inquiry brought no results. No one was willing to risk a trip to Warsaw. Even if they were not afraid of bombs, their horses on the way might be commandeered by the army. They could not afford that.

Nothing remained but to wait. Perhaps chance would bring us some unexpected means of transportation.

Days passed. Blue and golden days, with the sun shining bright in the cloudless sky, yellow leaves whirling slowly through the air, and the wide blue river flowing peacefully at the foot of the hill on which the house stood.

Most of the day I sat on the bench facing the lawn where the children romped and turned somersaults with gay peals of laughter. I tried to think and couldn't. My thoughts were like quicksilver. The moment I attempted to put my finger on them they would fall apart in tiny particles and run away. Useless. An old tune, so popular years ago, was running through my head with derisive obstinacy. "Blue Skies". . . I hated it! Because blue skies were all we had— blue, blue skies, with nary a cloud in sight—all that the Germans could wish for.

Oh yes. And blue birds—we had blue birds, too. At least four or five times every day they passed high over our heads, humming their infernal song. They flew in triangular formations, Warsaw-bound. Half an hour later they would return to the accompaniment of distant anti-aircraft fire.

Every time I heard the approaching drone I called the children and, holding them by the hand, I withdrew under the old poplar trees. As I walked across the lawn I could feel Mother's ironic smile following our retreat. Mother would not dream of leaving her comfortable seat just because a dozen or so German bombers were passing over her head. And she thought my precaution simply ridiculous. This made me angry.

"The trouble with you, Mother," I said accusingly on one of these occasions, "is that you have no notion of danger. I am afraid that if I take you back to Warsaw one of these days you are going to walk about the streets in the middle of the worst air raid. You are simply reckless. That's what you are."

"This is no way to speak to your mother," she rebuked me, and then added with a smile, "Now, look at me. Do I look a reckless figure?"

I eyed her critically. Well, no. With her pale face, finely chiseled features, and her austere black dress that had ignored fashion for the last twenty-five years and reached below her ankles, she looked like a fine old lady all right, but not exactly reckless.

"Perhaps you don't look it," I admitted, "but still you are. Remember the time during Pilsudski's coup d'état in 1926 when you went to church during the worst shooting in the streets? I was so furious when I found out about it that I ran after you. Bullets were whistling all around me and I kept repeating to myself, 'They will kill me. Serve Mother right. Serve Mother right. Why did she have to go to church. Why?' "

"It was silly of you. You should have stayed home. But that is beside the point. I don't see any reason why I should run away from planes which are obviously on their way to bomb Warsaw."

"They've bombed Konstancin, and Otwock and Wawer all right," I reminded her.

As a matter of fact it was not the Warsaw-bound planes I was so much afraid of as the returning ones. I had been told that the German bombers could not land without first releasing their deadly cargo. That's why if the anti-aircraft barrage around Warsaw should make it impossible for them to drop bombs on the city, they would drop them anywhere on their way back. Just to be able to return to their bases.

One heard so many stories these days! Newspapers had warned the civilian population that the German planes dropped, besides bombs and parachutists, poisoned candy, toy balloons filled with burning acid, and poisoned cigarettes. Even the brand of the cigarettes was mentioned, one of the cheap, popular ones, Klub. Of course, at the bottom of my heart I knew that this was nothing but crude war propaganda. Still, when it comes to one's own children, one wants to be on the safe side, and George and Ania were strictly forbidden to touch any unfamiliar object found on the ground. As for cigarettes, after two days at Aunt Flika's place my own supply brought from Warsaw gave out. I sent Leosia to the village store to get some.

"That's the only kind they have," she had brought me a package of Klubs.

"Now, you are sure you didn't pick them up from the road or something?" I asked her with a wink.

"Oh, no, Madam. The storekeeper took them out from a large stack behind his counter."

"Alright. We will see right away if they are safe."

I opened the package and lit one. The acrid smoke of cheap tobacco made me cough. I made a wry face.

"Judging by the taste they are certainly poisoned," I said with disgust.

George, who had gone with Leosia to the store and now stood in front of me, looked positively aghast.

"Oh Mommy, Mommy dear, please don't smoke poisoned cigarettes. You'll die. Don't. Oh, please."

Poor little Georgie! I grabbed him in my arms and explained that the cigarettes were not really poisoned, just bad.

"Why do you smoke them then?" he asked resentfully.

Why, indeed?

The children and I were not the only ones to seek the refuge of the poplar tree grove against the German raiders. The grove, Aunt Flika's greatest pride, covered over three acres and almost reached the waterfront. Two days after my arrival three riverboats moored alongside the grove under the huge branches which stretched far out over the water. The river, the captain of one of the boats explained, had become most dangerous. German raiders dropped bombs on the boats, or even swept down to strafe them with machine gun fire. This was a commercial line, and had no business being involved in war. So the Company had ordered him and his colleagues to go into hiding. This seemed a pretty safe place. He hoped the owner would not mind. No, Aunt Flika did not mind at all.

The narrow path that wound capriciously between the gigantic, moss-covered trunks was now constantly alive with small groups of sailors going back and forth to the village. Gay tunes of a Victrola[1] installed under a tree reached our ears as we sat on our favorite bench in front of the house.

The children and Leosia spent all their days at the river-front: the children inspecting the boats, while Leosia made sweet eyes at the sailors. She was a pretty thing with her naive hazel eyes and soft brown curls, and in no time the crews of the three boats were competing for her favors. For Leosia, I thought a little bitterly, this war had actually turned into a sort of jolly picnic, and I was sure she could not forgive me now my harsh order to leave her pretty dresses behind. Still, she seemed to do rather well with the four she had taken along.

No sooner had the sailors settled under the poplar trees than new faces began to appear in the grove. Refugees. They came from across the river in small rowboats, mostly men, but sometimes whole families with children and dogs. They camped in small groups under the trees, sitting and lying, eating provisions they had brought along. They never asked for anything at

---

[1] "Victrola" was a popular brand of phonograph record player manufactured by The Victor Talking Machine Company of the U.S.A.

the house except water, and never stayed longer than a few hours. Then sometimes they would recross the river, but more often continued on their way inland, eastbound. They never knew where they were going, just flying the menace of the advancing German army, but they brought news.

A big battle was in progress around Modlin, as the fortress was fiercely resisting the enemy's advance. So this accounted for the distant rumble of artillery fire we could hear even here! Two German tanks had broken through yesterday morning. They had passed on the road that led from Modlin to Warsaw (even from our side of the river we could see this road, a narrow, white strip) and had reached the outskirts of the capital. But here the poor civilian population met them with an unexpected reception. Men, women, even children, disregarding all danger, had thrown bottles of gasoline at the two tanks and succeeded in setting them on fire.

The brave people of Warsaw, it was just like them to do a crazy thing like that. Civilians against tanks! Our hearts swelled with pride. Barricades were being built on every road that led to the capital. Evidently Warsaw was not going to surrender. Thank heaven!

This was good news. But the refugees also brought horrible tales of bodies of women and children crushed by German tanks on overcrowded roads, of hundreds and hundreds of corpses lying in ditches wherever the German planes had swooped down to strafe fleeing crowds, of mothers carrying dead bodies of children shot in their very arms. Every time such horrors were reported I could see Mother's face wince. She was thinking of Franek, Franek, who at this very minute was probably tramping along some unknown, distant road, unless...

Mother never spoke of Franek now, but once she broke down and told me with a catch in her voice, "You know, I shall never forget the last time I saw him. That was only last Monday when he came here. We bade each other good-bye, and he promised to return in three days. I stood here at the gate post while he walked away toward the station. The sun was setting, and his hair had a golden gleam in it. And suddenly, as I looked at this tall, slim silhouette retreating rapidly, I . . . ," Mother's voice broke, ". . . some strange feeling clutched at my heart. I wanted to call him, and run to him, and hug him in my arms. I didn't do it, of course, but perhaps it was a premonition . . . "

I kissed her hand but couldn't find a word to say. She never mentioned Franek's name afterwards, but how she prayed! Every time we went to church together I watched her fine, white profile uplifted in prayer. The thin eyelids closed over her deep-set eyes, and her whole body was gently swaying to the inner rhythm of her prayer. The unearthly expression of her face made me feel almost uncomfortable. And when, the service over, she would reopen her eyes, there was in them a strange, lost look, as if she was returning from another planet and could not readjust herself at once to the surrounding world.

We spent much of our time in church. Every afternoon a special service for Poland was held, and all the village, the sailors, even the refugees came to take part in it. The little whitewashed church shook with our hymns, as if in defiance of the roar of the passing German planes.

Aunt Flika never went to church except on Sundays. Much to Mother's grief she maintained that praying was all right for those who had nothing better to do. Aunt Flika was busy. Her greatest concern right now was the fact that the plowing season was well on its way, and no one did anything about it. Fields lay neglected in the September sun, while the villagers stood on their thresholds and talked war.

"Why, the idiots," Aunt Flika fretted, "don't they know that their first duty is to the land that feeds them? War or no war, the land has to be plowed and sown. If it isn't there won't be anything to eat next year."

And setting a good example to the village she hitched the fat, twenty-two-year-old bay, the only horse that remained, to the plough, and proceeded herself to plow the ten acres of farm land that belonged to the property. I offered to help, but she pooh-poohed my suggestion.

"Do you know how to plow?" she asked me. "No? Well, then stay home or go to church with your Mother."

The next morning the whole village was out in the fields.

Sometimes among the civilian refugees who were now constantly crossing to our shore, a soldier would appear. To such soldiers Aunt Flika was unbelievably harsh.

"What are you doing here? Where is your regiment?" she would ask the man in a menacing voice that was in strange contrast with her tiny figure.

"I...I lost my regiment," the man would usually stammer sheepishly. "I am looking for it."

"The hell you are." Aunt Flika did not mince her words when she was angry. "You are running away from the enemy, that's what you are doing. No soldier has any business getting separated from his regiment. You report at once at Jablonna." She gave him the necessary directions. "Or I'll have you trailed by the gendarmes," she threatened.

Live soldiers were not the only ones to cross the river to our shore. One morning the body of a soldier with two wounds in his head was found in the bushes on the opposite shore and was brought over in a canoe. We all went to the funeral and followed the coffin, a crude, long box made of unpainted boards, to the little village cemetery overgrown with trees. Judging from the identification plaque found on the dead man's breast, he must have been a Little Russian[2] and come from some distant village in the marshes of Polesie.[3] His family would probably never learn where their son came to his final rest.

But our strangest visitor was yet to come.

One afternoon I sat on my favorite bench smoking. The hateful tune of "Blue Skies" was still humming in my head, and my thoughts were as elusive as ever. But the bench was a good observation point. The path that ran through the grove joined at the farther end of the lawn the road that led to the church and the village, and from where I sat I could see everyone who came or went to the river.

Suddenly I saw a large group of villagers emerge from the village end of the road. They seemed excited, they waved their arms and spoke in loud tones. Evidently they were headed for the house. My curiosity roused, I got up and went across the lawn to meet them.

"We've caught a monster, a wild beast," somebody called to me.

"It's a young bear," someone else added.

It was not a bear. It was a seal. How it ever got there was hard to imagine. It must have come from the Warsaw Zoo. But the Warsaw Zoo was ten miles away. The poor animal

---

[2] Little Russia (originally known as Little or Lesser Rus') was the name commonly applied to parts of modern-day Ukraine before the 20th century.

[3] Polesie or Polesia is one of the largest areas of swampland in Europe. Located mainly within the boundaries of present day Belarus and Ukraine but also partly within the territories of Poland and Russia, the swamps of Polesie are also known as the Pinsk Marshes, and the Pripet (or Pripyat) Marshes.

must have been crazed with fear to have found enough strength to travel that distance "on foot." Now I knew how wild beasts reacted to bombing. The poor seal was evidently exhausted, it lay limp in the arms of its captor, a sturdy peasant woman.

Aunt Flika was sent for and her advice sought. She decided to have the seal put in the fish pond at the far end of the vegetable garden. The seal, once in water, recovered strength enough to dive. The next morning Aunt Flika's manservant came to report that the seal had already eaten up all the fish in the pond. Obviously the exhausting march had not impaired its appetite.

While all this was going on, German planes continued to fly over our heads and the iron circle of war was apparently closing around us, for every day the rumble of artillery fire grew nearer and louder. Every night now a rosy glow lit the sky in the direction of Warsaw. And every night the glow grew larger, till at last it covered almost one third of the sky. Warsaw was burning.

And then, one evening as we sat on the porch waiting for the time to turn in—we were saving lights as the supply of kerosene was getting low, and there was no electric light in Aunt Flika's house—a blinding column of light rose in the direction of Warsaw and a terrific explosion rocked the house. We all jumped up, and Leosia broke into instant loud sobs. Leosia had the amazing ability to break into sobs at a second's notice. The children woke up, but they were not scared. They just called me to ask what was happening.

We never found out what the explosion was. We thought at first that one of the bridges had been blown up, but none was.

The shock, however, was too much for Leosia. The next morning she rose at dawn, and sailors or no sailors she ran to church to confess her maidenly sins.

From the collection of Stefan Mucha

"Every night now a rosy glow lit the sky... Warsaw was burning."

CHAPTER 11

Me, a German Spy?!

"I HAVE an idea," Mother said at breakfast one morning. "Now that we have the boatmen and their canoes here, why don't you take advantage of it? Perhaps you would be able to hire horses in the village on the opposite bank. If you find someone who would take us to Warsaw, the boatmen will take us and our suitcases across the river, and we could get to Warsaw that way."

"Don't be silly," Aunt Flika objected. "What do you want to send the child across the river for? There is constant shooting on the opposite bank, and everybody is running away. You don't want her to get shot, do you? Oh Iza, Iza, when will you at last make up your mind to stay here till the end of this war?"

But that was exactly what Mother did not want to do. In fact, she was more determined than ever to return home as soon as possible. Why, only the day before she had suggested to me that we should all go back to Warsaw on foot! How she expected Ania and herself, after the serious operation she had undergone only two years before, to walk ten miles was a mystery to me. But Mother never stopped at any obstacle.

"Alright, Mother, I'll go," I said meekly. I was still dreading the return to Warsaw, but I could not resist Mother's indomitable will.

Leosia was sent to the grove, and in less than ten minutes she produced a rowboat and a grinning, tan-faced boatman, oars in hand.

"It's awfully nice of you to take me across the river,"

I told him as I settled down in my seat and he pushed the boat away from the shore.

"Not at all, not at all," his white teeth flashed pleasantly in his brown face. "I have my own errands on the other side, too. The village store is out of sausages, perhaps I'll be able to get some across the river. Newspapers, too. And beer. A sip won't harm me, I'm sure."

I offered to pay for the beer.

The boat was silently gliding across the calm blue water. The sky was cloudless, and a bluish haze hung over the river in the direction of Warsaw. It had not rained for months now, and here and there sandbars lifted their lazy sun-bleached backs above the water level. The air was drenched with sunshine and calm.

Yet both the boatman and I incessantly scanned the sky.

"They like to swoop down and take aim at the boats with their machine guns," the boatman broke the silence, voicing our common apprehension.

"Yes, I know. What do we do, if they come?" I asked. "Jump in the water? I can't swim."

"It isn't deep here," he smiled. "You could easily wade across."

But no German plane appeared, and in less than ten minutes we reached the opposite shore. As I was getting out on the sandy beach I saw a man and a boy coming in our direction. They evidently were about to cross the river in the manner suggested to me only a minute ago, for they carried their shoes in their hands and their pants were rolled up far above the knees.

This bank of the Vistula was much lower than the one from which we came, and a high embankment ran along the river. Beyond it, perhaps a quarter of a mile away, lay the village. But as soon as we had climbed to the top of the embankment we found that we would not be able to take the shortcut. There was a road, right in front of us, leading to the Modlin highway, but a big sign at its entrance said: "No trespassing. Military site." An empty field fenced with barbed wire stretched to the right of the road, and way down, at the other end of the field, I could see two grounded planes hidden under a clump of trees. An air base.

We had to circle the field, but eventually we hit the Modlin road. A big sign at the entrance of the village told the name of the place. "Mlociny," I read. Mlociny, where Johnny had taken me out in his car! Was it only two weeks ago? Two months seemed more likely.

We soon found the village store and went in. I had no shopping to do, but the village store is usually the best information center. There were no customers in the store at this hour, and the fat woman who presided over the worn, wooden counter was not helpful. No, she did not know of anyone in the village who had horses for hire and would be willing to take us to Warsaw. People did not go to Warsaw nowadays. And those who went, went walking. There were barricades on the road.

I would not give up so easily, however. Perhaps a house-to-house inquiry would bring some results. I left my boatman to his beer, and went out. My companion promised to await me at the boat in an hour or so.

Outside, the main street seemed deserted save for a group of six or seven soldiers resting in the shadow of a tree in front of the red brick school building. Above their heads a radio set installed on the sill of an open window was pouring forth a steady stream of talk. The news, I thought, and quickly crossed the road to listen. It was not news, however, that was coming over the radio, but a long litany of names and personal information:

"Mary Zaleska advises her husband, Joseph, of Wloclawek, that she and her daughter Sophy are safely with her sister in Warsaw. Ladislaus Kuba of Radom asks for any information concerning his wife Adele and his three children, Barbara, Waclav and John, last seen on Tuesday, September fifth, on the Radom-Warsaw highway. . . " And so on.

It was a long and pitiful program. The radio was trying to help the refugees to locate their families. The war communiqués, one of the soldiers told me, would be coming in twenty minutes. I could not wait that long, so after exchanging a few remarks with the soldiers, I proceeded on my way.

I went from house to house, knocking on the doors. Nowhere did my knocking bring any response. The houses were empty. I noticed that in some of them the windows had been covered with boards. I understood now why the main street seemed deserted, the inhabitants had fled.

There was no use trying here. I turned into a side road and, walking between wicker fences, presently found myself in the real heart of the village. The houses along the Modlin road were for the most part prosperous-looking brick dwellings, but here the low, whitewashed, thatch-roofed cottages predominated. Each house had a tiny flower garden in front and an orchard in the back.

This part of Mlociny was not deserted either. Small groups of men and women, mostly women, stood in the narrow passes between houses, talking in low tones. They eyed me suspiciously as I passed. I stopped by two of these groups to ask about horses. They answered me reluctantly. No, they didn't know of anyone who owned horses and was willing to go to Warsaw. I knocked at a cottage door. A young girl opened it for me. She looked scared. All she said in answer to my questions was that the owner was away, and she didn't know anything. I continued to the next cottage.

This time it was a man who opened the door for me, a bewildered-looking villager of perhaps fifty, with ruffled hair and a deep-lined face. Here too, my call was obviously unwelcome. There was anxiety in the man's face as he gruffly answered my first question; his eyes kept evading mine and sliding over my shoulder, as if he were watching something on the road behind my back. And before I even had time to ask him another question, he slammed the door in my face.

What was the matter with those Mlociny villagers?

With a shrug I turned away from the door, and suddenly found myself facing a crowd of women brandishing sticks and pitchforks. Evidently they had silently followed me and were now blocking the path that led to the road. Twenty pairs of hostile eyes stared into my face.

A short, shrewd-faced woman with a heavy stick in her hand stepped forward and asked me in a menacing voice, "Say, you, what do you mean by snooping around this place? Wandering from house to house asking questions. And with a military gas mask, too."

With her stick she pointed to the mask flung over my shoulder. Of course it was not a military mask. It was the latest LOPP model for air raid protection workers, but the villagers of Mlociny could not be expected to be familiar with it.

So that was it. I had been taken for a German spy!

"I am not snooping," I answered in a placating tone. "I am just looking for horses to take me, my mother and my children back to Warsaw. I am staying across the river at T. with my aunt, Mrs. K."

152

On the other side of the Vistula everybody knew Aunt Flika; her name was equivalent to a password. But apparently her fame did not reach across the river, for the woman was unimpressed.

"That's your story. How do we know it's true? Show us your passport," she demanded.

"Certainly," I said with a smile, opening my purse. Ever since the war had started I never moved without my passport. But as my hand fumbled now in the bag it failed to grasp the thin, stiff cover. I opened the purse wide and looked inside. No passport. What on earth could have happened to it? And suddenly I remembered. Only this morning Ania had been playing with my purse. She must have taken the passport out, and left it on the table. I had not checked the contents of my purse before starting on this trip. I looked up now and saw those hostile eyes riveted on me, watching my every move.

"I... I am sorry," I stammered. "I can't find it... I must have left it home."

It sounded awfully silly, even to myself. There was a short pause, and then suddenly the woman's hand shot swiftly out and grabbed my right wrist.

"We arrest you," her voice sounded triumphant. "You are a German spy!"

Another hand, this one rather tremulously, took hold of my left wrist, and here I was, the alleged German spy, captive of the women of Mlociny! It was ridiculous, but it was not funny. I looked around at the faces surrounding me and there was hatred, implacable, blind hatred, in every one of them. The crowd was swiftly growing now. If somebody had thrown a stone...

Holding my wrist tightly, the woman who was the leader turned to her companions. "We will take her to the mayor," she announced. "He will know how to deal with a spy." It sounded ominous.

So we started in a big procession, I and my captors at the head, followed by the rest of the villagers, still brandishing their sticks and pitchforks. I walked fast—I did not want it to look as if the women were dragging me along—and I held my head high. But my cheeks were glowing. I had never felt so ridiculous in my life. Children were running after us, shouting "A spy, a German spy!"

We soon emerged from the side road onto the main highway. The soldiers with whom I had talked only twenty minutes before were still resting in front of the school building. "We've caught a German spy!" someone called to them, and they laughed aloud, but did not say anything.

Somewhere in the middle of the main street a man caught up with us. I recognized him instantly. It was the same man who had slammed the door in my face. He, too, was carrying a stick, and now took his place at the head of the procession, preceding me and my captors.

"This is unfair," I could not help reflecting with an inward smile, "after all, it was the women who had captured me. Why should he steal their show?"

At last we reached the village office, a white, one-story building. I was led inside by my two captors, the man with the stick preceding us through the door, while the rest of the crowd remained outside peering through the low windows. The room we entered was a typical village office with ordinances and posters hanging all over the whitewashed walls, and a high wooden counter which separated the officials' quarters from the outer office.

"Where is the mayor?" asked the man with the stick.

A young man seated at a desk on the other side of

the counter lifted a pair of china blue eyes from a sheaf of papers.

"The mayor went to Modlin," he said. "I am in charge of the office. What is it?" He rose from his chair.

"We caught a German spy. She was snooping around the village asking silly questions. Has no passport."

The china blue eyes scrutinized me for a few seconds.

"She looks German all right," the young man declared with conviction.

This was a little too much.

"No, I don't," I burst out with indignation. "I am one hundred percent Pole, and I look like a Pole. This is all a silly mistake." I proceeded to explain what had happened. But the young man was not impressed.

"How do we know your story is true?" he asked me.

"You have a telephone here. Why don't you call up the Manor at T. and find out who I am. Mrs. K. is my aunt."

"Sorry, the line is cut."

"What about Warsaw? I work at the Bank of Poland. They could identify me there."

"The line to Warsaw is cut, too."

I was at my wit's end. My only hope was that the boatman, not finding me at the boat at the appointed hour, would start a search and find me here. It must have been over an hour now since we parted at the village store. The young man, he was probably the secretary, gazed at me for a few seconds as if considering the situation, and then turned to a girl who all through our conversation had been typing behind the wooden counter.

"Miss Sophy, take this person into the mayor's room and search her."

At last the iron clutches of my captors released my wrists, and I followed the girl into a small office in the back of the building. The girl looked embarrassed.

"Will you undress, please?" she asked shyly.

"Certainly," I smiled at her. Now that the door had closed on my captors I had regained my composure. After all, the village officials could not shoot me without proper evidence.

As soon as I had taken off my blouse, the girl carefully examined my shoulders. I knew what she was looking for: bruises from parachute straps. A parachute opens with such a powerful jerk that the straps are bound to leave marks on the jumper's shoulders. Finding no damning evidence on my body the girl proceeded to examine one by one each of my garments, going carefully over every seam. I looked at her with open admiration. The civilian population all over the country had evidently been carefully instructed how to detect spies.

"Your shoes and stockings, please." She turned my stockings inside out, and finding nothing, took up my shoes. And here came the hitch.

My old sport shoes were of English make. Three years before, Olgierd had brought them from a business trip to London. As the girl tried to pull out the lining, to see whether there was any document or message hidden underneath, she saw the inscription on the inside label, "Regent Street." The "London" had been erased by long wear.

"Those are foreign shoes," she looked at me with sudden suspicion.

"Yes, English."

"How can you prove they are English?"

"The inscription is in English."

"Well, I don't know about this. I must ask. You can dress in the meantime."

She disappeared through the door which led to the outer office and did not return for over an hour. The whole village must have been pondering over my shoes. In the meantime I smoked the last cigarette I found in my purse, and then just sat there, in my stockinged feet, thoroughly bored and hungry. It was nearly three o'clock, the dinner hour was long over.

At last the girl opened the door and handed me my shoes.

"Those are English shoes," she announced as if I had not known it all along. "You better put them on and come to the other room. There is a man asking for you."

My boatman! I was in such a hurry that I didn't even bother to tie the shoestrings before I rushed into the outer office.

The boatman offered to vouch for my identity, but the secretary would not have it.

"The lady has been arrested and I have no right to release her before seeing her passport. Besides, she may get into trouble again on her way back."

Alright, the boatman would cross the river and return with my passport. I told him where the missing document was to be found, and begged him to hurry. I was getting pretty sick of the whole adventure.

Another hour of waiting. But now the secretary's attitude towards me had changed considerably. He asked me to sit down, and offered me a cigarette.

"Of course, if we have made a mistake we will apologize to you," he promised.

The waiting in the outer office was not as dull as I expected it to be. People came and went, asking questions, bringing documents to be confirmed by the office. A whole gallery of village types passed before my eyes. A tall man, he must have been a miller for there were specks of flour dust on his otherwise prosperous-looking suit, came in and leaned heavily upon the wooden counter. It was evident that he was an habitué, for the secretary got up from his chair and greeted him with a hearty handshake.

"Where is the mayor?" the man asked. He pushed back his cap and lit a cigarette with the air of one settling down to a bit of confidential gossip.

"Gone to Modlin. Will not be back till five."

"What did he go to Modlin for?"

"I'll tell you," the voice of the secretary grew confidential. "There was some monkey business again. This morning a messenger brought a written order to have the highway destroyed. You know, deep ditches cut across, all that. The order came supposedly from the General Headquarters in Modlin—it bore the seals—it looked all right to me. But the mayor is a smart guy. He would not obey the order till he had checked on it. He knows the commanding officer at Modlin so he called him up. And do you know what the commanding officer said?"

"What?"

"That the military authorities did not want to have the highway destroyed. They need it. The order was a fake. So the mayor went to investigate."

I had no time to listen to the rest of the conversation because at that moment the grinning face of my boatman appeared in the doorway. He had certainly made haste!

The secretary looked over my passport, and then returned it to me with a nod.

"It's alright. But still you have a German name." He was evidently going back to our old argument as to whether I looked German or not.

"You can have a German name and be a loyal Pole," I retorted. "Besides, this is my husband's name. My maiden name is Polish."

He was beaten.

"Anyway, we are sorry about the mistake we made," he said.

"Not at all," I was magnanimous now. "In fact, if you ask me, I have a deep admiration for those women who arrested me. After all, if I were a real spy I could have shot them, you know."

We parted with a friendly handshake.

The boatman had brought a friend with him, and now we were all three hurrying through the village. I was not tempted to linger in those streets which only three hours ago had witnessed the triumphant spy-procession with me taking the lead as the villain.

Once more we had to circle the air base, but before we had reached the river bank, the blue afternoon sky began to drone with German planes. And suddenly a terrific din of anti-aircraft fire burst all around us. We quickly took cover in a nearby grove of pine trees. Three little boys were already there, but as I soon found out, not for safety's sake. They were just playing hide-and-seek, and I had a hard time preventing them from running out into the road to observe the planes. The shooting lasted but a few minutes, and as soon as it was over I wanted to start out again.

"Wait a moment," the boatman stopped me, "shrapnel splinters will be falling now like hail."

We waited for another five minutes, I still fighting to keep the boys under cover, and then suddenly we heard a loud hiss, a metallic click and bang. Something had fallen on the hard road. It was too much for the three little boys and for myself, and we all ran out to take a look. It was a shrapnel splinter alright. At least six inches long, it had unpleasantly ragged and sharp edges. Two more splinters lay further down the road.

The little boys pocketed them with delighted shouts.

CHAPTER 12

Vadik

THE FAMILY had a big laugh over my "spy incident" as they called it, but Mother was disappointed. For, after all, once more I had failed to secure a means of transportation to Warsaw.

The next day, however, I was more lucky. Aunt Flika's provisions, some of them at least, were nearly exhausted. We used honey instead of sugar to sweeten tea and coffee, and were told to burn the lamp for half an hour only, when undressing, to save kerosene. Even salt had to be spared. None of these staples was to be found in the neighboring village store nor at the nearest railway stop. So I decided to take Leosia with me and walk as far as the next stop. It was a three mile walk, but it proved worthwhile. Not that the little store across the street from the depot was particularly well supplied. Most of its shelves were empty save for innumerable red packages of chicory, the favorite substitute for coffee. We got, however, ten pounds of flour, a package of candles and one pound of salt. No sugar.

"Come again Friday afternoon," the girl at the counter told us as we were loading our purchases in the big basket we had brought along. "I may have some sugar then. Mr. Skrzypkowski goes to Warsaw every Friday, and brings us groceries from there. Only don't be late or local people will buy up everything."

This was great news. Who was Mr. Skrzypkowski and where did he live? After securing the necessary information from the amiable store girl we went in search of our man. We did not have far to go. Mr. Skrzypkowski lived only a few houses away in a neat brick cottage. He turned out to be a jovial man in his early forties with a round red face, and shrewd squinting black eyes.

"Is it true that you'll be going to Warsaw Friday morning?" I asked, after telling him who I was and where I had come from. He, of course, knew Aunt Flika well. Everybody here did.

"To Warsaw? Sure I will," he answered, puffing his chest out proudly. "No one here," he indicated the village with a broad gesture, "would dare to go. They are all afraid of bombs. But not me. Business is business, I say. You've got to make a living even in wartime. Isn't that right?"

He was evidently immensely pleased with himself. Well, as far as I was concerned he was a hero. I felt about going to Warsaw pretty much as the villagers did. Obviously he was not a modest hero, but are all heroes bound to be modest?

Mr. Skrzypkowski was quite willing to take us to Warsaw, although he could not see why we should want to go there.

"You will not recognize the place," he assured me, "it's horribly destroyed." He spoke with such gusto about the destruction of the city that I had a slight suspicion that he was overdoing it a bit to impress his audience. It seemed as if every house that lay in ruins was a new feather in his cap, he, the man who went back and forth to the besieged capital!

He was starting for Warsaw very early on Friday, and therefore would not be able to come and get us at Aunt Flika's place the same day. He offered, however, to bring us to his village Thursday afternoon. We would spend the night there and start the next morning. This was Wednesday; day after tomorrow we would be back in Warsaw. One thing Mr. Skrzypkowski declined to tell me, and that was how much he was going to charge us for the trip.

"Don't worry, we will agree on that, lady," he assured me. But I did not feel so confident. I had heard about too many instances where horse owners in wartime asked sums even for short fares that ran into hundreds and thousands. What if Mr. Skrzypkowski should charge us more than either Mother or I could afford to pay?

It was with a strange mixture of exultation and awe that I walked back to Aunt Flika's place. Mother would be delighted, there was no doubt about it, and I was pleased to bring her the good news. And deep at the bottom of my heart I too rejoiced at the thought of seeing Warsaw again. I loved the old town and, like Mother, I had the feeling that once we were there everything would be alright.

But going to Warsaw was another matter. The prospect of entering the city under the threat of German bombers, finding our way through bomb-wrecked Praga,[1] crossing the bridge which in all probability was still the favorite target of Stukas, filled me with horrible apprehension. I had not yet recovered from the shock of my first bombing experience.

Mother's delight came up to my expectations entirely. She said she would go to her room and start packing at once, although, heaven knows, the few things she had brought along would not require more than twenty minutes to put away and we had more than twenty-four hours ahead of us. But Mother always believed in immediate action. Before going to her room, however, she told me her news.

"Do you know who is here?" she asked me. "Vadik."

---

[1] Praga is a district of Warsaw on the right bank of the Vistula River, while Warsaw's city center is on the left bank

Vadik was the son of one of her friends. "This morning, after you left, I was coming back from church, when quite unexpectedly an officer who was standing in front of the church ran to me and began to kiss my hands. I was startled, for I had no idea who it was. 'Don't you recognize me, Aunt Iza?' he asked. 'I am Vadik.' I had never seen him in a uniform before, and besides the poor boy looked terrible. He was dirty, and had not shaved for the last four days, he said. He was starved, too. Aunt Flika gave him a big breakfast and he is now asleep on the drawing room couch."

"What did he come here for?" I asked Mother.

"He brought a detachment with him. They are camping over there."

Mother's chin pointed in the direction of a cluster of maple trees on the other side of the lawn. Through the thinning yellow leaves of the surrounding shrubs I could see reclining khaki-clad figures and neatly stacked rifles. The stamping of hooves came to my ears, although I could not see the horses.

"It's good to see the regular army again," Mother said, and I knew what she meant. We had seen too many fugitive soldiers lately.

I did not meet Vadik till nightfall. All afternoon I was busy with the children, for Leosia, the fastidious Leosia who considered herself superior to any farm labor, had offered to dig potatoes for the soldiers' supper, and Vadik probably had his military duties to attend to. But after dinner, as we sat in front of the house, waiting as usual for the time to light the lamp and turn in, we saw a dark figure advancing across the lawn in our direction.

"Aunt Iza, are you there?" a pleasant low-pitched voice asked. "It's me, Vadik. Will you do me a favor? I brought you a letter. If you go to Warsaw will you call

Miss Mary K. and tell her to come to your house and get it? It's... it's very important for her and for me," he added hastily with almost boyish bashfulness. Miss K. was evidently his sweetheart.

"I'll be glad to do it," Mother said. "Come and sit with us. Here is Rulka."

I moved over to make room for him on the bench, and offered him a cigarette. But he declined to take it.

"That's practically the only thing we have plenty of in the army. We get two packs every day. You better take one of mine."

We lit our cigarettes and began to converse in low tones. The night was very still save for the distant rumble of artillery fire, and quite dark, even though the pink glow in the direction of Warsaw was quickly spreading over the sky.

I could not see Vadik's face, yet I was at once aware of a profound change in him. I had never known Vadik very well, but the little I'd seen of him left me with the impression of a languid young artist—Vadik was a painter—with a touch of the half-disillusioned, half-cynical man of the world about him. It was an altogether different Vadik that sat by my side now. There was a quality of simplicity and directness about him I had never suspected. He was friendly with an almost boyish friendliness that was most appealing.

In no time I found myself confessing the terror that had seized me during the bombing. I was still baffled by the intensity of feelings I had experienced at that time. There was nothing unusual about it, Vadik assured me, everybody feels the same terror when bombed.

"Don't I know it!" he said with a mirthless laugh. "I've been bombed eleven times within forty-eight hours. Nine times my company and I had to be dug out by rescue squads; I lost half of my men. It's a miracle I am still alive, a real miracle."

"Where was that?" I asked.

"Praga. You see," he continued, "I am a reserve officer, but I have a blue mobilization card, so I was never mobilized."

The holders of blue cards were supposed to report to their respective units on the third day of mobilization. By the second day of war, however (that was the third day of mobilization), the whole mobilization machine was completely disorganized, and that part of the plan was never carried out. Thousands of men awaited the blue posters, which would summon them to join their colors, in vain.

"Then came the fateful Tuesday when everybody was leaving Warsaw. By the way, do you know that it was I who called your brother and told him to leave? For myself I decided that I would rather fight than fly. So I put on my old uniform and went to report to the nearest infantry officer. I was given a detachment and was stationed in an orchard in Praga. For forty-eight hours we lived on green apples under constant bombing. That's when I lost half of my men. Then I was told to take the rest of my detachment and proceed in this direction, collecting fugitive men from other units as I went. Tomorrow we must be at Jablonna. The enemy has broken through and is advancing now on this side of the Vistula."

We knew that much; the artillery fire was coming now from that direction. I told Vadik about our intention to return to Warsaw, and he saw no objection to it.

"It really doesn't make any difference whether you stay or go back," he said. "There may be a major battle around here any day now, for all we know, and Warsaw is constantly bombed and shelled. The only advice I can give you is: whatever you do, for goodness sake don't flee. It's alright for a single man, but not for women and children. I've seen too many refugees. It's horrible. They start on their way decently enough in automobiles or horse carriages, with suitcases and all. And then they run out of gas, their horses are confiscated and they have to continue on foot. They leave their suitcases behind and within three days turn into the worse kind of tramps, barefooted, hungry, the children sick and dying, and all of them a constant prey to German bombers and machine guns. It's ghastly! Death is far better than such degradation."

For a minute he remained silent, and then got to his feet.

"It's getting late," he said. "I better go and see how my boys are faring. We are starting early tomorrow morning. Aunt Iza, you won't forget my letter, will you? And thanks for the comfortable nap on the drawing room couch. I certainly have not enjoyed anything as much in a long time. Goodnight."

With the easy gesture of the perfect man of the world he bowed over Mother's hand, raised mine to his lips, and vanished in the dark.

"What a nice boy," Mother said when he was gone. "Don't you think he is handsome too?"

"Well," I laughed, "I haven't seen much of his face tonight."

And I was never going to see it again. For the next day Vadik was killed. On his way to Jablonna, only two miles from Aunt Flika's house, a stray bullet got him. But we didn't learn about that till months afterwards.

CHAPTER 13

September 15: Home Again

MR. SKRZYPKOWSKI was as good as his word, and the following afternoon, Thursday, September 14, 1939, a long cart, driven by two fat horses and comfortably lined with hay, stood in front of the house.

We were not the only ones to leave. Mother's battle cry of "Let's go home!" had roused another set of refugees, a woman doctor and her two little boys. She was district physician of the local Sick Fund, and lived in the same village Mr. Skrzypkowski came from. They had arrived at Aunt Flika's place only three days before. Their little house built right on the highway had rocked constantly with explosions, and after four nights spent in a dugout she had decided to seek the refuge of Aunt Flika's giant poplar trees.

She was a brave little woman. Every morning, scared as she was of bombs, she set out on foot to make the round of her sick. But even so, her conscience was not entirely satisfied. What if anything happened to one of her flock of patients at nighttime? She wouldn't be there to attend the case at once. "I feel like a deserter," she told me once. Yet she was unable to make up her mind to leave the children and return to the house alone. One does not part with one's children at such times. Now, however, with us setting the example she decided to take her family back, too, and we were asked to spend the night at her house.

Aunt Flika was pretty disgusted with our departure.

"If you are bent on committing collective suicide, I can't do anything about it," she declared. "Just suit yourselves. I've never seen anyone as obstinate as your Mother," she added, turning to me.

"You don't have to tell *me*!" I laughed.

"And she's been that way all her life. Ever since we played together as little girls."

"Well, Auntie," I retorted, taking Mother's side, "if I may be quite frank, I don't think you are much better than Mother on that score."

"Who, me?" Aunt Flika exclaimed indignantly. "I at least am sensible."

I would not argue this point. Mother and Aunt Flika had a different kind of sensibleness, I guess.

Aunt Flika, however, had not much time to grieve over our inescapable doom. Two quartermaster officers had arrived that afternoon to commandeer grain, and Aunt Flika was busy fighting tooth and nail to save enough of her stock to last the household through the winter months and make spring sowing possible.

All the suitcases and bundles of our two respective groups were loaded on the cart, and Mother and the four children sat on top of them. The rest of us followed on foot.

The sun was already setting when we arrived at the doctor's house. The first thing that met our eyes as we entered the neat little apartment was a big radio set.

"Oh, a radio," Mother said delightedly. "Does it work? Let's turn it on!" Mother was a great radio fan, and for that matter, we were all starved for radio news. We tuned in on Warsaw and listened in silence.

It was horrible! A radio commentator had made a tour of all the fresh scenes of destruction and was now giving a colorful report of what he had seen. German bombs had struck one of the biggest hospitals that day, the Lord's Transfiguration in Praga, and the scenes that ensued were reminiscent of Dante's Inferno: sick and wounded trying to escape through windows; men with legs amputated only the day before, jumping out of bed and crawling along corridors; scattered bodies... No, it was too horrible!

But the next episode was even worse. A sixteen-year-old girl, Hanusia her name was, had gone out in the field to dig potatoes for the family. She was a pretty thing, with blue eyes and golden plaits of hair. She came out of the house confident and happy, humming a little tune. And then, as she was working in the field near Powazki,[1] a German raider swooped down from the sky and mowed Hanusia down with his machine gun. And there she lay in the open field, her basket half filled with potatoes, her golden plaits drenched with blood, her blue eyes still staring into the blue sky whence death had come...

It was too much. I could not stand it. I just couldn't.

"I can't listen to this stuff, Mother," I said. "I am going downstairs for a cigarette."

Outside the dusk had fallen, and only the usual curtain of reddish-gold light hung over Warsaw. The thunder of artillery fire seemed very close now, and with every explosion the windowpanes in the house tinkled slightly. A cold wind was coming from the direction of the river. I found myself shivering as I lit my cigarette.

I was depressed, terribly depressed. So this was the Warsaw we were going back to tomorrow. A Warsaw of fire and bombed hospitals, and youngsters killed in cold blood. I suddenly remembered what the girl with the deer-like eyes had told me on the train: "It is an inferno. A veritable inferno. You have no right to take your children there."

Oh, well, what was the use of backing out now? The war would get us anyway. I felt completely helpless. What ever made me believe that I and my family should survive this war? We would never be able to pull through it.

---

[1] A district of Warsaw northwest of the city center, which includes the Powazki Cemetery, one of the largest in Warsaw.

Somewhere inside me I could almost feel my soul tremble and shrink with apprehension and terror. In this darkness rocked by explosions, I felt small and lost and lonely.

But I was not going back upstairs, not now anyway. Let the man finish first with his tales of horror; I was not going to listen to any more of that!

I smoked one cigarette, and then another. I was on the point of lighting a third one, when I discovered that all my matches were gone. Reluctantly, I got up from the low fence on which I was sitting and went into the house. As I groped in the dark for the stairs, I heard the radio again. It was still talking, damn it!

But the moment I opened the door and silently sneaked into the room I noticed that it was a different voice that spoke over the radio now, a deep, friendly voice, one of those voices that go right to your heart.

"... And now that we have settled into this siege," it was saying, "what about opening a few cafés? Oh, no pastry of course; the flour we have is meant for bread, not for cookies. But a cup of coffee and some music wouldn't do us any harm. After all, we Varsovians love our afternoon demitasse, and we work hard, we fight hard, we deserve some recreation. And movies. I suggest that movies should be reopened, at least for an afternoon show..."

What was that? Who was talking about cafés and movies? I could hardly believe my ears. Here was someone who spoke in a perfectly normal, natural tone about perfectly normal, simple things as if life had not become one ghastly nightmare of fires and bombs and blood. Was there, could there be, any sanity left in the world after all?

"It's Mayor Starzynski," Mother whispered in my ear.

And the Mayor went on. In simple words, in this deep,

The body of sixteen-year-old Hanusia Mika, machine-gunned by a German fighter plane while picking potatoes in a Warsaw field, lies blood-soaked before her grief-stricken ten-year-old sister, Kazimiera.

From the collection of Zygmunt Walkowski

Stefan Starzynski (January 19, 1893 — October 1943)

Stefan Starzynski, the popular mayor of Warsaw, refused to leave the city with other state authorities and diplomats on September 5, 1939, and later became the symbol of the defense of Warsaw during the siege. After the Germans entered the city on September 28, 1939, Starzynski was allowed to continue his service as the mayor of Warsaw. He became one of the secret organizers of Sluzba Zwyciestwu Polski, the first underground organization in occupied Poland which eventually became the Armia Krajowa (AK or Home Army).

On October 5, 1939, Mayor Starzynski was arrested by the Gestapo and, together with several other prominent Varsovians, held hostage as a guarantee of the safety of Adolf Hitler during the German victory parade held in the city. The following day all of them were released.

On October 27, 1939, Starzynski was again arrested by the Gestapo and taken to Warsaw's infamous Pawiak prison. A few weeks later, in December, Starzynski refused to accept a rescue plan, claiming that it would be too costly to those involved in his escape. The final fate of Starzynski, mayor and hero of the Siege of Warsaw, remains unknown. According to the most probable version, he was transferred to a prison in Berlin and from there to Dachau concentration camp where he was executed in October 1943.

172

jovial voice of his, he discussed the daily problems of the besieged capital; he told of all that was being done for the defense; he admitted the difficulties, but said they would be overcome; he told of the splendid job done by the army, of the enthusiasm of the civilian population.

And as he talked the curtain of horror that all that afternoon had clogged my brain began to lift. The world was falling into focus, things looked normal once more. Not only that, little shivers of enthusiasm started to run up my spine.

And then Mayor Starzynski said something that made me sit up straight in my chair.

"I am addressing you now," he said, "all those who are outside of the capital, and cannot make up your mind whether to return or not. Come back, I tell you. Come back. We need you. We are working, we are fighting, we are doing our best to push back the enemy who so ignominiously has invaded our land. And we shall win! But we need your help. We need everybody's help. Every able-bodied man and woman is welcome in Warsaw. Come back!"

Suddenly, a strange feeling of elation seized me. Life once more made sense. It was alright. Fires, bombs, death itself were alright. They were all part of the splendid job of defense. And I, like everybody else, was asked to join in it. And I was going to. Yes, I was going back to Warsaw, going back as fast as Mr. Skrzypkowski's fat horses would carry me!

The world was still rosy with sunrise and silver with dew, when the next morning we started on our return journey. This time Mr. Skrzypkowski had brought around not a cart, but a comfortable open dray on rubber-tired wheels. This dray, he explained, was used in normal times to transport drugs and cosmetics from a nearby factory to the storage house in Warsaw. I was glad of this vehicle, for the jolts and jars of a regular cart were very bad for Mother. There were no seats in the dray, however, and we had to use our suitcases instead.

No sooner had we left the village than a group of five soldiers hailed us. They were going back to their regiment in Warsaw, and wanted a lift. Half a mile down the road another group of seven soldiers stopped us again and climbed on the dray. We were pretty crowded now. The soldiers chattered gaily with Mr. Skrzypkowski but I didn't feel quite so cheerful. In spite of the enthusiasm with which the Mayor's broadcast had filled me the night before, I was still mortally afraid of bombers, and it was with growing misgivings that I was now scanning the blue, innocent-looking sky. What if an enemy raider should come along? From above, our dray must look like a khaki-colored spot against the background of the white highway, a perfect target for strafing. And I had heard too many horrible tales of civilians who were massacred because they got mixed up with soldiers . . .

While I was brewing those morbid thoughts, Mother, who was sitting in front of me, suddenly turned around.

"I am worried," she said.

Mother, worried? That was something quite new. Was Mother beginning to realize what danger we were in? Was she, could she actually be, afraid of bombs and machine guns? It seemed hardly credible.

"Yes, Mother dear, what is it?" I asked sympathetically.

"You see," she said, "today is the fifteenth. And on the seventeenth I have to pay the luxury tax on the apartment. That's three hundred and fifty-four zlotys. And on the twentieth the mortgage rate on the Saska Kepa[2] house falls due. That's another three hundred zlotys. And I have

---

[2] Saska Kepa is a suburb on the right bank of the Vistula River in the Praga district of Warsaw.

only five hundred zlotys cash. Do you suppose the banks will be open?"

So that was what Mother was worrying about! A sudden impulse made me lean forward and kiss whatever I could reach of Mother, and that was her shoulder blade (the suitcase on which Mother sat was higher than mine).

"Mother, I love you," I said.

"What's that?" Mother asked, startled at my unexpected show of affection.

"Nothing, dear. I can assure you that the banks won't be open, but neither will the tax collector's office, nor the bank that holds the mortgage on the house. And I love you because you are worrying about those things at this precise moment."

"Of course I worry," Mother replied with conviction. "You know how I hate to be late in any payments I have to make."

The well-fed horses proceeded at a brisk trot and within fifty minutes of our departure we reached the city limits, where a party of thirty men or so were hard at work driving short bars of iron railing into the stone pavement of the highway. The bars were not put upright but at a rather sharp angle, their spiky ends facing outwards, towards Jablonna whence the enemy was evidently expected. A tank trap. A little further down the road a regular barricade was being erected.

"Look, Mommy," George exclaimed, "a derailed trolley!"

The boy was right. The streetcar, it seemed, was destined to form a part of the barricade, for it had been lifted from the rails and placed across the street. The mermaid painted on the car's side brandished her sword, as if ready to strike. Good old girl, she would show the Germans that she meant business, trust her!

We were now driving through Praga, the right-bank section of the city which so far had been subjected to the worst aerial attacks. Signs of destruction were in evidence everywhere. Small workmen's houses turned into heaps of ruins, a wooden church with its roof caved in, and endless blocks of big apartment houses staring blindly into space with row upon row of glassless windows. From one of the second-story windows a gay orange curtain flapped wildly in the wind. The houses, big and small, seemed deserted, and so were the streets, save for numerous detachments of soldiers. The civilian population had evidently fled the bomb-stricken section and sought refuge in other parts of the city.

We passed by the Zoo. Its gates were wide open, the enclosure down, and khaki-clad figures hurried to and fro. In the little pond to the right of the entrance, where only two weeks ago pink flamingos had stood in graceful meditation, saddled cavalry horses were drinking water.

The broad avenue that led from the Zoo to the Kierbedz Bridge was blocked by a gigantic barricade, so that we were forced to make a detour by way of a narrow cobbled street. Orchards stretched on both sides of it and through the picket fences I could see that they were full of soldiers. Was it here, I wondered, that Vadik had been stationed for those dreadful forty-eight hours?

Suddenly a fetid, nauseating odor assailed my nostrils. I looked around for the cause of it: a big pool of blood, still wet, stained the narrow sidewalk to our right and in the middle of it lay a steel helmet as full of holes as a sieve. I did not want the children to see this ghastly sight, so I tried to draw their attention to the other side of the street. This did not prove difficult, for right opposite the sinister stain a rolling kitchen had pulled up and a group of soldiers

From the collection of Sam Bryan, courtesy of Julien Bryan

Building a tank trap.

USNARA

Construction of a barricade in the Praga district of Warsaw.

From the collection of Stefan Mucha

Streetcars used to form barricades.

From the collection of Sam Bryan, courtesy of Julien Bryan

Polish troops regroup in Warsaw.

were clamoring for their breakfast. How they could eat in such surroundings was more than I could see.

At last we reached the bridge. It stood there, a testimony to poor German marksmanship. For, after all, the Stukas and Messerschmitts had been bombing it at least twice a day for the last two weeks, yet had failed to demolish it. True enough, we saw as we crossed the bridge two spots covered up with fresh wooden boards, evidently two light bombs had broken through the surface and plunged into the river, but one could hardly call that serious damage. The three other bridges which connected Praga with the rest of the city also seemed intact.

Once we had crossed the bridge we were in Warsaw proper. I was not familiar with Praga, I practically never went there except to take the children to the Zoo or to get on one of the eastbound trains. I had no particular feelings about the place. But here we were in the very heart of Warsaw, the Warsaw we knew and loved. I was strangely moved to see the old place again, and so was Mother.

We were greatly relieved to see that it was not in ruins. With the exception of two houses at the corner of Trebacka and Krakowskie Przedmiescie almost completely destroyed by a high explosive bomb, the familiar buildings looked pretty much as usual, even windowpanes were not missing. Yet the streets had an unaccustomed aspect, and this was chiefly due to an almost complete lack of traffic. No buses, no streetcars, no taxicabs, even no droshkies! You could have played ball in the middle of the once-crowded thoroughfares. Pedestrians, mostly in uniforms of some kind or another, hurried along the sidewalks, but their quick footsteps were not enough to fill the strange silence that hung over the broad avenues.

Suddenly, as we were passing the monument of Mickiewicz a loud hollow detonation shook the air. Involuntarily I crouched on my low suitcase, and Leosia emitted her preliminary sob, when Mr. Skrzypkowski turned around with a broad grin on his round face.

"Don't get scared," he said, "those are our heavy anti-aircraft guns."

This was surprising, for as far as I could see no air raid alarm was in progress. But, Mr. Skrzypkowski explained, air raid alarms were no longer sounded in Warsaw. With the German artillery shelling the capital day and night an all-clear signal would be pure mockery. People had to use their own judgment when to go out and when to take cover. Now, however, there was a lull in the artillery fire, we did not hear more than five or six explosions in the twenty minutes it took us to reach the house, and all of them were distant.

At last we entered our street. Mother once more turned around, her face beaming. "It's good to be back," she said.

Yes, it was. And the house stood intact. We already could see its yellow façade elaborately decorated in the fashion of the Gay Nineties shining in the morning sun. Not a windowpane missing!

While the superintendent helped Mother out of the dray, and the children and Leosia ran ahead to ring the apartment bell, I proceeded to settle my accounts with Mr. Skrzypkowski.

I was pretty sure he was going to ask me for a hundred zlotys, and was determined not to pay more than fifty. Fifty was plenty!

"Well, Mr. Skrzypkowski, how much do I owe you?"

The man began to scratch his head.

"Will fifteen zlotys be too much?" he asked.

Fifteen zlotys was less than three American dollars. Bless Mr. Skrzypkowski! The man was not only a hero but a philanthropist on top of it.

"No, I am sure it won't," I said. I was almost on the point of giving him a heavy tip, then thought better of it. Mr. Skrzypkowski had his horses and his business, while my Bank was gone. I could not afford to be too generous.

I caught up with Mother in the middle of the stairs, and we ascended the remaining steps together. On the landing Cook awaited us, more excited and voluble than ever. It was the second time she had thought we had deserted her, and once more we were turning up at the most unexpected moment. She was full of tales, but Mother would not listen. She brushed Cook aside and entered the apartment.

For a moment we stood in the dining room door surveying the old place. The family portraits gazed at us from the walls, the familiar heavy, carved-oak furniture stood where it had always stood, not a speck of dust anywhere, Cook who had a passion for cleaning had seen to that.

"Wind the clock please," Mother said.

CHAPTER 14

The Siege

AND THUS we settled into the Siege of Warsaw.

A big city, even when besieged and bombed, presents a lot of conveniences a country place like Aunt Flika's can't offer. Electric light, newspapers, and above all, the telephone. The first thing we found missing was gas; the mains had been shut off all over the city for fear of explosions. Oh well... we still had the old coal range.

I sat by the phone and called all my friends. I was relieved to find that so far all those who had remained in Warsaw (the majority had left during the evacuation) were alive and well. In good spirits, too. Amazing what a bracing effect this defense had on people.

Rose's baby had not arrived yet. She herself answered the phone.

"It's already two weeks overdue, you know," she told me, and then added with a flicker of her old humor, "the little wizard is probably afraid to take a peep at this blasted world. The doctor says that as long as it did not simply jump out at the first explosion, it has apparently made up its mind to play safe and stay where it is till the end of the war. Very sensible, I suppose, but not exactly comfortable for me."

"I should say not," I agreed. "Did you make any arrangements in case it should change its mind and arrive now?"

"Oh yes. I have reserved a room in a maternity hospital. And in case the whole business starts at night after the curfew, a trained nurse is spending the nights with me. There is also a doctor living in our house who has promised to help. He is an oculist to be sure but—," she broke off.

There was a muffled sound of an explosion in the receiver, then Rose's voice, suddenly small and anxious said hurriedly, "I've got to stop. They are starting shooting again, and the phone is right on the windowsill. Good-bye."

It seemed strange, for in our part of the city everything was quiet.

"Brave little Rose," I thought as I replaced the receiver. "She is certainly taking it well."

While Mother was doing her telephoning I glanced through the papers. I had not seen a newspaper in ten days and was famished for news. The Germans were attacking Warsaw from three sides, I noticed: south, southeast and the north. They had crossed the Vistula, and were closing in from the east, too. Fighting at some points was going on right in the streets within the city limits, with our soldiers repulsing fierce German attacks day and night. Suddenly an item prominently displayed on the front page caught my eye. "Warsaw to Bury a Hero," said the headline.

"The Warsaw Volunteer Brigade," I read, "organized only three days ago, has already suffered its first casualty. Feliks Drazynski, one of the first to volunteer in the brigade, lost his life while carrying on rescue work in a municipal building set afire by German incendiaries. Feliks Drazynski, a true son of Warsaw, for which he laid down his life, will be buried tomorrow with full military honors. The funeral service will be held at ten in the Garrison Church. The Mayor and the Municipal Council will be present at the ceremony...

"Feliks Drazynski," the paragraph concluded, "had been a ladies' hairdresser in civil life. His establishment was located on Krucza Street."

Not till I reached the last sentence did I realize that this hero Warsaw was going to bury with full pomp and ceremony was none other than my own Mr. Felix, the little baldish hairdresser who for two years had tended my unruly locks, and only two weeks ago had grieved over my decision to cut them off. I could still remember his last remark: "You can't expect a beauty parlor to flourish in wartime." No, war and hairdressing were not compatible, and now war had made a hero of Mr. Felix. It was strange to think of him as a hero. He was such an unassuming little man...

"I've telephoned Vadik's girlfriend," Mother announced, appearing in the hall door. "She will be here in ten minutes."

As a matter of fact, five minutes did not elapse before the girl came. Vadik, who was a painter, certainly had an eye for pretty girls. This one was a beauty. Smartly dressed, too. But she didn't seem a bit conscious of her attractive appearance. She looked upset and terribly worried.

She asked for the letter in an almost pleading voice, and her hand shook as she took it.

Mother showed her into Franek's room. "This room is unoccupied, you'll be able to read your letter in complete privacy."

The girl acknowledged this with a grateful nod and for half an hour there was not a sound from her. When at last she emerged into the hall again her face was stained with tears, and she was so flustered that she left her gas mask behind. One did not forget gas masks in these days!

I have often wondered since if she had had a premonition of Vadik's fate.

After the girl's departure I decided to go out. I was in a hurry to report at the Bank and start at once on some kind of defense duty. In spite of my eagerness, I had to muster

From the collection of Stefan Mucha

From the collection of Stefan Mucha

Warsaw is besieged...

185

USNARA

USNARA

. . . bombarded from all sides.

all my courage before I stepped out into the streets. This was the first time I was going to walk under artillery fire, and the prospect was not altogether reassuring. My apprehensions, however, proved unfounded. The enemy was giving Warsaw one of those short and infrequent respites, during which tense nerves relax, people who for days did not dare to leave the flimsy protection of a roof rush out into the streets to catch a breath of fresh air, and the whole besieged city seems to heave a sigh of relief and for an hour or two assumes an almost festive air.

Under the bright noon sun the sidewalks were crowded, people walked at a leisurely pace, talked, laughed, glad to be still alive, I suppose. I was amazed to see so many uniforms. Small detachments of soldiers marched up and down the streets, and as I peeked through doorways, I caught glimpses of army men and horses camping in the courtyards of apartment houses. A heavy machine gun pointed skywards from the second floor balcony of the house on the corner. Warsaw had become a fortress alright!

I noticed that the city was still full of refugees. Not that I saw in anybody's eyes that horrible, vacant "refugee" look that had haunted me during the first days of the war, but I was constantly stopped and asked the way to the City Hall, or Napoleon Square, or Nowy Swiat,[1] questions no resident of Warsaw would ever dream of asking.

All stores were open but no one seemed to be interested in any merchandise, save food. In front of every foodstore long lines of men, women and children waited patiently for their turn to enter. Some of these lines stretched for blocks.

---

[1] One of the most fashionable shopping streets in Warsaw, equivalent to Fifth Avenue in New York City.

"What do they sell in this store?" I asked a woman who stood in a line leading to a grocer's. There were perhaps sixty people ahead of her which meant at least two more hours of waiting.

"One egg, two herrings, half a pound of sugar and half a pound of salt per person. They say there might be some bread, too, but I am too far down the line, so I won't get any," she informed me in a cheerful, matter-of-fact tone.

So that was what Warsaw was down to: one egg, half a pound of sugar, salt, herrings, and perhaps some bread for the lucky ones! The food situation looked pretty bad indeed...

It was a long walk from our house to the Bank of Poland, so I decided to take a shortcut through Marszalkowska and the Saski Garden. I turned into one of the side streets and was walking rapidly when suddenly my progress was blocked by a barricade reaching to the second story of the neighboring houses. With a pang I realized that Marszalkowska, which is to Warsaw what Broadway is to New York, was not included in the innermost defense lines. So that was what the City of the Mermaid meant when it had pledged itself to fight to the last ditch! Barricades this side of Marszalkowska...

I had to make a detour of five blocks before I found a house with a double entrance through which I could enter the cut-off avenue. Another detour awaited me when I reached the Saski Garden, one of Warsaw's oldest parks. The park was closed to civilians, heavy artillery was posted among century-old trees where only three weeks before perambulators wheeled along graveled avenues, retired clerks napped in the sun, and sweethearts walked arm in arm...

At last I reached the Bank and here again a surprise awaited me. The janitor would not let me in.

"No outsiders allowed," he announced gruffly through the judas window of the big iron gate.

"But I am not an outsider," I protested. "I've been working in the Bank for the last eighteen months, and I came now to report for duty."

"I know you've worked here," he sounded a little mollified. "I've seen you every day coming in and out of the building. But you don't live on the premises now, do you?"

I soon found out what was the matter. After the evacuation the Bank had been closed to business, but forty or fifty families of lower officials and clerks had taken up their abode in the spacious Bank's basements which made excellent air raid shelters. The new tenants had organized their own fire brigade, rescue column and first aid squad and kept watch over the Bank's premises. And even more jealously they guarded large stocks of provisions laid aside for war emergency by the Bank Employees Cooperative Store. No, they did not want anyone's help (nor anyone's appetite either), I guess.

Well, that settled it. I was not wanted at the Bank. But since I was here, couldn't I at least go upstairs to my room and get some private papers I had left in my desk? I was thinking about the green turtle, too.

It was then that I learned about the bomb that had crashed through the Economic Research Department. The Bank, apparently, was a hot spot to live in. It boasted already of three bomb hits, and more were to come.

On my way home I dropped in to see Tomek's wife and sister. I was greeted with shouts of joy.

"Rulka! For Heaven's sake, how did you ever get back? We thought you had deserted us like the rest. You see, when Tomek was leaving (he finally decided to go with the Bank, you know) he told me: 'If you ever need advice go to Mrs. Langer. She will help you, I am sure.' Well, the very next morning I ran to your house, and they told me you were gone. I nearly wept when I heard it. My, what an awful day! *Everybody* was leaving Warsaw. Everybody! You weren't here so you can't imagine what it was like. Mad panic! We stood by this window and watched processions of people on foot, carrying suitcases, pushing perambulators, all evacuating. At one time we were almost on the point of joining the exodus. We would have, too, if it had not been for the baby. What luck we didn't go!"

I explained what had happened to me. I had known Krysia, Tomek's wife, for a long time but it was the first time I had met his sister, Ina. I remembered what Tomek had told me about her being on the verge of a nervous collapse and I was amazed to find her now composed and smiling.

"Meet Christopher," she said as an eighteen-month-old baby wobbled into the room and at once started to investigate the contents of my pocketbook. "Christopher, don't do that. He sleeps in the shelter but spends most of the day with us. You know," she added with a rueful laugh, "how crazy one is in wartime. When there was talk that Warsaw would be surrendered, everybody said that the Germans were going to kill all men, even little boys. I got so scared for Christopher that I actually borrowed some dresses from the janitor's wife and dressed him as a girl. Can you imagine? My, I am glad those crazy days are over!"

I promised to come and see them often, now that I was back in Warsaw.

Once home I sat again by the phone and called every friend and acquaintance I could think of in order to get some defense work information. "We need every able-bodied man and woman," Mayor Starzynski had said, and I was not going to sit with my arms crossed while this splendid defense was going on. But I was soon to find out that getting a defense job was no easy matter. Most of my friends had either joined the civic militia which had taken over the duties of the regular police, or else were working in hospitals. But the militia was by now fully manned, and the hospitals, although in sore need of trained nurses, did not care for amateurs like myself.

At last I remembered a women's defense organization I had been asked to join before the war. I had refused at that time, as I thought that all my time would be taken up by the Bank. Now, however, I was eager to turn to them. They, if anyone, would have openings. I found the address in the telephone book and after securing an introduction went to register.

But even here a disappointment awaited me.

"Are you an expert seamstress?" the brisk young lady who took my name, address and telephone number asked me. "We need women to sew for soldiers and hospitals."

I had to admit that I didn't know how to sew. Were there no other possibilities?

"Not right now. Perhaps later. What are your qualifications, anyway? Are you particularly good at anything? Cooking, nursing...?"

Again I had to confess that I had no such achievements.

"Well... What was your line in peacetime? Any specialty?"

"Economics, advertising and languages." It sounded so foolish that I could not help laughing. So did she.

"I am afraid that with those you won't go far these days," she said. "However, I'll see what we can do for you. If anything turns up, I'll let you know."

She called me that very afternoon.

"Mrs. Langer," she informed me, "there is an opening, but I don't know if you'll be willing to consider it. It's rather dangerous. Carrying food and cigarettes to the soldiers at the front. Would you take it?"

I hesitated for a second, then...

"I have two children, you see..., " I said apologetically.
She understood.

"I see. In that case, of course not. Perhaps we will have something else for you soon."

I told Mother about this proposal. Was I right or wrong to refuse?

"It's for you to decide," Mother said. "But I am awfully glad you did not take it. The only thing I really dread is that you should get killed in this war and leave me the children. I am too old now to bring up two small children alone."

Mother was a realist.

CHAPTER 15

Waiting for Horse Meat

"THE BUTCHER in Three Crosses Square is going to sell horse meat today," announced Cook, as she brought us our morning tea on the third day of our arrival in Warsaw.

She was addressing no one in particular and there was a deep tone of contempt in her voice, but to us the news was welcome. Here we were having our breakfast consisting of tea and one thin slice of bread per capita (and even that one thin slice was already considered a rare treat—bread was becoming practically unobtainable in Warsaw). At noon we would dine on a deep plate of cabbage soup, and at night... well, we would get another plate of cabbage soup.

We had been living on cabbage soup for two days now, and although no one complained, we were growing a little bit weary of this monotonous diet. The children's meals were supplemented with crackers, a piece of chocolate and sometimes half a glass of diluted condensed milk, but obviously such precious items could not be wasted on adults.

Of course, we still had our war reserves of canned ham and vegetables, dried peas, and even some rice, oatmeal and flour, but this siege looked as if it might last for several months, and in the meantime food conditions were bound to grow worse, not better. So we were determined not to touch our "iron rations" till the day when nothing, absolutely nothing, could be bought at the market or in the stores. "We eat today what we buy today," was a fast rule Mother and I had set on the very first day of our arrival, but so far our daily foraging expeditions did not fetch anything more than cabbage, which was grown on every empty building lot within the city limits and was therefore plentiful.

Under the circumstances, a good, juicy horse roast, or even a horse stew, seemed an attractive prospect.

"Oh, Cook," I exclaimed, "do buy some horse meat! It will be such fun to have meat for a change, even if it's horse flesh."

But I had forgotten what a dreadful snob in matters of food Cook was. She reveled in fine complicated dishes, she would gladly slave for hours over a sauce mousseline or a bit of fluffy French pastry, but when it came to simple dishes, "poor people's" food, she held them in deep contempt. Cook had already winced more than once at our daily diet of cabbage soup, and now, when it came to horse meat, she simply rebelled.

"Why, Madam, I'd rather die than touch horse flesh," she exclaimed. "It's dogs' food, not fit for human beings. I wouldn't eat it for anything."

"You don't have to eat it at all." I knew from long experience there was no use arguing with Cook. "We will eat it all up. Won't we, Mother? Won't we, children? All you'll have to do is cook it. And I *know*, Cook, that you will prepare a delicious dish even out of horse meat."

The last remark seemed to placate Cook a little.

"If Madam says so...," she said doubtfully. "But really, Madam, I can't stand in line for horse meat today. I reserved a place in the line at the grocer's on my way back from church. They are selling half a pound of rice today. I have to return at once, or I'll lose my place."

"That's alright," I reassured her. "I'll go for the meat. Just tell me which one of the butchers is selling it."

I had no difficulty in locating the butcher's shop. A line

of at least forty people already stood along the wall, although the door of the shop was closed. "The butcher went to the slaughterhouse at dawn, and is expected back with the meat sometime before noon," a young woman with a pink shawl wrapped around her head informed me as I took my place in the line. "When they open the store the line will move quickly."

I glanced at my watch. It was only a few minutes after nine. Three hours to wait. I settled comfortably, leaning against a wall, and lit a cigarette. I would not have dreamed of smoking in the streets of Warsaw in peacetime, but now I noticed half of the women standing in lines were smoking. Besides, I found a cigarette helped to quench the hollow feeling in the pit of my stomach I had begun to experience that morning. It was only twenty minutes since I had finished breakfast, and four more hours to wait for my plate of cabbage soup, and I was already hungry.

Overhead the sky was overcast for the first time in months, and strong gusts of wind chased heavy gray clouds. A constant though irregular rumble of artillery fire came from over the northern part of the city, but in our section everything seemed pretty quiet.

At my right stretched row upon row of the wooden booths of the fruit and vegetable market. Normally at this time of the year the booths would be piled high with pyramids of apples and pears, plums and tomatoes, cauliflowers, pumpkins, red cabbage, all the colorful September bounty. But now the booths were empty. Only one displayed a small pile of cabbage heads on a long otherwise empty counter, and this dozen cabbages seemed only to emphasize the desolation of the place. The vendor, a large fat woman, her head covered with a brown woolen shawl the two ends of which were crossed over her ample bosom and tucked under her apron, was engaged in a heated argument with a customer.

"What? Ninety grosze[1] for this small head?" the customer complained in a shrill indignant voice. "Why, this is outrageous! I've never paid more than ten grosze for a small head of cabbage. It's war profiteering, that's what it is!"

"Good Jesus! What are you talking about? Profiteering indeed," the vendor's face had turned red at the insult. "Do you think I am going to risk my life to bring you cabbage at ten grosze apiece? Last night when we went out in the field to cut that cabbage the son of our neighbor was shot in the field right next to ours. They could have just as easily shot my husband and me. And you want to pay ten grosze for that cabbage! Ninety grosze, I say, and that's my last word. Take it or leave it." Reluctantly, the customer paid and slipped the cabbage into her basket.

Many passersby stopped to ask what we were waiting for. "Horse meat," someone would answer, or "Horse cutlets" or "Horse roast," just for a joke. The passerby would consider for a while and then either join the line or pass on.

This was the way one shopped these days. You went out in the streets and looked for lines. You inquired at each what people were waiting for. Then you calculated the length of the line and the desirability of the eventual purchase, and joined the line that suited you best. Simple.

In the line people were either reading newspapers or talking. I was amazed at the friendly, cheerful spirit that was in evidence everywhere. Warsaw people were never noted for their friendliness. Warsaw was not Lwow

---

[1] Eighteen cents.

From the collection of Stefan Mucha

Three Crosses Square.

From the collection of Sam Bryan, courtesy of Julien Bryan

Vegetables are grown in all available open spaces.

USHMM, courtesy of Julien Bryan

Women sell food from baskets, in a rudimentary street market.

(Lemberg) where you had only to sneeze in the street to have four or five strangers call "Good health" to you. No, the inhabitants of the capital were always a little on the stiff side, rather morose and suspicious of strangers. But now, all the stiffness was gone. So were class distinctions. In the lines elderly gentlemen and cooks, factory workmen and smartly dressed ladies talked, laughed, passed bits of gossip and information, offered each other cigarettes and papers. Strange, how this siege seemed to bring out the best in human nature.

Ahead of me a little man in a gray felt hat and disreputable-looking raincoat was entertaining a whole section of the line. I tried to catch the jokes, but was too far away. I heard, however, the words "Hitler" and "Niemcy" (Germans) several times so I knew his witticisms must have been highly topical.

Behind me two women were talking:

"... She is so scared of shooting and bombing that she says she would rather starve than go out. She has not left the house since the siege began."

"Silly! Shooting has not been so bad in this part of the city."

"Sure. Did you hear that on Bracka two people were killed by a cannon bullet this morning? It fell right in the middle of the line to the Pakulski store. But here we have had no artillery fire so far. Anyway, she is so scared that she stays in bed all the time. Of course we can't let her starve, so I always bring her something every time I go out. I'll give her some of that horse meat, too. I hope she eats it, but you can never tell, she is such an old crank."

The woman in the pink shawl who had addressed me first was getting restless. She was fidgeting with her basket, walking a few steps out of the line, then returning.

"I left my four-year-old girl all alone in the house, and I am a little worried about her," she told me. "A neighbor has promised to look after her, but she has three children of her own. She is so busy, I am afraid she might have forgotten. It's so hard to take care of children nowadays. And this child of mine is so finicky with food. I have some oatmeal left, but she won't eat it. All she wants is eggs and meat. How can I get her eggs? I got one, yesterday, had to stand three hours in line for it. And today I thought I would make her a broth out of horse meat. Do you know if one can make broth out of horse meat?"

"No, I don't know, I am sorry. It seems to me the flavor would be too strong. But why don't you run home and see how the child is? I'll keep this place for you."

"Will you, really? Thanks a lot. I'll be back in a jiffy. I live not far from here." Half an hour later she was back. "The child is all right," she announced. "Has the butcher with the meat arrived yet?"

No, the butcher had not come, but something else came instead.

Rain.

Suddenly, almost unexpectedly, it began to pour, and moved by a common impulse, everyone in the line gave a cheer and clapped hands.

Rain. Good old, salutary rain. For over a month now we had been looking for it, wishing for it, praying for it in churches and homes. And at last it had come. Too late? Yes, perhaps. What good could rain do us, now that Hitler's motorized units had overrun more than half of the country and were at the very threshold of Warsaw? Yet, we could not help feeling relieved. There was something almost uncanny in this long spell of fine weather; it seemed as if even nature had allied itself to our foes. The Germans called it "Hitlerwetter." Now, at last, the spell was broken. Nature had resumed its normal course. Perhaps things would go better with us, too... One grows superstitious in wartime.

The rain was coming with a vengeance. Hard, straight, almost angry. Of course, no one was prepared for it. In those two months of drought we had forgotten what an umbrella looked like. In less than a minute we were all drenched to the skin. But no one left his post. After two hours of waiting in line you don't abandon your place just because you are soaking wet! We pressed closer to each other, closer to the wall, and with our feet splashing in water, we waited.

It poured for an hour. And then as suddenly as it started the rain stopped and the sun appeared between torn rags of clouds.

And almost simultaneously with the sun, the butcher appeared, too. He emerged from the low door of his shop, and in a booming voice shouted, "Sorry. Could not get any meat this morning. Perhaps there will be some this afternoon. Try again at four."

And he disappeared into the shop. For a moment the line swayed back and forth. Those who stood far away and had not heard the butcher's voice could not believe the news. Was this true? Would there really be no meat that morning? Perhaps if they waited half an hour, one hour longer... People had a tremendous faith in waiting these days. But finally all hopes vanished, and slowly, reluctantly, the line disbanded.

I looked at my watch. Twenty minutes after twelve. I would still have time to do some shopping before returning home for lunch. I had discovered the night before that my medicine chest needed a little stocking up. Wasn't war supposed to breed all kinds of epidemics? With two children, better be prepared for any eventuality.

I found the chemist's store dark, except for one electric bulb. The shutters were drawn. The chemist, a tall, bald, oldish young man in glasses was writing something in one of those big black books chemists always write in, while his assistant, a pert-looking blonde in an immaculate starched uniform, was studying the morning paper.

"Not many customers today," I remarked as I handed the chemist my list.

"No," he said. "There are no sick people in Warsaw nowadays. Dead—yes. Wounded—yes. But not sick. These bombings seem to have cured all the ills."

This, I reflected, was true, although I had not thought of it before. How many of my friends who used to complain about their bad livers, kidneys and hearts, never talked of them any more? And they seemed as fit as a fiddle. Only this morning Mother had told me, "I am surprised that my gall stones behave so well. You know that cabbage is one of the things I am absolutely not allowed to eat. Yet here I've been eating nothing else for the last two days, and it seems to agree perfectly with me." Perhaps, after all, there was something to be said for this bombing-and-starvation cure.

I was fumbling in my pocketbook for money when a long, piercing whine tore the air. A pause. Then a terrific explosion rocked the house. Five seconds later, another whine, another explosion. Then still another.

The German artillery fire was sweeping the square.

"If you don't mind, I'll stay here till this is over," I told the chemist, laying the money on the counter. I tried to say it with a smile, but my face felt strangely stiff.

"Why, of course. Take a seat. Or would you rather go down to the basement?"

"No, thanks. I'll be alright here."

"What about yourself, Mr. Waclaw?" the girl asked the chemist with a challenging smile. "You look a bit pale in this light. Wouldn't you prefer to go to the basement?"

"Don't be silly, Miss Lola," the man looked hurt. "I wouldn't think of it. But you better go. I really think you better."

"Me?" Miss Lola shrugged her shoulders with utter contempt. "I am used to artillery fire. Don't you know I have to cross half the town to come here in the morning and go home at night? How many times do you think I've been caught in artillery fire? A dozen, at least. It's no news to me!"

Nevertheless she had put down her paper and was listening.

All three of us were silent now, straining our ears, waiting...

Wheeeeeeew... Bang! Wheeeeeeeeeeew... Bang!

The "Bang!" no matter how close, was never half as terrifying as the whine of the shell. The shrill, long whistle seemed to go right through one's nerve centers. Every time it came I could feel something inside me shrink, shrink...

I also noticed that you could tell how far the shrapnel was going to fall by the sound of the whine. If the whistle was a long one it would invariably be followed by a distant, muffled explosion. If short, the nearby explosion would shake the house.

Farther... nearer... farther... farther... near... BANG!

"My, that was close!" Miss Lola exclaimed, as the house rocked, and the glass bottles and jars on the shelves began to tinkle. "It couldn't be more than a hundred steps from here."

But the closed shutters cut us off from the square. We couldn't see.

"Don't you want to go to the basement?" the chemist suggested once more. But both the girl and I shook our heads in mute protest. The man shrugged his shoulders and gave up.

The clock over the shelves struck half past twelve.

How long was this going to last? Would I miss my lunch? Shelling or no shelling I was hungry, and growing more hungry with every minute.

All at once the thought of lunch and home made me realize that the house, *our* house and Mother and the children were only two blocks away. And suddenly a dreadful apprehension seized me. What if . . . ?

For the next two full minutes I writhed and wrestled with growing panic. Every distant, muffled explosion sounded worse than the close ones. If I only knew what was happening at home, if I only knew...

And then I remembered the telephone and got up in a jump.

"Where is the telephone?" I asked so abruptly that I startled the poor chemist who was already pretty nervous.

"Why...why...," he stammered, "it's over there. In the corner."

My hand trembled as I dialed the number. For what seemed like ages I could hear the buzzer at the other end of the wire ring... ring... Was no one going to answer? My knees went weak.

At last there was the click.

"Hello?"

It was Mother's voice. As calm as ever.

"Mother," I panted, "are you all quite alright? I am at the chemist in Three Crosses Square and the artillery fire is simply terrible here. How is it there?"

"Why, of course we are alright. I've just finished giving George his French lesson and both children are in the kitchen now, playing. I am doing the accounts. Did you get the meat?"

"No."

"It doesn't matter. Come home as soon as you can, but wait till the shelling stops. And for Heaven's sake stop worrying about us. It's silly."

"Alright, Mother."

Relieved, I returned to my seat. The bombardment continued, fierce but irregular.

Suddenly the door of the store opened with a bang, and a messenger boy came in, whistling. He was pushing a bicycle in front of him.

"Here is the stuff you ordered from Motor." He threw on the counter a large parcel wrapped up in brown paper. "Don't mind I brought the bike in here, do you? I am afraid someone may steal it if I leave it outside. Bikes are in great demand today when there are no taxis or streetcars running."

He put the bike against the wall, then turned around, took off his cap, and wiping his forehead with his sleeve announced in a tone of deep admiration, "My, the mess they made of Mazowiecka! You wouldn't recognize the place. I am just coming from there. The two houses on both sides of the chemist are in ruins. Positively in ruins. Five people killed, eleven wounded. Gee, what a bloody mess!"

"They've been shooting pretty hard around here, too," remarked the chemist.

"I know. But Mazowiecka got it worse, I think. Well, I must be going. I still have all those to deliver," he pointed to a whole pile of brown paper parcels attached to the bike.

"Will you sign the receipt, please?"

He put on his cap, and whistling very loudly disappeared through the door, bike, parcels and all. Whistling must have been his method to keep his courage up, I reflected.

"There is a brave boy," the girl remarked as the door closed behind the messenger.

"A fool," muttered the chemist, shrugging his shoulders.

The shooting was subsiding at last. The shrill whine of the shells was no longer to be heard. A few distant explosions, then silence. It was over.

I glanced at the clock: twenty minutes to one. The whole thing had lasted only twenty minutes, and it had seemed like hours.

"I think I can go out now," I announced, rising from my seat. "Thanks and good-bye."

"You better wait a little longer. They may start shelling again," the cautious chemist warned me.

But I would not wait.

Outside, the big square with its monumental, half-Byzantine, half-Greek church squatting in the middle, was completely deserted. The sidewalks, still wet from the recent downpour, glittered in the sun. The big, empty square made me a little nervous. I began to walk very fast, almost to run. As I ran, I glanced to left and right, trying to catch a glimpse of signs of destruction. At first I didn't see any. Suddenly my foot stumbled on something that felt like a rock. I looked down, and saw that a shrapnel had hit the drive, torn off five or six square feet of the surface and had sent bits of asphalt flying all around. The sidewalk was littered with them.

I had to look under my feet now, for fear of falling down. A little further, the sidewalk was strewn with bricks and glass. I looked up and saw that a whole corner of a house had been torn off. It was the house in front of which I had stood waiting in line only half an hour ago. I ran faster. The next house had been hit halfway between the first and the second floor, an ugly, gaping wound. The one after that (it was a low, one-story building) had the roof caved in. Broken glass crunched under my feet. I had by now run almost the whole length of the square and still not a soul in sight.

And then from one of the narrow streets at my right two men emerged, carrying a stretcher. They, too, were running, but not as fast as I did. The stretcher must have been heavy. It was sagging...

With eyes that seemed at once strangely widened I followed their progress. They were running in the direction of Wiejska where several emergency hospitals had been set up. When I looked under my feet again, I gasped. I had nearly stepped into a big pool of fresh blood. *(Good God! It couldn't be human blood—not that much... Yet a dead horse would not have been removed so quickly. No, dead horses lay in the streets for hours—I had already seen them.)* I jumped over the pool and ran on, faster, faster...

I had reached our street now, and the signs of destruction were still in evidence everywhere. The china store on the corner had got it right plump in the middle. Debris of colored glass and gaily painted china littered the sidewalk. Two more badly battered houses. A caved-in roof. A hundred steps more, and I would be able to see our house. Again, something like panic seized me. It was more than ten minutes since I had talked to Mother on the phone. Anything can happen in ten minutes during a bombardment, and I had heard many a shell burst since I had put down the telephone receiver. As I was nearing the corner from where I could see the house my heart was in my throat, throbbing wildly, choking...

No, thank goodness, the house was alright. Not a windowpane missing. I heaved a sigh of relief and slackened my pace. People were appearing in the street now. From stores and doorways they emerged furtively, running in every direction. But I was not running any longer. I walked. Hadn't Mother told me not to worry? No, it would never do to return home panting, horror-stricken. I tilted my hat, and squared my shoulders. Two minutes later I was climbing the familiar, marble stairs.

"Is lunch ready?" I shouted. "I am famished!"

Chapter 16

Playing, Eating, Sleeping

THE CHILDREN had invented a new game. First Ania would take the wooden blocks—a last year's Christmas present from Hanka—and with infinite pains build a miniature city with walls, gates, and rather crooked towers and steeples.

When it was finished, George with a wicked gleam in his eye would shout, "And now I am going to bomb it!" He would grab a handful of other blocks—the ones with the letters of the alphabet painted in red and blue—and with a loud accompaniment of "Boom! Boom!" throw them at the newly erected city, till it lay in a heap of ruins. Ania would look on, smiling placidly.

When George destroyed her first city she had cried, but now she knew better. As soon as destruction was completed George would gather the blocks and build a city of his own, and then it would be *her* turn to bomb it. Yes, it was a good game, "history in a nutshell" I called it, and they played it for hours on end.

Cook did not approve of the game. "We have enough noise as it is," I could hear her mumble to herself, "without having those children raise such a racket with their 'boom-booms' and rattling blocks."

The children spent most of their time in the kitchen now because it seemed to be the safest place. The next door house protected it from the south, and the rest of the apartment from the east, the two directions from which the artillery fire reached our street. As soon as the sound of the explosions grew louder, or whenever we heard the ominous whine of shells tearing the air, I would order, "To the kitchen," and they would scuttle away like rabbits, dragging their toys behind them. There was no regular shelter in our house.

"Why don't you and Grandma come with us when we are sent to the kitchen?" George complained.

The fact was there were no comfortable seats in the kitchen, the place was cramped, and Mother and I just couldn't be bothered. Why, the children were sent to the kitchen at least five or six times every day.

Sitting on the kitchen floor, heads lifted, their blue eyes staring through the window at the sky, George and Ania would try to catch sight of the enemy plane or the big shells. They also tried to figure out whose batteries were firing, ours or the German.

With time George became quite proficient in telling the difference. It really was not hard to discern. If you first heard the explosion and then the whine of the shell, it was ours. If the whine came first and the "bang" afterwards, it was German. But to Ania it was always "ours"—she laughed at every explosion.

Sometimes firing would cease for an hour or two. Then I took the children out in the courtyard. The minute they saw the sun, caught a whiff of fresh air, they went wild. Like two colts turned loose on the first day of spring, they ran and jumped, raced and tumbled down, spinning around and around the yard till just watching them made me dizzy.

After that they would settle to their new and favorite outdoor game, collecting shell splinters. The ground was littered with them all over the town, and competition among the neighborhood kids was keen. It was Ania who got the prize piece, a splinter as big as her two hands and so heavy that she could hardly carry it. George never had such luck, his trophies were numerous but small.

At the first shot I would call them to come home.

"Just one more round, Mommy," they would shout, and depart in a gallop to the farthest end of the yard. Then reluctantly, they would return. Going out in the courtyard was such a treat, and it happened so seldom!

George resented my going out in the streets while shooting and air raids were in progress.

"Why won't you let me come with you?" he pleaded. "If it isn't dangerous for you, it can't be dangerous for me? And if it is dangerous for you, you shouldn't go out. I don't want you to get killed!"

"No, Mommy, please, don't get killed," interjected Ania. "I don't want you to die," she paused, a pensive look came into her eyes, "Not till I grow up and have my own children," she added.

"And then I can die?" I asked laughing.

She nodded gravely. "Yes, you can."

George had developed the disgusting habit of picking his nose. Was it boredom? Was it nervousness? I don't know. Anyway, every time I went into the kitchen he was hard at it. I tried to remonstrate, but it did no good.

At last in despair I told him, "You know, George, sixty years from now, when you'll be an old man your grandchildren will ask you, 'Grandpa, you were in Warsaw during that historic siege. Tell us about it. What did you do then?' And you will say, 'What did I do? Why, children, I picked my nose!'"

George emitted an uncertain chuckle. He didn't like the joke much. But it did work. He never picked his nose after that.

If George was often bored, Ania never was. She was busy. Terribly busy. Besides the new wartime games, she had her dolls to attend to, and she had always been a devoted mother. But even Stas's life, I noticed, was influenced by current events.

"How is Stas this morning?" I would ask her. "What is he doing?"

"He is standing in the bread line," she told me. "He won't be back for a long, long time."

And then one afternoon she announced proudly: "Stas has been killed by a bomb. We will bury him under the sofa."

The next morning, however, Stas was in the bread line again. Lucky Stas!

Both children had developed tremendous appetites. Gone were the times when Ania had to be coaxed to finish her plate of cereal and George asked to be excused before he had touched his dessert. Now, they never seemed to have enough. Was it because we all talked of food all day long? They gobbled up their huge plates of cabbage soup, they devoured their crackers and chocolate, and *always* asked for more. It made me mad.

"No. That's enough," I would snap. "Don't be such greedy little pigs!"

I remember reading about mothers who during famine periods used to suffer agonies whenever they had to refuse children food for which the poor little ones were asking. Sentimental hooey! Or perhaps there are really noble mothers like that. I wasn't. The simple question "Can I have some more, Mommy?" would send me into a fit of temper. What business did those kids of mine have to be always hungry nowadays? Their plates of soup were exactly twice as large as mine, weren't they? And they got two crackers and a piece of chocolate on top of that, too. It should have been enough, more than enough. They never ate so much in peacetime.

Hunger makes me mean, I guess. And I was hungry, very hungry, in fact, and growing hungrier every day. I was not so conscious of it between meals. But after every meal, and after dinner in particular, my poor empty tummy would rebel. It had been led to believe that it was actually going to be fed. Instead it was fooled. Fooled with a small plate of cabbage soup. And it protested. It asked for more, begged for more, yelled for more. Those after-dinner hunger pangs were the worst, they made me feel like crying.

Mother was hungry, too, although I didn't know it at the time. It was she who dished out the soup, two big, copious plates for the children, three medium-size plates for the two servants and me, and just a little bit at the bottom of the plate for herself.

Once I tried to remonstrate about it, oh, very feebly. She cut my argument short, rather sharply, "It's none of your business. Young people need more food than old ones. Besides, cabbage does not agree with me, you know that."

It was not till months afterwards that she confessed how much she had resented this self-imposed sacrifice. "Sometimes I felt like bursting into tears," she admitted, "and telling you all 'That's unfair. I am as hungry as anybody else. Give me some of your soup.'"

And still we did not touch our iron rations.

Ania was caught stealing pickled cucumbers out of our last and only can and was duly spanked. Not that the crime deserved such harsh punishment. But we simply could not afford to lose those cucumbers, they were Cook's main standby in camouflaging horse meat into something resembling beef stew. Besides, Ania's attitude in the matter was, to say the least, highly improper. At first I just scolded her. Then, ending my remonstrations in the classical, parental manner I asked her, "You won't do it again, will you, dear?"

She looked up, straight into my eyes.

"No, Mommy," she announced with conviction, "I won't do it when you are around."

Both children and I slept now in Mother's bedroom. Ever since the Germans had occupied Saska Kepa our front rooms had become unsafe. They lay directly in the path of the German artillery fire. The house across the street from ours was only two stories high, and presented no protection whatsoever.

"How thoughtless and selfish of people to build those low houses," I had grumbled while I collected our belongings, glancing furtively at the three big windows which seemed to invite enemy shells. This, of course, was a little unfair. The house across the street had been built in 1898.

At first we slept all four in Mother's bedroom, which was small and already overcrowded with furniture. No wonder that after one night Mother had enough of it.

"I like privacy better than my bed," she announced and withdrew to the dining room sofa.

I suggested that we should move her bed too, for the sofa was one of those mid-Victorian affairs, hard, narrow, extremely upright and absolutely unfit to sleep on. But Mother would not hear of it. Shift the furniture in the dining room? Why, this was unthinkable. Wasn't that the way it had stood thirty-six years ago, when as a bride she had moved into the apartment? She would rather sleep on the naked floor than move one piece of it, she assured me. Besides, she said, the sofa was quite comfortable. As to that, I had my doubts having, in my tender youth, spent several uncomfortable nights on it. But then Mother was a stoic, and I was not.

Altogether it was quite remarkable that we spent the nights in the apartment at all. Very few people in Warsaw did. Those who had no air raid shelter slept in staircases, or at best on the floor of their halls, just to be nearer the exit in case an enemy shell set the house on fire as, incidentally, many did.

Mother would have none of this nonsense. As she explained it to her friend Aunt Madzia, "My dear, if we all have to die, why should we go to so many inconveniences about it? I'd much rather be killed in my bed than in a staircase, wouldn't you?"

But Aunt Madzia would not be persuaded. She spent every night in the shelter.

"How absurd," Mother remarked. "You can't undress in a shelter, can you?" Mother never missed a single step in her many nightly preparations; she undressed, brushed her hair for fifteen minutes, went through all her ordinary ablutions. The only concession Mother made to the state of siege was in the matter of her corset. It was an old-fashioned corset with about eighty hooks and it took five minutes to put on. Mother wore it over her nightgown. "Just in case we should have to leave the house at nighttime. It takes so long to put on," she explained apologetically to me.

I undressed the children, too, mostly for psychological reasons. I wanted them to relax.

As for myself, I just kicked my shoes off and jumped into bed. At night the bombardment always grew worse, and I would lie in the dark listening to the shells. At every piercing whine, my whole body would grow rigid, and would not relax till I heard the explosion. Farther, nearer, farther, nearer, still nearer... What was I waiting for? The whine I would not hear, the explosion that would mean our house...

The bombardment did not seem to bother the children much, they slept right through it. Only sometimes when a shrapnel hit so close that it shook the house they would wake up.

"What is that? What has happened?" they asked, sitting up on the mattress on which they slept on the floor.

"Nothing. Just a shell," I reassured them.
"Ours?" Ania would murmur sleepily.
"Yes, darling, ours. Go right back to sleep."
Ours indeed! Good Lord!

CHAPTER 17

Grim but Determined, Warsaw Carries On

AUNT MADZIA came every afternoon to help us with the bandages. The professional nurse who lived in the apartment below ours was on night duty, and each morning brought us our daily assignment from the hospital in a big, black leather bag.

There was a whole story in those bandages. At first they used to be very clean and white, quite new looking in fact, perhaps used once and thoroughly washed afterwards. Then they grew yellowish and frayed, some had horrible half-washed streaks on them.

And then they were not real bandages any longer, just long narrow strips torn off from old sheets and pillow-cases, to be sorted out, sewn together and rolled into rolls which looked clumsy despite all our efforts to make them appear to be the real thing.

At last, one morning the nurse came upstairs with her black leather bag empty. Her ward had run out of clean bandages altogether. Whereupon Mother brought out her own old sheets and pillowcases, and we proceeded to make bandages out of those.

At any time, however, the bandages kept us pretty busy, and Aunt Madzia's help was most welcome.

Aunt Madzia was an old dear, anyway. As Olgierd once said, aunts were like wine: if they were really good they improved with age; if they were bad, they were apt to turn into vinegar. Aunt Madzia was certainly of good vintage. She was a jolly old soul, friendly, uncritical, and always immensely interested in all our little doings. Her ample bosom had served as a safe receptacle for many a family secret. She and Mother used to tease each other a lot.

"Had a good night at the shelter?" Mother would ask slyly, throwing Aunt Madzia a sidelong glance, while her fingers were busy with the bandages. "You don't look exactly as fresh as a rosebud?"

Unconscious of the trap that was being laid for her, Aunt Madzia walked right into it.

"Oh, my dear," she sighed, "I haven't slept at all. Not a wink. It was horrible!"

"Really? Isn't that too bad," Mother nodded her head in mock sympathy. "I, of course, slept like a top. But then, with you it is a matter of self-imposed sacrifice, this sleeping in the shelter. But do tell me, don't you feel a little foolish in the morning when you go back to your room and find no shell, no wreckage and your bed clean and comfortable, and untouched? It would seem like an awful waste of a perfectly good night to me."

Aunt Madzia laughed good-naturedly.

"Oh, Iza, you're so reckless. Dr. Sadowska insisted on sleeping in her bed too, and a shrapnel landed right in the middle of her room. Smashed up half the furniture and all that."

"It didn't kill her, though, did it?"

"No. She escaped without a scratch."

By now, however, Aunt Madzia was ready with a counterattack.

"Speaking of waste of time," she grinned, "are you still keeping these beautiful house accounts of yours? Entering every two grosze you spend? That would seem like a waste of time to me, when the house may be blown up any minute."

This time it was Mother's turn to retreat with a laugh.

"I know, I know," she admitted. "I sometimes laugh at it myself. Still, I am so used to them, I can't help myself. Besides, you know, we may survive till the end of the month, and then what a victory to close the month with a perfect balance. I really think it's worth trying."

Sometimes the two ladies would turn to the memories of old, happier times.

"Iza, do you remember the time when you and I came for the first time to this apartment? Thirty-six years ago, wasn't it? My, how time does fly! It was two weeks before your father and mother were married," Aunt Madzia turned to me. "Her trousseau had been sent ahead here, and I came to help her with the unpacking. We spent a whole afternoon here, while your father was at the office. Didn't we have fun, Iza? Still, I told your mother it was very unwise. Just imagine what would have happened if she had broken off her engagement at the last minute. Who would retrieve all those frilled bloomers, those starched petticoats put away among the masculine things?"

"You would," Mother looked at her old friend with an amused smile. "You were always the brash one. You wouldn't have minded going to a single man's apartment to retrieve anybody's petticoats!"

And so it went, every afternoon.

Between two and four the shooting was usually at its worst, and we talked and laughed a little louder to cover up the whine of shells overhead.

One afternoon Aunt Madzia, who had an uncanny way of noticing things, suddenly turned to me.

"What's the matter, Rulka? Anything wrong?"

"Not really," I smiled. "It's just... Well, if you must know, I just wanted to go to the bathroom. In fact, I've wanted to go to the bathroom for more than an hour now."

Both Mother and Aunt Madzia thought that very funny. "Why don't you go ahead?"

"I can't," I said soberly. "I never do when they shoot like that. Too afraid a shrapnel may get me there. Just imagine what an unromantic, unheroic death. I can't face it."

The two ladies burst into peals of laughter.

"Don't worry," Aunt Madzia assured me. "We will not put it in your obituary. We really won't."

"Cross your heart?"

"Cross my heart."

"Alright. You better keep your promise."

But as days went by Aunt Madzia's golden humor and good spirits began to wane. The fact was that Aunt Madzia, who all her life had been something of a gourmand, could not stand the privations of the siege diet. Hunger made her gloomy. Besides, one of her close friends, an old school principal, had been killed while looking out through her window, and that of course did not improve Aunt Madzia's morale either. Mother and I had sometimes quite a hard time to make her laugh. And then, one afternoon, Aunt Madzia exploded.

"My dear Iza, what's the use of it all?" There was exasperation in her voice. "The situation is awful, simply awful. Why do we go on, defending Warsaw? We are doomed. The Bolsheviks have occupied the east, the Germans have overrun the rest of the country, where is the rescue coming from? Nowhere. What's the sense of this mad defense, I ask you?"

"Why, Madzia, you shouldn't talk like that," Mother tried to remonstrate. "England is certainly going to help us. As a matter of fact, someone who listens to the British broadcasts told me only this morning that the British fleet has broken through Kattegat and Skagerrak and is expected any minute at Danzig. British planes have already been seen flying over Warsaw. Remember two days ago when there was an air raid and our anti-aircraft did not go into action? Apparently those were British planes flying overhead. Besides, if England and France start an offensive on the Western front . . . "

"Nonsense. They will do nothing of the sort. What do they care about us? They will let us stew in our own juice."

"Even if they do, don't forget Czestochowa and the miracle on the Vistula..."

"Oh Iza, you and your miracles...Don't be ridiculous."

"But I *do* believe in miracles," Mother insisted. "I believe that if we stick it out long enough the tide is bound to turn, something will happen. Our duty is to stick it out, not to argue."

"Yes, stick it out, till we all get killed."

"Maybe," Mother said gently.

It was true that the siege grew worse every day. When first we had returned to Warsaw, I had to go out of my way to get a look at the traces of bombardment. Now, signs of destruction stared at my face wherever I went: caved-in roofs, torn-off balconies and ugly, gaping wounds in the front and sidewalls of buildings. You never could foretell where the shell was going to hit; sometimes it would be the fourth or fifth floor, sometimes the second, sometimes the ground. In block after block yellow patches of fresh plywood sheets were replacing the shattered windowpanes. Whenever I met an acquaintance in the streets the first question would be: "How are you all? Have you any windows left?"

"Sure," I would brag, "not a single one missing."

"Impossible. How do you do it?"

"Ask the German artillery. For some inexplicable reason they always seem to miss our block. At any rate, we don't worry. The secondhand furniture store almost across the street from our house has a large supply of plywood, so we won't have far to go for it. And how are your windows?"

"The glass went last Tuesday. Yesterday the plywood fell out, too. We have to start all over again."

In the lines people no longer talked and laughed. Hunger and sleepless nights were beginning to tell. Red-rimmed eyes had a haggard look, faces were drawn, lips pressed tight. Strangers no longer answered jovially whenever you asked what they were waiting for. "I don't know," they would grumble, or "Why don't you see for yourself?" Others just shrugged their shoulders. Sometimes bitter quarrels would break out in the lines, and the members of the voluntary militia had a hard time maintaining peace and order.

People waited patiently enough, sometimes for hours, as long as the store was closed and empty. In fact, nothing at that time could move them from their places; bombers would roar overhead, artillery shells exploded in the vicinity, first aid squads hurried by carrying stretchers with wounded, and still the line stood unheeding, as if rooted in the pavement. But the minute the van carrying the daily supply stopped in front of the store there would be a mad scramble for the door. People pushed and pulled, trampled over each other's feet, fought with fists and elbows. Sleeves were torn off, coats ripped.

In the grim daily struggle for food, all human decency was forgotten.

There came a day when I no longer dared to stand in line. Besides, it was useless; lines were for the strong, the strong and the ruthless. Hunger is a bad master.

Then there were the little graves in the squares. I saw the first one on the fourth day of our arrival in Warsaw. It was in the small triangle at the crossing of Mokotowska, Krucza and Piusa. In the center of that triangle stretched a patch of grass, surrounded with a wrought iron fence and shadowed by a few bushes of lilac that grew in the middle. One end of that little lawn, I noticed, had been turned into a rubbish dump. At the other a little grave had bloomed out.

From the collection of Stefan Mucha

From the collection of Stefan Mucha

Signs of destruction appear throughout the city.

From the collection of Zygmunt Walkowski

From the collection of Stefan Mucha

Hundreds of makeshift graves fill Warsaw city squares...

224

From the collection of Stefan Mucha

From the collection of Stefan Mucha

. . . and municipal parks.

225

USNARA

Grim but determined, Warsaw carries on.

It was not much of a grave, a small heap of yellow dirt with a primitive wooden cross at the head and a glass of water with two or three flowers at the feet. A visiting card was pinned with a thumbtack to the cross, but I couldn't read the name. The next morning there were two more graves, then five... eight... ten...

And thus they grew, the rubbish pile at one end, the little graves at the other, with nothing but the cluster of lilac to separate them. At last one morning I noticed that the heap of rubbish had been removed, presumably to make more room for the dead. They needed it, too.

But in spite of all, life went on. Wreckage was removed, sidewalks swept clean, stores remained open and newsboys ran through the streets shouting the latest headlines. Telephones continued to operate, the radio bombed out of one station moved to another, gas and water mains were quickly repaired.

And every night at eight thirty the bomb-weary hearts of Warsaw still beat in unison. The Mayor addressed the city at that hour and Warsaw drank in every one of his simple, heartwarming words. And as the Mayor's voice boomed from every loudspeaker in town, stooping shoulders would square once more, chests swell with pride and red-rimmed eyes sparkled again. The ordeal of the interminable day was forgotten; Warsaw once more became conscious of its strength and purpose.

For Starzynski not only spoke to the people of the capital, he spoke on behalf of the city itself. He had a right to do so, no man alive had ever done as much for the capital as he had. Warsaw was his lifework, his one and only passion. And we all knew it. Election after election we all had backed him at the polls, regardless of political convictions, because everyone knew that with Starzynski, Warsaw was not a matter of politics but love. He had cleaned the municipal administration of graft, he had turned public utilities into models of efficiency, he had built, remodelled, adorned the streets, filled the squares with flowers.

And now, in one magnificent gesture of defiance he was throwing that beloved city of his open to enemy bombs. He, who for years had striven and slaved to give it comfort and beauty, now, with the same boundless energy and zest, led it to its destruction.

And still now as ever the people stood behind him. For they knew, and he reminded them every night, that destruction, hunger, even death no longer mattered. Something bigger was at stake.

Poland's honor. Poland's fate.

As long as Warsaw stood the country was not defeated, there still was hope. Warsaw was not a city any more, it was Poland itself. And in that hour of supreme test the proud Mermaid would not, could not fail . . .

Hungry, grim but determined, Warsaw carried on.

CHAPTER 18

The Malachowskis

EVERY DAY on my way home from the food lines I dropped in at the Malachowskis. They lived only one block away from us, on the same street, and hadn't I promised Tomek Malachowski to look after his wife and sister?

On the whole the little household was faring pretty well. They, too, still had all their window glass except for a small round hole in the bedroom pane, where a shrapnel splinter had broken through and had snugly settled in the curtain, enmeshed in its fringes. Young Christopher's pale little face had become almost transparent from staying too much in the dark shelter, but his mother did not seem to notice it. The two girls had grown much thinner, and Ina was delighted about it.

"Just look at this," she would say, showing how loose her skirt was. "Don't you think my figure has improved? All the family used to tease me about being so fat. Now, before this is over I'll be as slim as a sylph."

Both girls were very busy. After Tomek's departure Krysia had become the LOPP captain of the house. It was she who appointed the night watchmen, inspected the attics, supervised the shelter. In addition, the kitchen of their tiny apartment was constantly used by soldiers stationed in the house. They brought their soup to be reheated, asked for hot water, borrowed pots and pans.

The entire second floor of the house was occupied by a military court-martial. It was a ghastly neighbor to have. Once as I was entering the gate I saw a soldier led out of the house by two men in the uniforms of military police. They really were not leading him at all, they dragged him. And the soldier was sobbing, sobbing loudly, like a child. Outside a truck was waiting, with another member of the military police at the wheel. It was not even a military truck, the words "Asko—Laundry and Dry Cleaning" were still painted on its side.

I knew what that car meant. A short drive to the Citadel, and then the firing squad. The man was a deserter.

For a second I stared at the little group, my heart wrung with pity and horror. Ever since that first bombing at the railway station I had felt a guilty compassion for all deserters. The sight of posters listing the names of men court-martialed for desertion made me wince. During those agonizing moments I had learned what mortal fear could do to one. And here was a man who was going to die just because he couldn't face death. It had been too much for him. He couldn't take it, yet take it he must.

Oh well, what was the use of thinking? Quickly I ran up the few steps that led to Krysia's apartment, and rang the doorbell.

As days went by the little household began to acquire new members. One morning a young student opened the door for me. "Zbyszek Malachowski," he introduced himself. He was Tomek's first cousin and had been bombed out of his house. Next appeared Krysia's two girlfriends, Zosia and Ida. Their apartment had not been bombed but it was on the fourth floor, facing the Vistula and German artillery fire. Quite untenable, in fact.

After the two girls came a beautiful Irish setter. Zbyszek had found him in the street. The poor dog must have lost his master a long time ago or else had been turned loose by unsympathetic servants. He was terribly emaciated and there was a painful look of fear in his lovely brown eyes. Zbyszek proceeded to feed him out of his own meager rations, and by the end of the second day the young beast

From the collection of Sam Bryan, courtesy of Julien Bryan

From the collection of Sam Bryan, courtesy of Julien Bryan

Destruction wrought by German artillery and bombs forces many Varsovians to live and worship on the streets.

From the collection of Zygmunt Walkowski, courtesy of Julien Bryan

The Royal Castle burns fiercely.

had recovered enough spirit and strength to bounce all over the two tiny rooms and upset the furniture twenty times a day.

Last to appear was the cat. It was a nondescript stray cat, and I never found out who introduced it to the family. Anyway, it was there, always sitting on the windowsill, philosophical and unperturbed.

With so many inhabitants the two-room apartment had become a lively place, and in spite of everything there was something cheerful about it, too. I loved to come here, even though there was usually no place to sit except the floor; all chairs were littered with refugee belongings. The girls spent most of their spare time making cigarettes for the wounded. Zosia had discovered one of her brothers, a cavalry officer, in the Ujazdowski Hospital, wounded in the leg. The wound was not serious, but it had become infected, and Zosia was constantly in and out of the hospital, taking over cigarettes and bundles, bringing back military gossip. The latter was not cheerful. Our crack cavalry regiments had been decimated, and the casualty list grew every day.

One morning I found Ina alone. Her cheeks were flushed.

"Guess where I've just been?" her voice was quivering with excitement. "My house! My own apartment on Wilanowska. I needed some warm things for Christopher and myself, so I decided to go. It was awful. They are fighting only two blocks away on Czerniakowska, and I heard machine gun bullets whistling all around. And hand grenades bursting! You can well imagine how scared I was. However, I got there alright, and back too."

"How did you find the apartment?"

"The apartment? It's a mess. A shrapnel has hit the kitchen. One wall is down, everything lies on the floor. And the place used to be so neat. It seems to me many things are missing, it looked as if the apartment had been looted. But I had no time to investigate. Just grabbed the things I needed."

"Where are Krysia and the others?" I asked.

"Krysia and Zbyszek went to the line at Meinl. Apparently Meinl is selling cocoa today. And Zosia is at the hospital. She had just had word that the Ujazdowski had been bombed again, and her brother was wounded for the second time. Right in his bed. Imagine!"

"Seriously?"

"I don't know."

This had been a day of bad news. The Royal Castle had been bombarded again and practically demolished; a shrapnel had hit the roof of the old cathedral. And now again the Ujazdowski. This must have been the fifth time the Ujazdowski Hospital was showered with shells.

For a minute or so neither of us spoke, we just looked at each other.

And then, casually I asked, "How long, do you suppose, this will last?"

Ina's glance did not waver. "Anyway as long as there is still a single Varsovian alive."

And this was the girl who at the beginning of the war was on the verge of a nervous collapse!

CHAPTER 19

We Take in the Grudas

WE HAD our own refugees now.

One morning while Mother was still in church, someone rang the front bell. It was not the family ring, one long, one short, but as I chanced to be passing through the hall I opened the door myself: a man, a woman and two little girls about George's age stood on the landing. The man was carrying two suitcases, the woman a large can of cucumbers.

"Yes?" I asked hesitantly. I didn't recognize them at first. The woman stepped forward.

"Mrs. Langer, it's me, Mrs. Gruda," she announced in a shrill whimpering voice. "We just met your Mommy." (If there is anything I hate, it is to have Mother referred to as 'your Mommy.') "She was on her way to church and she told us we could come here. You see, we were evacuated from our house last week when the Germans occupied Saska Kepa. So we went to stay with Mr. Gruda's brother on Twarda, but the house on Twarda was bombed. Good Lord, what a bomb that was." She proceeded to give me a full and detailed account of wreckage and casualties wrought by the bomb. "After that we went to stay with friends who live on Leszno. And then the house on Leszno was struck, and so I say to my husband, 'Look here,' I say, 'perhaps Mrs. Rayska will take us in.' So we take the children and the suitcases again, and right in front of the church we meet your Mommy, and she says, yes, we can come, and so here we are, and— "

"Come in," I opened the door wide, cutting short the flood of explanation. I knew that Mrs. Gruda, once started, would never stop of her own will. "Better take the suitcases in here," I turned to Mr. Gruda showing him into Franek's room. "I suppose it's where my mother means to put you up."

This, of course, was not a very warm welcome, but then how could I help it? I had never met the other members of the Gruda family, but I knew Mrs. Gruda, and could not stand her.

Mother had two little villas in Saska Kepa and Mrs. Gruda was managing them for her. She was supposed to collect rents, pay taxes, bills and suchlike. On every first of the month she would come and settle accounts, and whenever Mother was away it was I who had to deal with her. How I hated those visits! First, she was always late for our appointment, sometimes one hour, sometimes two. As I was always in a hurry to be off to some party or another, it made me mad. But the minute I would decide "Drat the woman...I won't wait any longer" and was about to put on my hat and give her the slip, she would appear at the door, perspiring and panting.

"Well, Mrs. Gruda," I would say, trying to hide my annoyance. "Let's get it over quick. You promised to be here at seven you know, and it's almost nine."

That would start the first flood, the flood of explanations. But I wouldn't listen.

"Never mind, never mind," I would interrupt. "May I have the bills?"

Then would come the inevitable fumbling in the bag, a desperate search for bills and receipts. And all the while the whimpering voice would be droning at my ear, "Oh my, oh my, where is that water bill for Zakopianska No. 17? I know I took it. Why, it was lying on the dining room table only this morning. No, it was on the bureau. That's just the trouble with those maids. I told my Kasia not to move my papers. 'Never touch them,' I told her. 'It's none of your business, and how can I find the bills when they are no longer where I myself have put them?' "

Sometimes a bill would be missing, and that meant another one of Mrs. Gruda's visits within a day or two. The prospect made me perspire while I watched Mrs. Gruda fumbling in her bag.

At long last the bills, dirty and crumpled, were produced, and I would start to add them up; I couldn't trust Mrs. Gruda with the figures. While I struggled with the sums, that worthy woman, having discharged her duties to her complete satisfaction, would sink her plump body into an armchair and embark upon the recital of one of her domestic tragedies.

For all my dislike of her I had to admit that poor Mrs. Gruda did not have an easy life. Mr. Gruda, by all accounts, seemed to be pretty much of a wastrel. He drank, spent all the family money on horses, and lately was carrying on an open love affair with a neighbor's servant girl. It was all very sad, very sad indeed. But couldn't I really be spared any details of that rather sordid backstairs romance? Apparently I could not. Her ample bosom heaving with grief and indignation, Mrs. Gruda would serve me every juicy bit of it, and as she talked her heart would swell with self-pity till finally it overflowed in a torrent of tears and imprecations against "that scoundrel who brings such shame upon my poor innocent children and myself." It took Mrs. Gruda ten minutes to get over her fit of tears, and by the time she had wiped her eyes and risen to her feet it was ten o'clock and my evening was ruined.

Those scenes were re-enacted with painful regularity on every first of the month all through the summer, and I often wondered how Mother could stand it all year around. It may be that Mother had found a method to deal with that dejected spouse. For my part nothing I could do (and I was pretty rude at times) would prevent Mrs. Gruda from unburdening her soul upon my innocent and completely unwilling shoulders. I came to a point where the very sound of her whimpering voice gave me the creeps.

And that was the refugee Fate was sending us now!

Well, I suppose one does not choose refugees in wartime.

I had gathered from Mrs. Gruda's confidences that her husband had deserted her months ago, and was therefore surprised to see him turn up with the rest of the family. War must have brought them together, I thought. As I ushered the Grudas into Franek's room I gave the "villain" a quick glance. He was a small man with a pointed sallow face, a tiny black moustache and furtive eyes; not much of a sheik. He reminded me of a rat more than anything else.

But the children were charming. I took them by the hand and led them to the kitchen where George and they soon became fast friends over the wooden building blocks.

Mother returned from church shortly after.

"Those Grudas are here," I told her gloomily. "The bombs seem to follow them around. They've already been bombed out of two houses, and I could bet they will bring a bomb on this house, too."

Mother gave me a sympathetic little smile. She knew my dislike for Mrs. Gruda. "I know they will be a nuisance," she said apologetically. "But I couldn't very well refuse them hospitality, could I?"

"Of course not. After all, they are refugees, aren't they?"

Mother soon had matters well in hand. The Grudas were given Franek's room which was practically shellproof. (Anybody in Warsaw could tell you that a shrapnel never pierced more than two walls, and Franek's room was beyond my room and the hall, thus offering a three-wall protection. Of course, if the shrapnel chose to hit the doors it would be another story, but this was the usual margin of unsafety. Only the kitchen was absolutely shellproof, and even the kitchen was open to aerial bombardment.) Besides the room, they were offered the use of the kitchen. I also introduced them to the bathroom and went even so far as to offer them the biggest cake of soap I could find. My nose told me at once that the unfortunate family had not washed since they had left their own house.

As to provisions, they were told to fend for themselves; we simply could not take on four more mouths to feed. And they had enough money, they said.

The arrangement worked out quite well, much better than I expected.

We did not see much of the Grudas. Mr. Gruda spent most of the day in the food lines where, being a man, he had far more luck than any of us. He brought back a loaf of bread once, and offered Mother half of it. This was a magnificent gesture on his part. Mr. Gruda, however, had good reason to show Mother his gratitude. Three years before, while it was still he, and not his wife, who managed Mother's small estate in Saska Kepa, he had embezzled three months' rent and lost it on the race track. Mother had refused to prosecute him for it. "He hasn't enough money to repay me anyway, and it won't do his children any good to have a jailbird for a father." Instead, she turned over the management of the property to Mrs. Gruda. That half a loaf of bread represented the compound interest on Mr. Gruda's debt of gratitude.

Another time he brought a pigeon. It was one of those gray and rainbow-colored pigeons which used to whirl in large flocks around the churches, the Public Library, the Technical School. The poor bird had one wing broken by a shell splinter and was terribly skinny; no one fed pigeons in Warsaw any longer. Even so, however, the pigeon was quite a treat. It was equally divided among the four children and though there was no more than one morsel for each, they greeted it with shouts of joy. After George and Ania had eaten their portions I was given the bones to chew. They were good, too.

Mr. Gruda also helped me with the windows. All windows in Warsaw had double panes, and we were advised over the radio to take out the inside panes to save them from destruction. With Gruda's assistance I managed to unhinge all the lower parts of the windows in the two front rooms. We hid them behind the sofa, carefully wrapped up in rugs. But the upper windows resisted all our attempts to remove them from their hinges. "If you are bound on suicide, you stupid things, just stay where you are, and you'll see," I grumbled, giving up any further attempts at last.

I proposed to Mother to remove the inside windows in the three back rooms too, but she refused. "Single windows are all right in summertime, but now that winter is approaching we will be cold." Mother was determined to ignore the threats of bombardment.

In the meantime Mrs. Gruda had taken abode in the kitchen, where Cook and she spent long hours discussing the bloodcurdling stories they had collected in the lines. I no longer dared to enter the kitchen lest I hear some more gruesome details concerning the girl who, descending the steps of the Savior's Church, had her head torn off by a shell, or the woman who lost her mind and jumped screaming into a burning house.

There were more of such stories every day, and both Cook and Mrs. Gruda seemed to revel in them. While one talked the other would listen attentively, nodding her head in mute appreciation of the horrors described. Sometimes one or the other would utter a deep sigh and exclaim: "Oh God, have mercy upon us," or, "Now, you see. Didn't I tell you the world was coming to an end? What will become of us all?"

Whether the world was coming to an end or not, however, Cook and Mrs. Gruda did not let it interfere with their daily duties. While their minds and tongues were engaged in a veritable orgy of war atrocities their hands were as busy as ever with cooking, washing, mending. Meanwhile the children were playing on the kitchen floor. With four partners instead of two the new bombardment game became more exciting than ever, and sometimes a happy burst of laughter provoked by a particularly well-aimed missile would rise above the voices of the two women telling their gruesome stories.

When it came to real bombardment, however, I soon noticed how different was the reaction of the Gruda children from that of my own two kids.

To George and Ania the sound of close artillery fire was the source of pleasurable excitement. Their eyes would sparkle, their cheeks grew rosy, and they would talk excitedly, discussing whose artillery was firing, how big were the guns. At such times George would go into a lot of technical details he had picked up, God knows where, and his constant chatter would get on everybody's nerves.

Not so the Gruda children. The minute they heard a nearby explosion they would huddle in a corner, crouching on the floor, both hands pressed to their ears, eyes shut tight.

Poor youngsters! They knew all too well what bombardment means. They didn't want to see or hear any of it.

CHAPTER 20

September 23: My Birthday

ON THE day the Grudas arrived I had an urgent telephone call from Rose. I used to phone her every day to find out how she was getting along. I was surprised, therefore, to have her call me. Her voice sounded anxious.

"Look here, Rulka. I wonder if you would help me. The baby, I think, has at last made up its mind to come, and I want to get to the hospital. I've called the hospital at Zlota where I have engaged a room but the telephone doesn't answer. I suppose they've been bombed. I can't go to Omega because it's full of wounded. The hospital of the Elizabethan Sisters is right on the front line. And I don't know of any other. Could you suggest something?"

"Wait a moment. Yes, I can. Ania was born in Sano on Lwowska. As safe a spot as any in town. I know the doctors and the nurses there. Let me call them and find out."

After a bit of telephoning everything was arranged, and Roman himself took Rose over to Sano. She called me from there to tell me that everything was fine, except the food—the hospital's provisions were running very low, and as Rose put it, "I am probably going to starve before the baby is born. The family, however, is organizing a rescue party. They may save me yet." I promised to visit her the next day. Lwowska was a little safer than the street on which Rose had hitherto lived, but even at that, the visit would require some effort.

Ever since the German artillery had started shelling our part of the city in earnest I was loath to go off any distance from home. It was not only that one felt so much safer under the protection of a roof and walls than in the open streets. What worried me most was the eternal uncertainty as to what might happen to the house while I was away. What if on my return I should find the house destroyed and Mother and the children dead, or taken to a hospital? Every time I came back from a more distant shopping trip my heart would be in my throat as I neared our street, and not till the yellow stucco façade was in sight did the pang subside. No, it was no fun.

When it came to visiting Rose, however, I felt a vague sense of duty about it. I had promised Roman when I saw him last, on that distant day of the bank's evacuation (Could it be less than three weeks ago? Three months seemed more likely!) that I would come and see his young wife, and I had not done it yet. As long as she was staying with Roman's mother it really didn't matter, but now the poor child was all alone in unfamiliar surroundings, about to have a baby right under the bombs and mortally worried about a beloved husband constantly exposed to danger. No, I must go to see Rose.

But I had reckoned without the Germans.

The next day—this was September 23, and incidentally, my birthday—the Germans chose to send over Warsaw squadron upon squadron of bombers. They flew very high and only a few dived to drop bombs. Not a concentrated attack, just a few indiscriminate bombs here and there; just enough to keep us constantly on our toes. And they kept it up from nine o'clock in the morning till nightfall. Certainly not a day for paying calls.

Twice that morning we left the apartment and, carrying our suitcases, herded on the landing of the kitchen stairs. In case the house were struck by a bomb it seemed safer to be nearer the exit. Our suitcases had been ready for weeks, waiting under the kitchen table. Each contained two changes of underwear, a suit of warm clothing and a blanket. Money and jewelry we carried in small linen bags on our breasts.

The landing was crowded with people from other apartments. From every dark corner peered pale, anxious faces, and the passage was crammed with suitcases and bags. As I stood there, holding the two children by the hand, I was only conscious of the throbbing roar of the engines overhead, the pounding of my own heart and the vibration that shook the house. Otherwise my mind was a complete blank; no fear. Was I getting used to the bombers? I thought so... that day.

As soon as the roar of the planes subsided into a gentler drone we returned to the apartment and our normal occupations.

"I don't think I'll go and see Rose today," I told Mother after our second exodus to the landing. "Perhaps tomorrow will be better."

This, of course, was nothing but wishful thinking. I should have known by then that "tomorrow" was always worse than "today."

"Yes, I really think you had better stay home today," Mother agreed. Coming from Mother this was something.

Fate, however, had decreed otherwise.

Right after lunch I went to fetch Aunt Madzia, but as she lived almost next door this could hardly be called going out. I was back with her in less than five minutes. No sooner, however, had we settled to our daily assignment of bandages, when Leosia came to announce that Gosposia was in the kitchen and wanted to see me.

Gosposia had been our cook for three years, and a braver, more devoted soul I've never seen. We were all very fond of her, and I would never have let her go, if it were not that after Olgierd's departure for the United States I had decided to break up housekeeping and move to Mother's. At that time both Gosposia and I had wept bitter tears on each other's shoulder and ever since she had come every month to see me and report about her progress in other households.

"Something has happened to Gosposia and she is sobbing something terrible," added Leosia. "But neither Cook nor I can make out what's the matter."

In the kitchen I found Gosposia huddled on a low footstool, her face hidden in both hands so that only the back of her head with the big knot of hair showed above the broad, fat shoulders that were shaking with sobs.

"What is it, Gosposia, dear?" I asked, stroking her head gently. "Why do you cry?"

She lifted her round face, usually so jolly, now covered with tears and puckered like a child's.

"Oh Madam, they are dead... my darlings are dead... that awful man... and my sister-in-law, too... wounded... and the pigeons, and the dogs, such lovely dogs, Madam!"

It took me some time before I got her story straight. In fact there was not one story, but two.

The first referred to Gosposia's sister-in-law. Gosposia, who was living now on the outskirts of the city, got worried over her family and for the first time since the siege began had come all the way over to the center of the city where her brother, a hairdresser (a fact she was immensely proud of) lived and had an establishment. She had found the apartment gone, two shells had torn the upper story of the house to pieces. Neighbors had informed her that both her sister-in-law and her niece were at the hospital.

"Are they seriously wounded?" I asked.

"The neighbors say they will recover."

"And what about the baby?" I knew that Gosposia's niece had a child.

The baby had miraculously escaped and the neighbors were taking care of it.

"Well, Gosposia, it isn't so bad then. It might have been worse. You shouldn't cry, not really. The way you act one would think that all your family were dead."

"Yes, Madam," admitted Gosposia, and then burst into tears again. "But the pigeons... and the dogs... all my darlings are dead!"

And now came the other story which, in Gosposia's eyes at least, was far more tragic than the first one. Gosposia's master had departed during the general evacuation and had left her behind to watch over the apartment and the dog, a lively, "perfectly darling" fox terrier by the name of Coco. Gosposia didn't mind that: all the other masters in the house—one of those big cooperative apartment buildings inhabited mostly by state employees—had left, too, and she had made many friends among the remaining servants. Besides, she had plenty of provisions.

Everything would have been fine, if it were not for one gentleman—"a horrid man, worse than Hitler"—who had stayed behind. This "devilish person" had instituted himself the ruler of the whole house, and what a ruthless tyrant he was! He first commandeered all the provisions for the soldiers who were stationed nearby. Gosposia managed to hide most of hers ("the soldiers don't need them, Madam, they have their rolling kitchens—it was just his silly whim"). But as he was searching the apartments for hidden victuals, she could never tell how long she would be able to hang on to them.

Next he decreed that in a city where there was not enough food for men, no dog should remain alive. Gosposia fought tooth and nails to save Coco, but to no avail. The poor doggie was snatched from her and shot with the others in the courtyard under her very eyes. It was a dreadful memory, poor Gosposia shuddered at the very thought of it, and burst into a fresh fit of sobs.

And then, this was the last straw, he shot all the pigeons. For anyone who didn't know Gosposia this would sound like a minor offense, but to Gosposia pigeons meant everything; they were her hobby. Anywhere we lived she would find pigeons to feed, or rather the pigeons would find her. I did not approve of the hobby. The house management always complained that the walls under our kitchen windows were dirty, and would we please discontinue feeding pigeons on the windowsill? Every time after such a complaint I would talk to Gosposia about it, and she would promise to discontinue her favorite pastime. And the next thing I knew, the pigeons would be on the windowsill again. "They came for their dinner," Gosposia gingerly explained, "and I just couldn't disappoint them." Gosposia simply could not live without her pigeons.

And now her own window had become a death trap for her little pets. If it were not for her, they wouldn't come to the house where the dreadful man lay in ambush, and shot them one by one. At last there was only one left, and she stopped leaving crumbs for it, hoping that, perhaps, it would quit coming and thus escape destruction. But it came just the same, and . . . yes, the brute shot it, just as it was flying away hungry and disappointed. No, Gosposia would never forgive that man, he was a monster, a beast . . .

At last Gosposia's sobs subsided.

"I'll be going home, now," she announced, wiping her eyes. "It's done me good to see you, Madam, and the children, and tell you all about it."

"But Gosposia," I protested, "you cannot go now. Don't you hear them buzzing?" The drone of the planes overhead was audible all through our conversation. "It's awfully far to your house. Why don't you stay here overnight?"

I threw a furtive glance at Cook. There existed a long-standing feud between the two women over some recipe that did not turn out the way it should, and I was afraid Cook might protest. But she didn't bat an eyelid. After all, this was war; even the most bitter kitchen feuds were forgotten.

Gosposia, however, refused my invitation. She was in a hurry to get home, and who could tell whether tomorrow air raids wouldn't be worse?

Besides she had her provisions, why should she eat our insufficient food?

And suddenly Gosposia's countenance beamed with a wide grin. "Look here, Madam," she exclaimed, "why don't you and Leosia come with me? I'll give you half of my provisions."

"Why, Gosposia, that's impossible! You'll need them yourself."

"Oh no, Madam, I have far more than I need. I can give you rice and flour, cream of wheat and grits. And sugar, too. Besides, that awful man can take those things anyway. I much rather you had them. Let's take some baskets and start right away. Leosia can help you."

"Would you come, Leosia?"

"Sure, if Madam does. I wouldn't dream of going all that way all by myself, but with Madam it will be different."

What temptation... rice, flour, grits... yes, but those planes overhead... four miles to walk in a pretty fierce air raid. Should I go or shouldn't I?

"Wait a moment. I'll ask Mother."

I returned to the dining room and explained the situation to the two ladies.

"You can't go," Aunt Madzia declared at once. "Four miles in this air raid? That's pure madness. No flour is worth such risk."

"As far as risk goes we have just as much chance to catch a bomb here."

"White flour," Mother said dreamily.

"And rice," I added.

"And cream of wheat," Mother continued. Then suddenly turning to me, "No, Rulka, I can't advise you in this matter. It's for you to decide."

"All right," I said, "I will go. And if I get killed... Well, Auntie, it's my birthday today, you know. It's rather smart, I think, to die on one's birthday. She lived thirty-three years. Not a day more, not a day less. Neat."

I didn't think, however, that I was going to be killed. Ever since I was a child two numbers had persisted: twenty-three and sixty-seven. All documents I ever possessed bore one of these numbers, or both. And every time I was handed a cloakroom check I would give it a curious glance: twenty-three or sixty-seven would be on it as often as not. So, ever since I was sixteen I strongly believed that I would marry at the age of twenty-three (which I did) and live till I am sixty-seven (which possibly I still may do). If my hunch was right, I still had a margin of thirty-four years. The only thing I didn't like about this business was leaving the house. What would we find on our return?

We set out in pretty good spirits, chatting gaily. Leosia and Gosposia felt safe, they said, because I was with them, and their presence in turn gave me an unexpected feeling of security. There is nothing like companionship in times of danger.

The drone overhead was continuous but distant; we didn't see the planes. The streets were empty, even bread lines had dispersed by that time. Only in the square two men were working, digging a grave. The body, an old woman, lay alongside, a poor little heap of rags, very flat and peaceful. It wasn't even covered with a sheet—these were days of hurried burials. Without stopping we crossed ourselves, whispered a short prayer and hurried by.

A little further down the street we came upon a dead horse. All the flesh had been removed by the hungry inhabitants of the neighboring houses, and the bare, bloody carcass with the head and legs still covered with skin and stiffly stretched out made a ghastly sight.

"We can't go through Nowowiejska," Gosposia announced, "it's barricaded. We will have to go around."

For all her roly-poly appearance Gosposia was a pretty brisk walker, and as both Leosia and I had long legs we made good progress.

"If we continue at this pace, and nothing stops us, we will be in Gosposia's house in less than an hour," I remarked.

If nothing stops us... Five minutes later the drone of the planes drew nearer, grew louder, and suddenly the roar was upon us. We ducked into the nearest doorway.

We found two people already hiding there, a girl and a neat-looking, elderly woman dressed in black. The old lady immediately produced from her pocketbook a folded newspaper, spread it on the lowest step of the staircase, and sat down.

"I always carry a newspaper with me," she announced. "One can never tell nowadays on what dirty stairs one is going to sit."

Being not so thoughtfully provided for, we sat on the bare stairs and waited. Five minutes, ten minutes. The throbbing of the engines continued. We weren't really

USHMM, courtesy of Julien Bryan

From the collection of Stefan Mucha

As Warsaw runs out of food, starving Varsovians resort to eating horses killed in the bombings ...

251

From the collection of Stefan Mucha

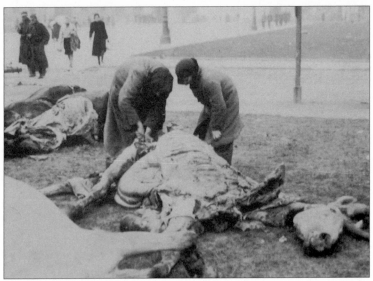

USNARA

... often the horse carcasses are stripped of flesh where they have fallen.

scared, but annoyed; we were in a hurry to be on our way. At last the noise began to subside.

"You'd better wait a little longer," the old lady warned us, "they are apt to come back."

She was right. We hadn't gone more than a hundred yards when the roar was upon us again. Once more we had to duck. This time the doorway was empty, dark and had a musty smell. Standing there we heard the crash of a none-too-distant explosion. But it was too late to turn back now. We had to continue on our way.

From then on we literally ran from doorway to doorway, catching our breath only when we ducked to let the planes pass. It was all right as long as there were houses and doorways to hide in. But at a certain stage of our trip we had to pass through a street where on both sides only high walls stretched for the length of three blocks —the Warsaw Water Station. And again the roar of the bombers caught up with us there. We ran like mad. At last, panting and exhausted, we reached a building, one of those grim, modern government office buildings. I was about to throw myself into the open door, when suddenly a sentry I had not noticed before barred my way.

"Sorry," he said. "This is a military site. No one is allowed to go in."

We were in a fix. A military site, German bombers overhead, and no other building in sight.

"Can we at least remain here on the porch?" I asked. The porch had a little roof, and a roof, no matter how flimsy, seemed more secure than the open street. The sentry had no objections to that. So we stood huddled to the wall, waiting. Nothing happened and we continued on our way. Altogether we stopped in seventeen doorways, and it took us three full hours to reach Gosposia's house.

Gosposia at once proceeded to fill the bags and baskets we had brought along. A bag of flour was produced from under the bathtub, a sofa cushion yielded sugar, a hatbox brought forth rice and grits. Poor Gosposia, she had carefully stowed away her precious provisions. Loaded to capacity, we started on our way back.

The return journey was pretty much the same, save that the heavy baskets hampered our movements when we ran. Very soon our arms and shoulder blades became sore, but we didn't mind. We were proud of the bounty we were bringing home.

Only once we didn't go into hiding when the roar overtook us. We were in the open again and this time we caught sight of the planes. They flew in a formidable triangle, gleaming like silver in the rays of the setting sun. Our antiaircraft artillery was trying to reach them, little fluffs of smoke rose all around the glistening birds of death. This is always a fascinating sight, and forgetting all danger we just stood there watching. No, the planes were too high, the little fluffs could not quite reach them. And suddenly the leading plane dropped something. A bomb...? A second of breathless suspense. No, it wasn't a bomb. It fell very slowly and all at once split into hundreds of sparks. The sparks descended unhurriedly, whirling in the quiet evening air, growing larger as they neared the ground... rectangular. They were leaflets!

"Wonder what they have to say this time?" I mused.

We were soon to find out. In the crowded doorway where we took refuge once more fifteen minutes later, a man asked, "Did anyone see the leaflets the Germans dropped a short while ago? They say that this is their last warning. If Warsaw does not surrender at once, they will destroy the city completely—raze it to the ground. Not one inhabitant will survive!"

"Let them," a woman said darkly. "They've done enough damage already." Others just shrugged their shoulders. German threats...

It was already dark when we reached the house. Mother opened the door for us. "I am glad you're back, I was beginning to get worried," she said.

Mother, worried? To be sure our trip had taken us over five hours. But it was worth it.

"Just look, Mother, what we brought. I'll bet you've never seen such splendor."

Only then I noticed that the hall was dark.

"No electric light," Mother said. "It's gone. So is the water."

"Water?" I gasped, and then very low, "Good Heavens, that's the end."

Electricity didn't matter, we still had candles, and so had everyone else. But without water we were at the mercy of incendiary bombs.

"Is it only our street which has no water, or is it all over town?"

"All over town. The filters were bombed this afternoon. The radio says it will take at least several days to repair them. It's lucky the bathtub is filled with water."

A tubful of water. What good would that do in case of fire? Again I could feel something inside me shrink, shrink. The Germans may make their threat good yet...

That night for supper we had noodles, the fruit of our expedition. A warm glow spread through our bodies, it was wonderful to be replete once more.

"I don't think I ever ate so much in my life," Mother said with a contented sigh.

But even though satiated I did not feel happy. We were eating in the kitchen. The light of the single candle flickered constantly. Shadows were dancing on the walls —the place looked strangely gloomy. And the German artillery had started its concert again.

Wheeeeeew! Bang! Wheeeeeew! Bang!

It was going to be a hot night. And no water... Fires would spread all over town, and there would be no way to check them.

Suddenly Mother's voice roused me from these grim thoughts.

"Please, Cook," Mother was saying, "don't give me such strong tea, or I won't be able to sleep tonight!"

Chapter 21

September 24: The Church of the Savior Burns

ALL NIGHT long the German guns kept up their terrific pounding. It was unlike anything we had ever had before; "hurricane fire" is what they call it, I guess. And now it was morning, and the bombardment still went on, and on, and on... Not a moment of respite.

Mother said she had slept pretty well through it all.

"I have developed a system, you see," she told me. "You know that my right ear isn't very good. So as soon as they start shooting I turn on my left side, and with the good ear pressed to the pillow I hardly hear a sound."

I wished I had a deaf ear to turn to the German artillery fire. As it was, at least half a dozen times I had fallen off into a doze, only to be awakened by a terrific crash that seemed to be no more than a few hundred yards away. I hadn't even taken my shoes off that night, and I got up sore and terribly tired. Washing would have refreshed me, but our tubful of water was too precious to be wasted on mere cleanliness. I dabbed at myself and the children with eau de cologne, and as it was Sunday we set off for church.

The church was just around the corner, and we didn't walk there, we ran, keeping as close to the walls as possible.

The church was packed with people, but a strange hush hung over the crowd. There was no usual shuffling of feet, coughs, whispers of prayers. Very few lips moved. People just stood there, silent, motionless, hunger, fatigue and tension written on every face...

And then at the altar the priest intoned the Supplications, the deep bass of the organ answered somewhere from the back, and suddenly the whole church burst into that most dramatic of all human pleas:

> *God Thou Holy—God Thou Mighty,*
> *Mighty and Immortal,*
> *Have mercy upon us!*

It was like the supreme cry of distress. It beat at the walls, shook the roof, fought its way to the Heavens.

It wasn't God that answered; it was the German artillery. Wheeeeeeeeew—Crash!

But still the hymn continued, stronger, more insistent, swelling in prayer, in hope, in despair. . .

> *. . . from hunger, fire and war*
> *Deliver us, O Lord.*

Crash!! (This was terribly close.)

> *. . . from sudden and unexpected death*
> *Save us, O Lord!*

No, it was too much, too much. I couldn't stand it any longer. The candlelight on the altar began to dance before my eyes, everything became blurred, and two heavy tears rolled down my cheeks. Others followed. I was crying, help-lessly, like a baby.

It made me terribly ashamed, for no one else wept. All around me people knelt with eyes on the altar, their faces transfixed, and sang, sang as if their hearts were going to burst:

> *We sinners implore you, O Lord*
> *Have mercy upon us.*

But there was no mercy. The bombardment continued, furious, inexorable. Suddenly there was a commotion at the door, quick footsteps ran along the aisle, and I saw a man disappear into the door of the vestry. A minute later the crowd opened to let pass a group of three people, a priest and two men carrying candles. With majestic slowness the little procession proceeded to the door, down the church steps and at last disappeared into the empty street.

Viaticum for the dying... Have mercy upon us!

"I think I have had enough for today," I announced on my return from church. "I am not going out again."

But no sooner did I settle down to the rolling of bandages when the telephone rang. It was the Women's Defense organization with which I had registered on the first day of our arrival in Warsaw.

"Mrs. Langer," a voice said, "are you still looking for a defense job?"

"I certainly am."

"Well, I think we have something for you this time. Will you come to the headquarters and see Mrs. S.?"

"When?"

"Right away. Can you make it?"

"Sure." I couldn't help a slight note of defiance creeping into my voice. They did pick out the right time for an appointment, didn't they? Well, a defense job is no soft job anyway; bound to involve danger, I might as well get used to it at once. Besides, I had only five blocks to go. Five blocks under hurricane artillery fire. Oh, well...

I told Mother about it. She didn't protest, but I could see by a slight contraction of her eyelids that she didn't like the idea of my going out again. However, "Good luck" was all she said.

I felt proud and terribly excited as I descended the stairs. At last I was going to join the ranks of those who actually did something for the defense of Warsaw. Rolling bandages was nothing but an old woman's task, anyway.

I braced myself as I stepped into the street. Funny how a straight back helps to keep fear down. Chin up! I wish I knew how to whistle. "Left-right, left-right," I kept repeating to myself, as I marched at a military, rhythmic pace down the deserted windswept streets. The bombardment continued as fierce as ever, and every time a shell whistled over my head I couldn't control a violent start. Twice I broke into a run but checked myself in time. No, running would not do, it made one panicky. "Left-right, left-right..."

Three more blocks to go. I turned into Aleje Ujazdowskie. The broad avenue with its lovely deep perspective of trees and beautiful buildings looked strangely desolate. Not a soul in sight. In the middle of the thoroughfare lay a dead horse, twigs and branches torn by splinters littered the sidewalks. In the midst of them rested a dud bomb, a big one, too. Carefully I circled it. "Left-right, left-right..."

In one of the narrow borders of turf on which trees grew, a little grave had sprung up. So it wasn't enough to have graveyards in every square? Were the streets going to be changed into cemeteries too? "Left-right, left right..."

Two more blocks to go. Wiejska was strewn with glass. Shells must have hit here recently, for glass was usually removed almost at once. Bloodstains dotted the sidewalks. No wonder, Wiejska had been turned into a street of hospitals. One more block. A hundred steps... fifty... twenty... At last I was there.

I had to step over a pool of blood before I reached the door. Two women stood talking in the vestibule. I asked them where the blood came from.

From the collection of Zygmunt Walkowski

"Were the streets going to be changed into cemeteries too?"

From the collection of Stefan Mucha

A Polish cavalry officer is buried under the sidewalk—his curved saber rests on top of the grave.

Graves by the roadside in the Praga district of Warsaw.

A soldier's grave on the sidewalk at the junction of Aleje Jerozolimskie and Marszalkowska, two of the main downtown streets.

From the collection of Sam Bryan, courtesy of Julien Bryan

A priest rescues a precious altar crucifix from the ruins of his church.

From the collection of Sam Bryan, courtesy of Julien Bryan

Sacred church statues do not go unscathed.

"A man was killed on the doorstep half an hour ago," one of them informed me in a matter-of-fact tone. "The body has not been identified."

There wasn't a single windowpane left in the whole building, and with the wind outside the drafts were terrible. I climbed up the stairs, and proceeded through innumerable corridors bustling with girl scouts and women in semi-military uniforms.

At last I located Mrs. S.'s office. I had known Mrs. S. in pre-war days. She was then an attractive woman of thirty-five, smartly dressed and affecting rather heavy makeup. There was not a speck of makeup on her face now, and she wore a semi-military uniform, a khaki-colored blouse with a leather belt and a navy blue, pleated skirt. This sober costume clashed somewhat with an extremely long and unmilitary-looking cigarette holder she was waving in the air as she talked to the woman seated at the opposite desk. Little feminine habits will persist in spite of any siege...

"Here is Mrs. Langer," Mrs. S. said cheerfully as I entered. "Mrs. K., didn't I tell you she would come?" She gave me a wink.

Apparently this summoning me right in the midst of a bombardment had been something of a test. I was glad I passed it. After all, it might easily have happened that I should not be there at all, and through no fault of mine, either.

I was offered a seat, a cigarette, and told what was expected of me.

Apparently the military authorities were getting worried over the widely spread defeatist propaganda carried on in shelters. The women's organization had been asked to help in detecting the source of it, and I was going to be put on the squad to which the job would be assigned. Officially, we would visit the shelters looking for cases of typhoid fever (which were numerous). Unofficially, we would listen to conversations and report our findings. It was all going to be strictly confidential, with a special code, a mysterious telephone number to be used only in particularly urgent cases, passwords, and whatnot. Altogether quite exciting for anyone interested in that kind of espionage work.

Personally, spying never appealed to me. However, if this was to be my defense job, I was determined to carry it out to the best of my abilities. I asked about methods to be used but was told that I would have to work them out for myself. The whole thing was at an experimental stage.

"When do I start on my first round?"

"Tomorrow at nine AM. Mrs. K. will telephone you."

I was given the code and telephone number, and dismissed with a friendly "Good luck" and a wave of the long cigarette holder.

I was less heroic on my way home. The first shrapnel that whistled over my head sent me scurrying into the nearest doorway. From then on I ran, ducking frequently. Nevertheless I reached home in less than fifteen minutes, and felt pretty pleased with myself. After all, I had done it. I had gone out under heavy artillery fire and got a defense job. Mentally I patted myself on the back.

I told Mother about my job, but only a part of it: inspecting shelters for cases of typhoid fever; the rest was a deadly secret. She, again, refrained from any comments.

"Is Aunt Madzia coming this afternoon?" I asked.

"Wait a moment, I'll call her up and find out."

Mother went to the telephone in the hall, leaving the dining room door open so I could listen to the conversation. Aunt Madzia was evidently hard to persuade for I heard Mother say, "Come now, don't be so timorous. We will give you a cup of coffee. Real, good, hot coffee, with sugar. Do come."

"I'll go and fetch her," I called from where I sat. Mother repeated my message but it apparently did no good.

"Well, if you don't think my coffee is worth risking your life for, I feel very much insulted but what can I do about it? See you tomorrow, I hope."

Mother was just replacing the receiver when there was a terrific crash. I saw the front room door fly open, I saw Mother crouch, then I heard the tinkle of broken glass.

"Mother, are you hurt?" I cried.

"No, but the front windows are gone."

A bomb had crashed somewhere near and we hadn't even heard the plane! We all ran into my room to see what was hit. It was the secondhand furniture store almost across the street from our house.

A column of dust was still rising from the wreckage. It was lucky that this was Sunday and the place was almost sure to be deserted.

"And here goes not only our window glass but the plywood that was to replace it," I remarked.

George, who had followed us from the dining room, ran to the kitchen to tell the Gruda children all about the bomb that had destroyed not only our windowpanes but the plywood too, all in one stroke.

We cleared the debris which littered the floors, and carefully closed the doors to the two front rooms through which the cold wind blew now as it pleased.

The afternoon without Aunt Madzia dragged on interminably. Mother and I were working on the bandages but we didn't have much to tell each other, and even the radio no longer kept us company, the German bombs had at last succeeded in silencing it too. This was a real blow, for it meant that tonight we wouldn't hear Mayor Starzynski's daily broadcast. It was during the Mayor's talks that one braced oneself to carry on through the following night and day. And now, when the siege had grown worse than ever, we would no longer be able to hear his stirring words.

The bombardment did not relent for a minute.

I was growing restless. Would that hateful afternoon never end? I wished it were over. Why? I don't know. I didn't expect the night to be any better. But that was just the way one felt in those days. During daytime one wished for night, but when night came one couldn't wait for the daylight to return. Just like a man in pain, who cannot find comfort either in time or space.

That Sunday afternoon the suspense was particularly unbearable. From time to time I glanced at the dining room clock. It ticked as usual, but I could have sworn the hands did not move. For hours it was three ten. Then for hours again three fifteen. A longer afternoon I've never lived through.

At last dusk began to fall. Mother got up and went into the front room to fetch fresh sheets for bandages. Suddenly I heard her call, "Rulka, come here a minute, will you?"

I went into the front room. Mother was standing on the balcony that overhung the street, and I joined her there.

"Look," she said.

The Church of the Savior was burning. It was burning like a torch with huge flames leaping high in the sky. The two gothic steeples, sharply outlined against the red and golden background of flames, looked more graceful, more ethereal than ever. Taller, too. Never was the Church of the Savior bigger, more imposing and more beautiful than in this hour of final destruction. It was a glorious and horrible sight. For a long time we watched it in silence.

"I saw it built," Mother said at last in a low, strangled voice. "It was the year before you were born. I used to sit on

The Church of the Savior, circa 1920s.

From the collection of Stefan Mucha

After the siege, "the other steeple still remained upright, like an accusing finger pointing skyward."

270

this balcony waiting for your father to return from the office. And every day I would watch those two steeples rise higher in the sky. They are going now..."

Again we relapsed into silence. Suddenly one of the towers, the right one, collapsed, sending a gigantic column of flames high into the sky. But the other steeple still remained upright, like an accusing finger pointing skyward.

"Let's go inside," Mother said finally. "What's the use...?"

As we returned to the dining room I glanced through the window. On this side, too, the sky was tinted with a rosy hue. It couldn't be the glow from the burning church, the dining room windows pointed to the north.

Somewhere in that direction other buildings had also been set afire. And there was no water to quench the flames.

The bombardment had ceased at last, but the silence that fell over the city now was perhaps even worse. Tension grew with every minute. We were waiting, waiting...

What were we waiting for?

CHAPTER 22

September 25: Black Monday

SEPTEMBER TWENTY-FIFTH, 1939. No one in Warsaw will ever forget that day.

Eight o'clock found us already on the back stairs landing, suitcases, gas masks, coats and all. I can still see myself leaning against the wall, trying to shield the children with my body, "Like a hen and her chicks," George had said, smiling up at me from where he crouched on the floor.

Wave after wave of German bombers swept overhead. They flew so low that at times it seemed impossible that they should miss the roof. What on earth was our anti-aircraft artillery doing? Not a shot, not a bark. Here came another wave. The roar of the motors grew deafening, the walls trembled. Now. . . ?

Crash! A nearby explosion rocked the house, then another, and still another. We heard the tinkle of broken glass. But thank goodness, it wasn't our house. Not this time. Not yet. And the roar of the planes was growing fainter, more distant. . . ("You'll live to be sixty-seven, you'll live to be sixty-seven," I repeated to myself, but I didn't believe it anymore.) The roar came back once more. Louder, louder. . . Now. . . ?

And thus for hours.

Three times that morning we tried to return to the apartment and resume our normal occupations (I still half expected a telephone call that would summon me to my new duties), and three times the roar of the bombers chased us out onto the landing again.

And then a little before eleven the bell in the courtyard began to ring.

German generals plan the final assault on Warsaw.

"September twenty-fifth, 1939. No one in Warsaw will ever forget that day."

From the collection of the Museum of the Polish Army, Warsaw

The Germans bomb Warsaw relentlessly.

From the collection of Stefan Mucha

A road leads straight into burning Warsaw...

USHMM, courtesy of Julien Bryan

...where fires consume hundreds of buildings during this day.

Fire!

There was a patter of running feet. Someone shouted from downstairs: "Quick! The back of the house is on fire. Bring all the water you have. Quick!"

I told Leosia to remain with the children on the landing, and ran back to the apartment. Mother and Cook followed me. We grabbed buckets and filled them in the bathtub. No time now to spare the last of our water. It splashed all around as we ran back and forth, back and forth... A human chain was organized in no time; buckets passed from hand to hand.

"What has happened?" I asked a man, as I handed him my full pail in return for an empty one. "Couldn't they extinguish the incendiary?" Incendiaries were easy to extinguish. Just one shovelful of sand or dirt would do the trick.

"No. The man who was in the attic watching for them was killed when a high explosive hit the house at the back. They found a new way," he added bitterly. "First a high explosive, then an incendiary. It works."

Up and down the stairs. Back and forth, back and forth... It was a relief to be running, carrying buckets. One had no time to think of the bombers overhead.

I was just returning to the bathroom with two empty pails when I heard someone knocking at the front door. I handed the pails to Cook and ran to open the door. Krysia Malachowska, panting and hatless, was standing on the threshold.

"Look here, Rulka," she was talking very fast, trying at the same time to catch her breath, "do you know that all your side of the street is on fire? You better bring your mother and your children and come at once to our shelter. We will be glad to have you."

I gasped.

"Do you mean to tell me that you've run all this way through a burning street and under the bombs just to invite us to your shelter?" I could hardly believe it.

"Yes, of course. Come as soon as you can. I've got to run now. I am needed at the house."

She was already descending the stairs.

"Thanks!" I cried after her.

Of all the invitations I've ever had! And it was *I* who was supposed to take care of Krysia and Ina. But I had no time to think about it now. Fires don't wait. Back and forth, back and forth. Up and down the stairs...

At last the tub was empty. Nothing but a little mud from dirty pails remained at the bottom.

"No more water," Mother said philosophically. "At least we've done our duty."

I ran out into the courtyard to see if I couldn't help with the fire out there. But I was not needed. There were enough men working on it. They worked with spades now. Not a drop of water remained in the whole house and they were filling buckets with dirt. It was the fourth and third story of the back wing that was burning. Not a big fire, either. Just a lot of smoke and a few flames coming out of the windows. I returned to the apartment.

A man had followed me from the landing and was standing now in the middle of the kitchen. An elderly, neatly dressed gentleman, but I'd never seen him before.

"Don't lose your heads, ladies," he kept repeating. "For Heaven's sake, don't lose your heads. A level head is the most important thing at such moments. Keep quiet. Don't lose your heads."

"No," I assured him with a smile. "We don't intend to lose our heads." I could see that the poor man had completely lost his. But Mother, who was as cool as a cucumber herself, could not conceive that anyone could be unnerved to the extent of walking into a stranger's apartment uninvited. She beckoned to me.

"Get him out of here," she said as soon as we were out of the man's hearing. "What is he doing in our kitchen anyway? I am sure he came here to steal something."

"Why, Mother," I laughed, "don't you see that the poor man is half-crazed with fear? He is no more a thief than you or I."

"Well, get him out anyway. I don't trust him."

I returned to the kitchen and offered the man a cigarette. A smoke perhaps would steady his nerves. He accepted it gratefully but I had to light it for him, his hand shook so.

"My daughter has completely lost her head," he told me after taking a few puffs. "I wanted her to come and stay with us on Nowogrodzka. But no. She insisted on my coming here. Crazy woman. Why aren't we on Nowogrodzka now? We would be safe. It all comes from losing one's head!"

I doubted that Nowogrodzka would be any safer now than our own street. But here was my chance to get him out of the place.

"Don't you think you better go and see how your daughter is faring?" I asked. "I am sure she needs your company."

"Yes, I guess you are right," reluctantly he turned towards the door. "But, ladies, for Heaven's sake don't lose your heads."

After he was gone Mother and I went back to the dining room. The Grudas were still on the landing, but Cook, Leosia and the children had returned to the kitchen. Ania was going to take her midday nap on Cook's bed.

"I am a little tired," Mother said. "Let's rest for a while. Perhaps in half an hour Cook can get us something to eat." There had been no breakfast for us that morning.

Mother lay down on the sofa, while I threw myself into

an armchair and lit a cigarette. We didn't talk, just relaxed. There was no sound of bombers overhead, or perhaps we didn't listen...

The orange lightning cut through my consciousness like a whip. Then the terrific jolt of explosion. The long, rumbling noise of crumbling walls, the tinkle of broken glass.

Mother, the room, everything disappeared in a cloud of dust...

I half rose from the chair and peered in the direction of the sofa.

"Mother, are you alright?" I called. Something was moving behind the curtain of dust.

"Yes. Are you hurt?" Mother's voice sounded muffled and distant.

"No, I'm alright."

And then one single thought, one single word flashed through my mind: *the children!*

The children were in the kitchen and the kitchen lay beyond the dark, long passage whence the explosion had come.

I jumped to my feet and blindly ran in the direction of the door. The door was gone, my groping fingers encountered only splinters. I pushed past them and began to fight my way along the dark corridor. A big, heavy wardrobe had fallen across the passage and was barring my way. With one desperate heave I pushed it back. How, I don't know.

The floor was littered with bricks, mortar and junk. My feet stumbled, climbed, slipped again. Something big and soft like a curtain wrapped itself around my head. I tore it off and saw with dismay that the back of the passage was filled with daylight: the wall between the corridor and the bedroom had tumbled down.

At last the kitchen door! Someone from inside was trying to push it open, but the door, held by the debris on the floor, would not yield. I grabbed the handle and gave a terrific jerk. The door opened a little, just a crack. I could see Leosia standing on the threshold, livid and sobbing.

"The children!" I screamed.

"The... children... are alright," she answered between sobs. "But Madam... this... awful bomb... "

I did not listen any more. I had at last succeeded in opening the door and was now standing in the middle of the kitchen floor holding George and Ania pressed hard to me. My knees were shaking.

Poor kids! For the first time, their eyes were wide with fear.

"See, Mommy?" George showed me a small cut in the thigh from which a few drops of blood were running down his leg.

"It's nothing, darling," I tried to reassure him. "We will take care of it later. Only don't touch it with dirty fingers."

But George was disappointed. He *wanted* to be wounded.

"It's real deep," he insisted.

"Look here, Madam," Cook, gray-faced and shaky, brought me a piece of broken glass perhaps two feet long and half a foot wide. "That's what we found on my bed where Ania was lying. It slipped right *under* her. If it had fallen *on* her... " She did not finish, but I knew what she meant. It was a miracle the child was still alive.

Mother had followed me through the wreckage in the corridor and was now standing in the door surveying the scene. Although the kitchen windows were smashed, there wasn't as much dust here as there was in the dining room.

"The bomb must have hit the house next door," Mother remarked, "and we probably got only a small part of the load." She turned towards the corridor, as if looking there for the corroboration of her statement. At once I saw her shrink back.

"Fire!" she exclaimed. "Smoke and sparks are coming through the windows!"

She meant the two small corridor windows so close to the wall of the house next door that they did not let any light through. They had let the bomb in, though, and now they were letting in the fire. And not a drop of water in the house!

Smoke was already filling the kitchen. Again we grabbed our suitcases and coats and moved out onto the landing. This time, however, we descended the stairs and stood on the ground floor landing. It was better to be as near the exit as possible. German bombers were swarming overhead again.

I had lost sight of Mother when we left the apartment, but now she appeared at the door which led from the courtyard.

"I went to see the fire captain of the house, but he won't do anything about it," she told me with a trace of bitterness in her voice. "All he said was, 'We have no water, what can we do? Let it burn!' Yes, let it burn !"

Poor Mother! Not for a second had she hesitated to give the last of our water that morning, and now that her own beloved apartment, the apartment in which she had spent thirty-six years of her life, was catching fire, all she got for an answer was a rude "Let it burn!" Yet the fire captain was not to blame. What could he do?

"What shall we do now, Mother?"

"We can at least save some of the things."

"How?"

"Take them down to the cellar. I don't suppose the fire will get there."

"Alright."

Once more I left the children with Leosia and followed Mother back to the apartment. Cook went with us, too. She was determined to save our precious provisions, and also her own belongings. Up and down the stairs, up and down again...

George wanted to go down to the cellar with me, he offered to carry my candle. I let him, once. The air in the cellar was cold, damp and musty, like in a tomb. And the very sight of the tiny barred windows, so small that not even a child could climb through them, made me shudder. No, anything better than to be buried alive here! The planes were still roaring over the roof...

"No, George, you can't go back in the cellar again. Stay where you are, that's a good boy." I myself was running back from those catacombs as if the devil was at my heels.

Up and down the stairs, up and down... Bedding, clothes, precious old books...

"Mother, where is the case with silver? The big one?"

"I've already carried it down."

"You didn't!" That case must have weighed at least a hundred and fifty pounds!

"Yes, I have. Will you take those chandeliers down for me?"

"Mother," I said, "if ever you decide to take the big dining room cupboard down to the cellar, will you *please* let me help you?"

But my irony was entirely wasted on Mother. She was too busy.

I was just taking out Franek's suits from the wardrobe when a small procession passed furtively across the dining room towards the hall door. Mr. Gruda, carrying two suitcases, Mrs. Gruda with the can of cucumbers, and the two children.

"Leaving?" I asked, not without sarcasm. The birds of ill

omen had brought a bomb on the house and now they were departing. Didn't I tell Mother it would be so?

"Yes," Mr. Gruda answered. "We've just remembered that Countess Plater lives not far from here. Mrs. Gruda used to work for her. Perhaps she will take us in."

Woe to Countess Plater! If her house had not been bombed already it was sure to be hit that afternoon. This, however, was none of my business.

"Mother, what about the pictures? Shall I take them down?"

"No. The dampness of the cellar would ruin them anyway. They will have to remain. Perhaps after all ... "

I knew what Mother meant. Smoke and sparks continued to pour through the corridor windows, but nothing so far had caught flame. There still was a flicker of hope, however faint.

"What else do we take down?"

"Let me see... I think we have already carried down all the more valuable things. And there is still so much stuff left." She looked around.

"Mother..., " I hesitated, "would you mind if I took the children and Leosia to Krysia's shelter now? There seems to be a lull in the raid..."

"Why, of course, go ahead!"

"Will you come too?"

"No, not now. Let me stay a little longer here," she pleaded. "I will surely come, in an hour or so."

"Alright, Mother, don't forget the address." I gave it to her.

I collected my little party. Leosia was to carry her suitcase and mine, and keep an eye on George. I took the children's big suitcase in my left hand, threw the children's bedding over my right arm and with my free hand grabbed Ania's little paw.

"Let's start. Keep close to my heels."

I did not glance back at the house. We started off confidently enough. The blue sky over our heads was calm and empty and Mother's soothing influence was still upon me.

How the house on the left burned! Huge flames leaped from every window from top floor to ground floor. Running, we crossed the street. Faster, faster. If only we could reach Krysia's house before the planes returned ... At my side Ania ran shouting with laughter, she always loved to run tugging at Mommy's hand. Poor Ania, she didn't know that this time we were running for dear life, not for fun. The wind blew off my hat.

"Mommy, your hat," George shouted from behind.

"Forget it. Don't stop," I called back.

If only ... Oh God! If only ... But no. Even before we reached the corner the bombers were upon us again.

Vrrrrrrrrrr ... !

Mad panic seized me once more. Cold sweat broke out all over my body. It was the end. They would drop the bomb now. No use running ... No use trying to escape ...

And still I ran. But it was like in a nightmare. My feet were of lead, they hardly moved at all. The suitcase weighed a ton, Ania and the bedding another ton, blood was hammering at my temples, burning houses danced before my eyes ... no, I could never do it, never! My lungs were bursting for lack of breath, I could not go on. And still I ran ...

The house, Krysia's house, was at last in sight. One more desperate effort, and I reached the door. I did not stop. The shelter was at the other end of a small courtyard. Fifty more steps under the menacing, roaring sky and we were there.

As I threw myself into the entrance Ania's hand slipped from mine, and the poor child fell tumbling down the short wooden stairs. She landed all in a heap, shrieking with fright, her knee bleeding. Fortunately Ina stood at the bottom of the stairs. She grabbed Ania in her arms and soothed the child's desperate sobs.

"Whoever heard of throwing children down the stairs," an angry man's voice said in the dark.

George passed me like a flash and ran down the stairs. Thank Goodness, both the children were safe!

I remained on the top step, leaning against the doorframe, unable to move, to speak . . . I had not yet recovered my breath, my knees felt weak, my whole body trembled. Ina had taken the children into the shelter and I could hear her talking to them.

"I have a wound," George was announcing proudly. Poor kid, at last he had found a sympathetic audience.

After a while I recovered enough strength to go down. The shelter consisted of a big basement room dimly lit with one flickering candle. At least forty people lay, sat and crouched on the cement floor. Soldiers were coming in and out. Ina had spread a blanket in the middle of the floor where a little empty space remained, and George and Ania lay on it motionless and silent. They were exhausted. I covered them with their coats. Ania's eyes were closed, but George's stared blankly at the ceiling.

"Where is Leosia?" I asked him.

"I don't know, I think she remained in the doorway," he answered in a whisper. He did not move.

Once more I returned to the top of the basement stairs, and through the open door began to call, "Leosia! Leosia!"

"Stop that hysterical shouting!" an angry voice said again. "Don't you know people's nerves are on edge."

"I am sorry," I mumbled.

I guess my voice must have sounded hysterical. My whole body was still quivering, my teeth chattered.

"You are cold," I heard Ina's gentle voice at my ear. "Here, take this coat." She wrapped her own fur coat around my shoulders.

"Thanks, dear. I guess I am pretty jittery. You know we had a bomb and a fire in the house, and running here under the bombs nearly finished me off."

"Yes, I know," she nodded. "George told me about it."

I continued to worry about Leosia. What on earth could have happened to the girl? Why didn't she come? I gathered the little that remained of my courage, and catching a moment of comparative calm ran once more across the courtyard.

I found Leosia hidden in a dark recess of the front staircase. Her whole body pressed to the wall, she sobbed and whimpered with complete, hysterical abandon.

"Poor child," I said, touching her shoulder. "I am glad I found you. Come along, I'll take you to the shelter. They are not flying right now."

"No, no," she sobbed, drawing away from me. "I won't go... I won't move from here... No... no... "

"Alright, stay where you are," I was annoyed. "When you've recovered from your fit of tears you can come alone. The shelter is just across the yard. You can't miss it."

I returned to the children and sat down on the floor by George's side. Both he and Ania still lay motionless. The flame of the candle flickered, big shadows danced on the walls. All around me people were talking in low tones. Three or four children played noiselessly in one corner. In another a woman lay propped up on a pillow. She was moaning. "She has pneumonia," Ina whispered in my ear. The muffled sound of explosions came through the thick walls.

"Mommy... "

I turned around. George's big, weary eyes were looking at me.

"Yes, darling?" I leaned over him.

"Mommy, when will this end? I am so tired... I don't think I can stand it any longer..."

"Why, George, don't be silly," I tried to make my voice as cheerful as possible. "Don't you know we are going through the worst bombardment history has ever known? And you say you can't stand it! Why, you'll be proud all your life you've been in it!"

George was instantly interested.

"Is it really the worst? Worse than Madrid?"[1] George was an astute newspaper reader.

"Much worse. In Madrid they never bombed for more than five or six hours. And today," I glanced at my watch, "it's six. They've been bombing for ten hours already, and it isn't the end yet."

"I see," George was favorably impressed. "The worst bombardment in history," he repeated.

Again we were silent. After a while George told me he was hungry (no wonder, none of us had eaten anything since last night). Couldn't I give him something to eat?

"I am sorry, darling, I have nothing."

But Ina had heard George's plea and two minutes later appeared with a plate of cabbage soup. George sat up and took a spoonful but immediately made a wry face. "It's horrible," he whispered to me, "cold and bitter and smoky. I can't eat it." The boy was right; the soup was not only cold but dreadfully burned. Ania wouldn't eat it either.

"Well, I guess you'll have to wait till Cook comes. She has provisions in her suitcase," I told them.

---

[1] During the Spanish Civil War of 1936-1939, Spanish Nationalist forces led by General Franco, supported by Nazi Germany and Fascist Italy, used heavy bombers to lay siege to Spain's capital city, Madrid.

Why weren't Mother and Cook here yet? I was beginning to get worried. Hadn't Mother promised me to leave the apartment one hour after we did? It must have been around four when we ran here, and it was half-six now. What had happened to them? The bombardment still continued.

Leosia had at last decided to come to the shelter, and was sitting now on the corner of the children's blanket. She was no help whatsoever, and the children were growing restless. What could I do to keep them quiet?

I told George and Ania to sit close by my side and began to tell them a fairy tale: "Once upon a time there lived a little boy and a little girl..." It was a long winding tale full of fairies and gnomes, and secret passages in the mountains, and magic golden shovels on which one could fly, like an airplane...Yes, it was a lovely tale, and the children listened to it with rapt attention. But I could not concentrate on the fairy yarn I was spinning before their tired, bomb-weary eyes. Anxiety was gnawing at my heart. Why didn't Mother come? What had happened at the house since we left? At last I could stand it no longer, I broke off in the middle of a sentence.

"I am sorry," I said in my normal, not my "fairy tale" voice, "I'll tell you the rest later. I must go now and see what Grandma is doing."

"Oh, Mommy, but you can't," George protested. "You must tell us first what Puck told the little boy when they hid behind the Queen's throne."

"No, not now." I really did not know what Puck was going to tell the little boy. I touched Leosia on the arm. "Try to rouse yourself and keep an eye on the children. I am going out to see what has become of Mrs. Rayska and Cook."

She nodded but did not lift her head.

Once more I ran across the courtyard. I noticed that the big front door was wide open, and people, lots of people, were passing in front of it. Men, women, children. Some carried suitcases, others bundles. They advanced rapidly, silently, all in one direction, away from the center of the city. Although it was already night the street was as bright as if it were noon. I stepped out of the door and peered in the direction of our house.

From the corner of Wilcza onward the whole street was one raging sea of flames. And Mother was there, right in the middle of that burning block! I knew now why she hadn't come, she had been trapped in the fire. Mother, Mother dear! I *must* rescue her...

I leaned forward as if to run, took a step, and drew back. I couldn't do it. I couldn't face that raging sea of flames. I just couldn't.

It was preposterous, monstrous. There was Mother, my beloved, brave Mother, my best war companion, perhaps at that very instant dying in flames, and here was I writhing in an agony of shame and fear, unable to move, to run to her help.

"You cad, you cad!" I kept repeating to myself, clenching and unclenching my fists in helpless rage. But it was no use.

"You can't leave the children," a voice inside me was saying. "Who will take care of them? Leosia? She is worse than useless." But I knew that it was not the love of the children that was holding me back. It was low, dastardly fear.

And still in front of me silent crowds were flowing down the street.

"Nowy Swiat is worse...," I heard someone say. And then, "Marszalkowska is burning too..."

From the collection of Stefan Mucha

From the collection of Stefan Mucha

Clouds of smoke obscure the sky as far as the eye can see.

From the collection of Sam Bryan, courtesy of Julien Bryan

From the collection of Sam Bryan, courtesy of Julien Bryan

A raging sea of flames engulfs the city long into the night.

Once more in a last desperate attempt I threw myself forward, ran a few steps... Panic seized me. I was back in the doorway. I couldn't do it. Slowly, reluctantly, I turned back. I didn't go to the shelter. Instead I turned into Krysia's apartment. Krysia was alone, rolling cigarettes. Heavily I leaned against the wall.

"Well...?" Krysia looked up to me.

I was too miserable to hide my shame and despair.

"Our house is burning, the whole block is burning, and Mother is there, caught in the fire, and I can't go to rescue her. I can't! I tell you I can't!"

Krysia didn't say anything. She just looked at me and there was contempt in her eyes. *She* had gone that morning under bombs to fetch us—we, who were practically strangers to her.

I closed my eyes. I could see Mother surrounded by flames, choked by smoke, fighting desperately to get out of the apartment, failing... Mother dear, will you ever forgive me?

The bombardment had ceased and silence hung all around us.

And suddenly in that silence a clear voice asked somewhere in the doorway, "Can you tell me where Mrs. Malachowska lives?"

It was Mother's voice.

In one leap I was in the doorway. "Darling!" Sobbing and laughing, I covered her hands with kisses.

"I am glad you heard my voice," Mother said. "I remembered the number of the house but had forgotten the number of the apartment. Here, take this, it's heavy." She handed me her bag.

Breathlessly I told her the story of my fears and betrayal. She dismissed it with a shrug. "You couldn't have left the children, anyway," she said. "No, I had no trouble getting out of the house. In fact the apartment is not burning yet, although flames are already entering through the windows. I tore all the curtains off, and hung relics of saints on all the walls. Perhaps *they* will keep the fire out. Can you find me a chair? I am a little tired."

Darling!

Now that Mother was with me, everything was alright once more. I had recovered my old spirits. I could talk and laugh and joke again. And all the while I watched Mother's serene, pale face with loving eyes. But she didn't even notice...

And there wasn't much matter for laughter, either. Mother told me what had happened at the house after we left. The elderly gentleman who had that morning wandered into our kitchen had finally, it seems, completely lost his mind. His daughter had vanished somewhere during the confusion that followed the bomb and this proved to be too much for the poor man. He went in circles round and round the courtyard repeating in monotone: "I must take my life away. Will someone hand me a gun? I must take my life away. Will someone hand me a gun?" No one, of course, handed him a gun, and when Mother left he was still in the courtyard, walking in circles. The old lady who lived on the third floor had also vanished, leaving a note behind: "I am going into the unknown." No one knew where she was and her old husband was frantic.

Mother had remained in the apartment all that afternoon, sorting things out, taking them down to the cellar. She simply could not tear herself away from the old place. That's why she came so late. Cook was busy, too, but she would come soon. The fire captain had told Mother to leave the apartment door unlocked, so he could keep an eye on the fire. "I do hope no one will loot the place," Mother said. Looting of burning houses had become very frequent lately.

"I am hungry," Mother whispered into my ear at last. "Do you think we will get anything to eat?"

The burnt cabbage soup reappeared once more. It was reheated, however, this time, and we managed to swallow it. Mother had brought some crackers with her, and she told me to take them to the children. It was decided that Mother would sleep in the apartment, while I spent the night with the children in the shelter.

I found the shelter completely dark. Sounds of snoring came from every side. In the corner the woman with pneumonia was still moaning. I struck a match to find my way. Someone touched me.

"Madam, it's me." It was Cook. She was crouching on the floor, leaning on a suitcase.

"Oh Cook! I am so glad to see you here," I whispered to her.

The children were no longer in the middle of the floor where I had left them. Christopher's nurse had given them her cot; an empty chair stood by the side of the cot, evidently prepared for me. Carefully I stepped over sleeping bodies and made my way to it. The children were not yet asleep.

"Mommy, I can't sleep. They snore so terribly, and Ania kicks me all the time," George whispered to me.

"What can I do, darling? It's war. You can't expect to be comfortable in wartime." I gave them the crackers and they munched them in silence.

What wouldn't I give to be able to stretch out! Every muscle of my body ached with the effort of all the carrying I had done that day. But there was not an inch of free space on the floor. Somebody's leg protruded even under my chair.

As I curled up on the hard seat I heard the first whine of a shell. German artillery was starting bombardment again. But I did not care. The children were with me, Mother slept under the same roof only a hundred yards away... let them shoot...

Almost at once I fell into a heavy, dreamless sleep.

CHAPTER 23

September 27: Warsaw Surrenders

MANY PEOPLE maintained afterwards that the second day of the all-out bombing of Warsaw was even worse than the first one. Perhaps it was so. Thousands were killed that Tuesday.

For my part, however, I don't remember a single explosion. Nor a single roaring plane. Maybe my brain did not register them any longer. The fact is I lived through that day in a state of semi-consciousness in which time, among other things, no longer existed. It neither dragged, nor flew, it simply wasn't there. Yet some memories remain very vivid in my mind.

The morning cocoa, for instance. We all stood crowded in the little kitchen, flooded with sunlight. The stray cat was sitting on the windowsill. I can still see the comfortable curve of the cat's back outlined in a halo of sunlight against the dusty pane. Krysia was pouring out hot cocoa in dirty cups and glasses (there was not enough water to spare for dishwashing), and handing them out to us. I could hardly wait for my turn. It was a very simple mixture, just cocoa and hot water; no sugar, no milk, still it tasted good. Hot, too, it warmed you up inside, and we were all cold. I took two glasses to the shelter for the children. Cook and Leosia got theirs, too.

After breakfast someone suggested bridge. There didn't seem to be anything else to do, so we dragged out a table and began to play. Krysia, Zosia, Ina, Zbyszek and I. Never before did I have such luck. Two little slams and one big slam almost in a row.

"Phenomenal, phenomenal," Zbyszek kept repeating.

"It's because we don't play for money," I assured him.

We laughed at Zosia who was constantly mixing up her suits. Meanwhile Mother had sneaked out of the apartment. She returned some time later, loaded with stuff. We were still playing.

"What's that?" I asked.

Father's picture, Franek's diploma and, of all things, the family genealogical tree!

"Yes!" Mother's face was beaming. "I've been in our apartment. And, can you believe it? It still stands as it did. No fire. And the fires on both sides of the house are burning much lower today. Perhaps, after all... I can hardly believe it. It seems too good to be true!"

"But Mother, how can you go out on a day like this?" I said reproachfully.

"I had to know what was happening at the house. And on my way back I went to Uncle Joe's apartment. You know, he told me some time ago that if ever we needed a refuge, we could always come to him. I thought perhaps Cook and I could go there. There is such a lot of us here, it's hard on Mrs. Malachowska. But no. At Joe's it's even worse. Do you remember the long dark passage that leads from the hall to the kitchen? Well, he has twenty-two people in there. Twenty-two! Just lying on the floor. And among them two cases of pneumonia. Alicia and Aunt Mura. I am afraid we will have to remain here, if Mrs. Malachowska doesn't mind."

Mrs. Malachowska did not mind. She told Mother she was delighted to have us. But six extra people were no small trouble for a tiny household like hers. It was lucky Cook had brought some of our provisions.

The rest of the day I spent with the children in the shelter. Ania was having a grand time. She had discovered three other little girls about her own age, and was playing hide-and-seek with them in the dark. She had learned two new nursery rhymes and a soldier had given her a long stick of candy. Yes, life in the shelter was lots of fun to Ania, too much so, in fact. People all around were complaining of the noise she made, but it was so hard to keep her quiet!

George was frankly and horribly bored. I took him for a while to Krysia's apartment where he promptly buried himself in a detective story he found on the table. Certainly not a book for him, but it was his only solace and I did not have the heart to take it away.

People came in and out of the shelter. Some even ventured out into the street and brought back news. Horrible, gruesome news—of death, and wounds and destruction.

But I would not listen. That day I was completely numb to the outside world. I refused to worry and could not even understand why everyone made so much fuss when it was discovered that the pile the soldiers had left in a corner of the shelter covered with sacking was nothing but hand grenades. What difference did it make? If a bomb hit the house we would be blown to pieces anyway, and if the bombs spared us, hand grenades don't go off as easily as all that, and the children had been warned not to touch the pile. What was the use of fussing?

Not till night did my fears return. I had decided to sleep this time with Mother in Krysia's dining room. Krysia had spread cushions on the floor under the table where quite a bit of empty space remained, and this was going to be my bed. And a grand bed it was. The cushions slipped a little from under me, but they were soft, and how wonderful it was to be able to stretch out. I was just wallowing in the luxury of it when all at once a strange noise coming from under the floor caught my ear. "Shhh, shh, shh," it went. What was that? Krysia's apartment was on the ground floor, no one lived underneath. And suddenly I remembered what Cook had told me that afternoon. Last night a time bomb had exploded in the house on Three Crosses Square where a court-martial was located. There was a court-martial in this house, too... It must be a time bomb!

Mother was already asleep. I could hear her peaceful, even breathing. No one else in the apartment stirred. And I did not raise the alarm. Paralyzed with fear, holding my breath, I waited for the bomb to go off... It never did. I had forgotten that a carpenter had a workshop in the basement.

The next morning we woke up conscious of an unusual silence. No bombs, no planes, no artillery fire. The stillness was uncanny. But it was a relief. The Germans at last were giving us a respite.

The house at once began to bustle with activity. People were leaving the shelter, children were allowed to go out and play in the courtyard. Mother and Cook ran at once to our old house, and Krysia called me into the empty kitchen "for a conference."

"Rulka, you must help me out," she said, "our supply of water is almost gone, and we have to get some more. I wanted to send my maid to get it, but she says she won't go unless one of your maids goes with her. She says she is not going to work and risk her life for other people's maids when they can do it themselves. You must make Leosia go with her."

Bother! The notorious "servant problem" cropping up at such a time! But I had to admit that both Krysia and her maid were right, there was no sense in one girl doing all the work and taking all the risk while the other sat idly in the shelter. The walk to the nearest pump was both long and dangerous. A single girl could not bring enough water for fourteen people. I promised to talk to Leosia.

I might have saved myself the trouble. The little coward burst at once into tears and declared that she would rather die "right here on the spot" than go out to fetch water. No, no, she wouldn't go.

Alright. In that case I would go myself. I took two empty buckets from the kitchen and started at once.

"Don't go through Frascati Park, Madam," Christopher's nurse warned me. "It's full of dead."

I hadn't even reached the corner, when Zbyszek and Ina passed me, running like mad.

"Don't bother about the water now," they shouted to me. "Wedel is selling chocolate and crackers, we are going there. Come along!"

I took the buckets back to the kitchen and started once more. Destruction stared at me from every side.

Some houses were still burning, others lay in ruins. The chemist's shop where I'd listened to my first artillery bombardment was one horrible, mangled mess. Thousands of white, pink and green leaflets and stationery covered the pavement in front of the church, evidently blown away from a bombed office. In the square four corpses awaited burial, lying in a row on the ground: two wrapped up in sheets, the third in a faded green blanket, the fourth, evidently a soldier, covered by a military coat. A group of men were hurriedly digging graves, more graves...

My eyes searched for familiar stores around the square. Stores where I had bought all my life. None remained. Those which were not burned or bombed had been looted; empty, glassless show windows gaped in utter desolation. Wasn't there a single house left on this side of Bracka...?

I took it all in with only half my mind. The other half

was constantly on the watch, conscious only of the blue sky overhead, whence death might come any minute. But I reached Wedel's store without a single plane appearing. The sky was still, the sun shone bright on the tragic, destroyed city.

I was surprised not to see a line, the street was practically empty.

"The line is in there, inside the building," a civil militiaman who stood in front of the store informed me. Oh yes, there was a line alright. It started at the door and continued up the stairs, winding around the staircase.

"You'll have to go up to the end of the line," another militiaman directed me, and I began to ascend. Somewhere on the fourth floor I saw Ina and Zbyszek; we grinned at each other. The end of the line was not yet in sight. Fifth floor, sixth floor, seventh floor, I counted the flights as I climbed. Would that line never end? Eighth floor. This was the top landing and at last the end of the line.

Panting, I leaned against a wall. There was a skylight above my head, the glass shattered. A girl by my side was reading a magazine. "I got it in there," she pointed to an open door. "You can have one, too." I peered through the door. This must once have been a cozy studio, now it was a sad scene of wreckage. Overturned furniture, broken lamps, torn curtains. A pile of dusty magazines and books lay on the floor. I picked up an old copy of the French *L'Illustration* and returned to the landing. Slowly, very slowly, the line moved downwards.

From time to time I glanced at the skylight, but the sky was still. If only we could get down to the third or second floor, I would feel safer. But even before we reached the fourth, word came up the line: "No more packages today. The store is sold out." We were told to disband. It was

From the collection of Stefan Mucha

"Destruction stared at me from every side."

From the collection of Stefan Mucha

Destruction...

From the collection of Stefan Mucha

...and the dead.

disheartening but no one complained. Standing in line had become something of a lottery, anyway. Sometimes you won, but more often you lost, and as long as you didn't lose your life, it really didn't matter.

I wondered if Ina and Zbyszek had got their chocolate; I didn't see them anywhere. As we filed out through the door we were handed slips of blue paper with numbers on them. These would give us priority in tomorrow's line. It was something, anyway.

I was halfway between Wedel's and Krysia's house when the roar of a low-flying bomber sent me scurrying down the ruined streets. A shelter, any kind of shelter...!

But there was no shelter anywhere. The doors of bombed houses were already boarded up. Other houses were still burning. Nothing, no place to hide. I had to run two full blocks before I found a doorway. By that time I was nearly done for. Black spots danced before my eyes, blood was pounding at my ears, my weak knees would not support me any longer. Heavily, I slumped to the floor. There I sat, huddled up till the noise died away and everything was calm again. At last I rose to my feet, and weak and exhausted resumed my way. My heart was still beating wildly, but I had recovered my self control.

I was humiliated by the panic I had felt only a while before. Would I never get used to the sound of roaring planes? Would I always lose my head the moment I heard them? It was humiliating, absurd. The plane, I noticed only now, had not dropped any bombs.

I met Mother right in front of Krysia's house. Her face was radiant.

"Good news," she called to me. "Good news!"

"What is it?" I asked eagerly. In one instant I had forgotten the plane, my panic, my weariness...

"Come inside the house and Zosia will tell you herself. She's just back from the hospital."

We both ran into the house. Zosia was standing in the middle of the room swinging her hat in one hand. She talked breathlessly, and seemed beside herself with excitement.

"Yes, good news!" she shouted. "The colonel told me himself. The British have landed at Gdynia. And General Bortnowski's army has broken through at Radom, and is marching to the rescue of Warsaw. They are only thirty miles away. They'll be here day after tomorrow. Yes, it's good news, tell it to everyone you meet!"

She was almost hysterical.

"Oh, Mother!" In wild joy I clapped my hands, jumped up and down, hugged Mother in a passionate embrace. Mother's face was beaming, too.

"Yes, at last... at last...," she repeated. And then, "Let's go and tell Madzia about it. We haven't seen her since Saturday, we might as well see how she is faring. The poor thing was so scared, so depressed, she will be glad to learn."

Aunt Madzia's house, two houses beyond ours, was only half burned. The left wing where Aunt Madzia's apartment was had escaped flames and bombs. A crowd of people, both civilians and soldiers, stood in the courtyard talking in hushed voices. They were looking at the burned wing. Smoke was still coming out of the windows.

"Wait here, Mother," I said. "I'll go and see if Aunt Madzia is home. If she is out, there is no sense in your climbing four flights of stairs."

I ran upstairs and knocked at the door. No one answered. I knocked again. Nothing. I returned to the courtyard.

"She is out," I told Mother. "I wonder where she went?"

In the crowd that stood in the courtyard I noticed a girl I knew. She was an acquaintance of Aunt Madzia, too.

"Do you know by any chance where Miss Szeligowska is?" I asked her. "No one answers the door."

The girl looked at me absentmindedly.

"Miss Szeligowska?" she said in a harsh, indifferent voice. "She is dead."

"Dead?" I repeated. "But that's impossible. Her apartment is untouched."

"I know. But when the fire started in this part of the house," she pointed to the smoking windows, "she and her cousin ran away to a friend's house on Wilcza. A bomb got them there. Fourteen people were killed, and their bodies are not recovered yet. Only this young lady escaped."

A girl with a terribly bruised and swollen face stood at her side. With a pang I recognized Vadik's pretty fiancée.

"Yes," the girl said now, "and I only escaped because I went out into the hall to light a cigarette. And even at that I was buried under the ruins for four hours before the soldiers dug me out."

She spoke in a shrill, hysterical voice, a voice I had never heard before. It was obvious she had not recovered from the shock yet.

I turned around and looked at Mother. I knew what the death of Aunt Madzia meant to her. Her best, oldest friend...

She stood silent and motionless, only one corner of her mouth quivered a little.

"Poor Madzia," she said at last. "Poor old Madzia..."

And then with a supreme effort she lifted her head. Her face brightened.

"Anyhow, we are bringing you good news." Her voice was firm and clear. "Help is coming! The British have landed at Gdynia. General Bortnowski's army has broken through at Radom and is marching here. They will be in Warsaw in two days' time."

A strange silence greeted Mother's words. No one spoke.

"It's true," I insisted. "We've heard it from high military quarters."

Suddenly an officer stepped out from the crowd. His face was contorted with grief and rage.

"You crazy women!" he shouted. "How can you go around repeating such monstrous lies? Don't you know Warsaw has surrendered?"

Warsaw Mayor Stefan Starzynski (third from left) surrenders the city to the Germans.

The defenders of Warsaw lay down their arms in large numbers.

CHAPTER 24

Bitter Days

OH! THE bitterness of those days...

So it had all been for nothing! The thousands of victims, the gallant effort, the supreme sacrifice, the destruction, all for nothing.

In the streets people wept. Others went around with stony faces. Through the devastated city the wind blew gusts of dust and ashes. The smell of smoke still hung in the air...

For nothing!

That afternoon all over town posters appeared on the battered walls, announcing the capitulation of Warsaw. They were signed by the Mayor and the Chief of the Military Forces in the capital. In sober terms they stated the reason for surrender—the destruction of the water supply. Gave the terms—soldiers would be disarmed and allowed to return to their homes, only officers were to be taken prisoner—and appealed for peace and order. Twenty-four prominent citizens had gone to the Germans as hostages.

Lack of water, of course. A town of over a million inhabitants could not go on defending itself without an adequate supply of water.

But if so, some people said, why didn't we surrender on Sunday, when the filters were already destroyed? Why didn't Warsaw spare itself those last two days of inhuman slaughter and destruction? Think how many lives, how many buildings would have been saved...

Yes, that was true. But if Warsaw had surrendered on

Cena **10** gr.

Czwartek   Dnia 28 września 1939 r.

KURJER WARSZAWSKI

ROK SETNY DZIEWIĘTNASTY

WARSZAWO!

Po 28 dniach zmagań po nie prawdopodobnych ofiarach i poświęceniach uratowałaś swój honor do ostatniej chwili.

Uratowałaś Warszawo Honor Polski.

Tysiące rannych i zabitych z pośród ludności cywilnej, całe ulice w gruzach, najpiękniejsze, najwspanialsze, najdawniejsze gmachy świadczące o niezniszczalności ducha Polski — nie istnieją.

Wojska nasze po bohatersku broniły swych murów zmagając się z przeważającą liczebnie i technicznie armią niemiecką. Cokolwiekbądź się stanie i jakie nas dni czekają, musimy pamiętać o tym, że miasto nasze, stolica Polski, musi się z tych gruzów podnieść. Aby to osiągnąć, potrzebne nam są niezwykłe siły ducha energii i wytrwałości fizycznej.

Nie dajmy upaść swej woli i nie ulegajmy często roztrzęsionym wskutek ostatnich przeżyć nerwom. Zimna krew, wytrwałość i praca to program nasz na dni najbliższe.

Stawajmy wszyscy na swoje posterunki pracy. Starajmy się jaknajprędzej zaleczyć ciężkie rany stolicy i jej życia społecznego.

Ciężkie być może czekają nas dni i ciężka praca. Niechaj nas krzepi w tych godzinach próby pamięć na bohaterstwo przeszłych pokoleń polskich. Niechaj nas krzepi wiara Ojców naszych.

Niech żyje Polska.

Nie ma miejsca na swary

Polska przeżywa ciężkie, tragiczne dni. Dziś nie ma miejsca ani czasu na wypominanie sobie win wzajemnie. Dziś musimy żądać od każdego Polaka, aby wszystkie urazy partyjne zapomniał. Cały wysiłek musi skierować do jednego celu:

dla POLSKI.

Każdy z nas musi spełniać swe obowiązki z wytężoną siłą. Nie wolno nam tracić nadziei, ale też trzeba zapomnieć o winach przeszłości. Gdy nadejdzie dzień, odpowiedni, wówczas zbadawszy i dobrze rozsądziwszy może będzie trzeba powołać tego czy innego do odpowiedzialności. Dziś jednak nie ma winnych i nie ma tych, którzy mieli rację. Są tylko Polacy karni, posłuszni, z poczuciem odpowiedzialności za przyszłość.

NIECH ŻYJE POLSKA!

Niech żyje Prezydent Mościcki. Niech żyje Rząd Rzeczypospolitej.

From the collection of the National Library, Warsaw

September 28, 1939—Warsaw has surrendered.

WARSAW!

After 28 days of struggle, after unbelievable sacrifice and devotion you have upheld your honor to the very end.

Warsaw, you have upheld the honor of Poland.

Thousands of injured and dead civilians, whole streets in ruins, the most beautiful, the finest, the oldest buildings, testimony to the indestructibility of the Polish spirit, are no more.

Our armed forces have heroically defended their ramparts against the numerical and technical superiority of the German army. Whatever may happen and whatever awaits us, let us remember that our city, Poland's capital, will rise from these ruins. In order for this to happen we need to display exceptional courage, energy and physical endurance.

Let our resolution not flag and let not our nerve, badly shaken by recent events, fail. A cool head, resilience and hard work are our immediate goals.

Let us all attend to our places of work. Let us with all haste heal the grievous wounds that the capital and its everyday life have suffered.

Hard days may well lie ahead, as may hard work. In these hours of trial let us draw strength from the memory of past heroic Polish generations. Let us draw strength from the faith of our Fathers.

Long live Poland!

This is no time for quarrels

Poland is now experiencing difficult and tragic days. Today is neither the time nor the place for blaming one another. Today we must demand that every Pole forget any party political slights. Our whole effort must be focused on a single goal:

POLAND

Each and every one of us must do his duty with all his strength. We must not lose hope, and we must also forget the mistakes of the past. When the right day comes, then, after careful inquiry and thought, we may bring to book those who deserve it. Today, however, there are no guilty people and there are no righteous people. There are only disciplined and obedient Poles who feel responsible for the future.

LONG LIVE POLAND

Long Live President Moscicki.

Long live the Government of the Republic.

Translation of announcement from the Kurjer Warszawski, *September 28, 1939 (immediately preceding).*

Sunday, Warsaw would not have been Warsaw, the gallant City of the Mermaid.

Cities, like nations, like human beings, have to remain true to their own natures. Warsaw had pledged itself to fight to the bitter end, and to the bitter end it had fought. It had done its duty. Perhaps, some day, history would acknowledge the fact, repay for all the death and destruction.

Perhaps...

In the meantime a wave of bitterness surged throughout the city. Bitterness against the old government that had flown to safety, leaving the people to their fate. Bitterness against the army that had not held the enemy back. Bitterness against Great Britain and France who had not come to our rescue... Old class hatreds revived. If Warsaw had been Paris, the barricade built against Hitler's army would have served other purposes... But Warsaw is not a city of revolutions. National insurrections, yes, but not social revolutions.

Besides, there was no time for it. The grim problem of living, living without food, water, and in bomb-wrecked houses, was facing everyone.

The German army did not enter Warsaw at once. They gave the city a week to clear the barricades, repair its water and light system, and bury its dead. This was more easily said than done. The barricades disappeared very quickly, it's true, but two full weeks passed before the first electric bulb shone in the German-occupied Hotel Europejski (in our apartment the electric light reappeared on November 27, two full months after the capitulation). It took the repair crews ten days of day and night work before the first water mains were reopened in some parts of the city.

As for the dead...

It was never accurately established how many people perished in the Siege of Warsaw. Probably it never will be. The first statistics said seventeen thousand. Later thirty, eighty, a hundred and twenty, a hundred and eighty-five thousand... All I know is that when the father of one of my friends died of heart failure in December, the manager of the Powazki Cemetery told the family that this was the one hundred thousandth funeral they had had since September 1. And Powazki was the rich people's cemetery. How many more went to Brodno where poor people were buried? How many more still lay under the ruins?

Every day I passed the house on Wilcza. Aunt Madzia's body had not yet been recovered. Every day I had to go by the house on Mokotowska where four of my schoolmates, one with a three-month-old baby, were buried under the ruins. Every bombed house contained dozens of bodies.

And yet this was not the worst. The worst were houses like the one on Koszykowa, only three blocks from where we lived, where seventy-two people were trapped in the shelter. Everyone knew they were there, still alive, yet there was no way of getting them out; a seven-story building had collapsed blocking the entrance. Seventy-two people doomed, condemned to the agony of slow death in the dark. I would make long detours to avoid the sight of this house, but how many others like that one did I pass every day, unaware?

Silent crowds flowed endlessly along the ruined streets. Haggard, ashen, incredibly dirty, for clouds of dust from the bombed houses whirled constantly in the air, and there was no water to wash. The number of people wearing bandages was incredible, every third or fourth person had one. Acquaintances greeted each other with a new greeting: "My dear, I am so glad to see you alive!"

Polish soldiers are herded out of Warsaw under German guard.

USNARA

Varsovians are given a week to clear the barricades...

From the collection of Zygmunt Walkowski

...and bury the thousands of dead.

From the collection of Stefan Mucha

From the collection of Stefan Mucha

"Silent crowds flowed endlessly along the ruined streets."

From the collection of Stefan Mucha

Thousands join the daily queues for water...

USNARA

... and for basic food supplies if they can be found.

Yes, a familiar face, even one you hardly knew at all, had suddenly become precious. Too many dead...

Sometimes a small detachment of soldiers would march down the street. They carried no arms. People stood still and looked after them. Those gallant khaki uniforms... Rumpled, torn, dirty... We would see them no more. A dirty sleeve would hastily wipe a tear from some grime-covered face...

It took me weeks before I saw and grasped the extent of destruction wrought by German bombers. What had they done to my beautiful city, of which I used to be so proud? What had they done? Nothing remained of it.

The Royal Castle, the beautiful palaces, the monumental government buildings, the old Opera House, the stores, the cafés, all gone. Nothing but a huge cemetery of twisted, charred ruins, a ghost of a city. When for the first time I walked through Nowy Swiat and the Krakowskie Przedmiescie, I cried.

And yet even while my eyes filled with tears at this sight of wanton destruction, something deep inside me was singing, "I'm alive, alive! I'm alive! I won't be killed now." I was ashamed of it. What did it matter if I were still alive in the face of this tremendous tragedy?

But somehow it did matter, and I couldn't help it anyway. Something inside me was swelling, expanding, filling my whole being with wild joy, the glorious joy of being alive!

No one who hasn't faced death can know what that joy is.

On the same afternoon on which the capitulation was announced we returned to the old apartment. It wasn't very safe yet, houses on both sides of ours were still burning, but Mother couldn't wait to be home once more. She had been almost sure for a while that she would lose it. It made her the more eager now to be back inside those old, beloved walls.

Ania was the only one who was sorry to leave the shelter. "Mommy," she begged, as she skipped along the street tugging at my hand, "when bombs fall again, and all the houses are burning again, we will go back to the shelter, won't we?"

Only now, on our return to the apartment, did the desolation of the place strike me fully. "It's cold!" That was the first reaction. The big, glassless windows seemed enormous, and every gust of wind blew new clouds of dust into the rooms. Everything was so covered with it that you couldn't tell the color of the furniture. The plaster had fallen off the ceilings in all the rooms leaving ugly, raw patches. The floors were littered with glass, plaster, debris and knickknacks that had fallen off the tables and shelves. Broken curtain rods, overturned chairs, a shattered mirror—the place looked a sight. Only the old dining room clock ticked on unperturbed, as if nothing had happened.

"Look," Mother pointed to the smashed door which hung lamentably on one hinge, and then to the big arm-chair where I had sat when the bomb fell. "Look—it's only three steps from this door to the chair. And the chair stands right in front of it, too. It's a wonder you were not killed!"

Yes, it was a wonder. Probably the high back of the chair had saved my life. But then, I suppose everyone in Warsaw who had survived the last two days of siege had a miraculous escape of some kind. The problem right now was not how I escaped death, but where were we going to sleep that night? It was pressing, too. Dusk was already

USNARA

The once beautiful Royal Castle Square which has stood at the heart of Warsaw since the 17th Century...

From the collection of Stefan Mucha

... is reduced to rubble within the first four weeks of the war.

From the collection of Stefan Mucha

From the collection of Stefan Mucha

Nowy Swiat, Warsaw's most fashionable shopping street, lies in ruins.

From the collection of Stefan Mucha

From the collection of Stefan Mucha

Street after street of destruction...

From the collection of Stefan Mucha

From the collection of Stefan Mucha

From the collection of Stefan Mucha

From the collection of Stefan Mucha

From the collection of Stefan Mucha

From the collection of Stefan Mucha

falling and we wouldn't be able to do much by candlelight. The bedroom where one of the walls had crumbled down was out of the question. The dining room or one of the front rooms with their big, empty windows? We might as well have slept outside. We decided upon Franek's room. It had only one window, and a small windowpane, through some freak of nature, had escaped destruction. We stuffed the rest with blankets; that one pane would give us enough light in the morning, anyway.

But the blankets did not keep the wind out. Our teeth were chattering as we went to bed, and although we used all the blankets, coats and furs we could find around the house, it was hours before I got warm enough to go to sleep.

At six o'clock the next morning we awakened with a start.

The bell was ringing. Fire!

We leaped out of bed. The children were dressed in a jiffy and dispatched with Leosia back to Krysia's house. Mother and Cook were to take care of the suitcases while I ran out to learn where the fire was. I found the fire captain in the courtyard.

"Where's the fire?"

"There." He pointed to the roof. Thick columns of smoke were coming out of one spot, right over our apartment.

"What will you do about it?" I asked. (Would he do anything at all—I wondered. Although a chimney sweep by profession, he did not seem to be a particularly lucky choice for a fire captain.)

"I'll see," he said meditatively, still looking at the smoke. "Perhaps we can tear the roof off."

"Did you send someone to the regular fire department?"

"No. Our district fire department on Nowy Swiat has been bombed out."

"But there must be another one left," I insisted. "Do you know where the nearest one is?"

"Yes, Plac Unii."

"All right, I'll go there."

It is a twenty-minute walk from our house to Plac Unii, but I covered the distance in ten, even though I had two barricades to climb.

The sergeant to whom I reported the fire was polite but noncommittal.

"You probably have dozens of fires right now," I told him. "Will you be able to come soon?"

"We will do our best. Right now we have eighteen fires on hand, and two of our engines were smashed. However, we certainly will come as soon as we can."

They did come. Forty-eight hours later.

On my return I saw two men working on the roof whence smoke continued to rise. In the apartment, I found Mother alone, lying on the sofa.

"It seems rather pointless to start putting the place in order right now," she said, as if apologizing for her idleness.

It did seem pointless. I sat down and lit a cigarette.

We waited. Nothing happened. We waited some more.

Nothing. Again I went outside. The smoke continued to rise, but there was less of it. At last we got bored with waiting, sent Cook to bring the children and Leosia back, and started to clean the apartment. What a job! We carried out bucket after bucket of debris but there still seemed to be as much of it as before. There was no use wiping the furniture, new dust was coming in constantly.

"We will never get the place half clean till we do something about the windows," Mother remarked. "And water, if we only had water..."

Around noon I remembered the blue slip from Wedel's candy store and ran for the line. By that time we had all forgotten the fire. As I hastened along the streets I almost ran into Jule, Roman's brother.

"Say! I am glad to meet you," I exclaimed. "How is Rose? How are you all?"

He glanced at me, then turned his eyes away. I noticed that his face had a strained expression; he was very pale.

"Rose is alright," he said slowly. "She has had her baby, a boy. She is with us now. My mother is alright, too. But . . . ," his voice broke, "Roman is dead."

"My God!"

For an instant we stood silent, not looking at each other.

"How?" I whispered at last.

"He was driving the ambulance last Monday when a bomb hit right in front of the car. He and his companion were both killed instantly."

"Does Rose know?"

"Not yet. I am just coming back from the hospital where they told me about it."

"You mustn't tell her," I exclaimed.

Jule made a desperate gesture. "How can we keep it from her? She is frantic with worry. It's she who sent me to the hospital."

"My God," I whispered once more. There was nothing more to say. We shook hands and continued each on our way.

Roman dead! I couldn't believe it. Our office rooms were just across the hall from each other, and every day after the daily press résumé was sent out he used to come and sit on my desk, discussing the latest political and Bank news or telling me all the little funny things Rose had said and done. Roman dead! I remembered now the last time I saw him in the Bank that day of evacuation, when, seized with sudden apprehensions, I had kissed him good-bye. I never saw him afterwards.

How he had hated war! It was so utterly incompatible with his dream of living in a quiet, provincial town with plenty of books and Rose... Poor little Rose. Jule was probably telling her right now. How would she take it? How will she ever be able to stand it? They had been so absurdly in love with each other...

Back home I told Mother of Roman's death.

"Poor Janinka," she exclaimed. Janinka was Roman's mother. I was thinking of Roman's wife, Mother... of his mother.

We worked like slaves that afternoon and went to bed exhausted. It was still dark when something woke me up suddenly.

The fire bell was ringing again.

I propped up my head on my hand and listened. It rang and rang. Would I have to get up? Mother was not stirring. My whole body was numb with fatigue, and at last I was warm. Must I really get up? Forget it! I turned around and went back to sleep.

At eight o'clock I woke up out of my own free will.

Mother was already sitting up in bed.

"Did you hear the fire bell this morning?" she asked.

"Yes, I did. But I was too tired to get up. Did you hear it?"

"Of course. But I was too tired, too. And I thought it would be a shame to wake you all up."

We looked at each other and laughed. If anyone had told us only two weeks ago that we would ignore a fire-alarm...

But the old place did not burn down after all.

CHAPTER 25

The Nazi Occupation Begins

THE GERMANS did not march into Warsaw as triumphant conquerors. They sneaked in, unobtrusively, in small groups, like thieves.

We were terribly busy all that week after the capitulation. There were so many things to be done: debris had to be cleared, water had to be brought (the nearest well was at least a mile away from our house, and we had to stand two hours in line before we even got to the pump), something had to be done about those gaping windows, and done in a hurry for the weather was growing increasingly cold.

And then there was still the food problem. Now that the siege was over we didn't even have fresh horse flesh from killed horses. The iron ring of the German army was still closed tight around the city and did not let any supplies in.

We were so busy, in fact, that we had forgotten the Germans would ever come. The first sight of enemy uniforms in the streets of Warsaw was a dreadful shock.

The children and I were just coming back from a walk. I had told George and Ania on my return from that running trip to Gosposia's house about a house I had seen on my way: the house itself was untouched, but a shell must have passed quite close to it and the impact of the air had ruffled the tiles of the roof; they all stood up on end. This gave the whole house a funny appearance, like a man's head with hair raised by fear. The children had insisted on seeing it now, and as they needed fresh air (they had both grown thin and pale) I had decided to take them that afternoon. We were passing through Lwowska when suddenly I caught sight of three Germans coming down the street towards us.

Blue uniforms, silver wings on collars and sleeves—they were fliers. They walked slowly, looking around as they went, evidently admiring the destruction they had wrought. As they drew nearer I peered at their faces with horrified curiosity. What were they like, those monsters who had brought wholesale death and destruction upon us? Why... they were mere kids! Blue-eyed, pink-cheeked, snub-nosed, they didn't look more than sixteen, and as nice as nice could be. The sight of these childish faces gave me a worse shock than any criminal face would have done.

And then a wave of bitter resentment swept over me. Not against those boys. No. They were innocent. Kids of that age have no imagination. They were told to fly, to drop bombs, to machine-gun everything in sight, and they did as ordered. To them it was probably a glorious, rather dangerous sport. But the man who sent them... this so-called civilization of ours which made that insane tragedy possible. Why did men invent automobiles that turn into tanks, planes that turn into bombers? And weren't we proud of these inventions? "The soaring human genius conquers air and space!"

Yes, and puts lethal weapons into children's hands, too.

After that afternoon I saw German soldiers whenever I went out. There were more of them every day. Their trim, gray-green uniforms struck a sharp contrast against the background of the ruined city and its shabby, haggard-looking inhabitants. The Germans were evidently impressed by the sights they saw: they walked slowly, looking around, many snapped cameras at the ruined buildings. They tried to be friendly to the civilian population; perhaps it was a matter of policy, perhaps plain human decency and pity.

From the collection of Stefan Mucha

"The first sight of enemy uniforms in the streets of Warsaw was a dreadful shock."

From the collection of Stefan Mucha

From the collection of Stefan Mucha

"I saw German soldiers whenever I went out..."

From the collection of Stefan Mucha

From the collection of Stefan Mucha

"... There were more of them every day."

From the collection of Stefan Mucha

USNARA

*Adolf Hitler salutes his troops in Warsaw during the Nazi victory parade
held on Aleje Ujazdowskie, October 5, 1939.*

One day in the square I saw an officer watching the burial of a small child. He was an elderly man and his eyes were full of tears. He noticed that I was looking at him and quickly turned away.

The Germans began to distribute bread and soup in the streets. This created a sharp division of opinion among people and caused endless arguments.

"This is our bread," the party of empty stomachs maintained. "They've stolen it from us. We might as well take it back. Why should we make them a present of it? The more we take from the Germans, the better."

"No," shouted the defiant spirits. "Rather die than accept anything from German hands. A movie camera stands by each bread truck. They take pictures of German soldiers distributing bread to Polish people. They will show it in Berlin and abroad with the caption, 'Hitler, the benefactor of Warsaw civilians.' No. We've starved for over a month. We may starve a few days longer till food is brought to Warsaw."

Mother and I never could decide which of the two parties was right. Yet, somehow, no one in our household ever stood in line for German bread.

One afternoon Ania returned from her walk with Leosia, flushed and excited.

"I've met a Hitler," she announced (every German was "a Hitler" to Ania), "and he wanted to give me a chocolate bar. But . . . ," proudly, "I didn't take it."

"You don't like Hitler, I see," I said, amused.

"No. He is naughty. He killed my Aunt Madzia." Ania had adored Aunt Madzia.

The next day I took George to help me carry water. Of course he could not carry much but he begged to help, and even half a pitcher of extra water meant a lot in those days. We were assigned one glassful a day per person to wash in, and considering the dust that lay everywhere it was really nothing. George, like any other little boy of eight, did not mind a dirty face and hands, but Ania, who was a dainty little thing, asked constantly to have her hands washed and had to be refused.

The well from which we took our water was at the bottom of a large garden, and I let George wander around while I stood in line. I didn't really mind standing in line, even though the path that led to the well was muddy and my feet were soaked through in no time. It was a rest to be standing in a garden, with the pale blue October sky overhead, and breathe the fresh leaf-scented air instead of smoke and dust. The bombed houses, in particular, had a peculiar sweetish smell that was nauseating. As it was almost noon the line wasn't very long; most of the people got their water supply in the morning.

A German soldier came out of a nearby building carrying a steaming bowl of soup. I saw him advance towards George, and extend the bowl towards him. George drew back.

"Take it, take it!" I heard the soldier insist in German.

George blushed to the roots of his hair, smiled, violently shook his head and turned away; no German soup for George, either!

The soldier shrugged his shoulders and advanced toward the line. Two schoolgirls stood behind me. He offered the soup to them. Giggling, they accepted and began to eat ravenously. The rich smell of the soup came to my nostrils and made me feel faint (we were still very hungry). I was proud of George.

The soldier in the meantime had returned to the building, and now reappeared once more, carrying a pail. He went straight to the pump, ignoring the line,

From the collection of Stefan Mucha

Hungry Varsovians reluctantly accept food from German field kitchens.

From the collection of Stefan Mucha

The water lines seem to stretch for miles.

From the collection of Stefan Mucha

A German soldier supervises water distribution.

and pumped the pail full of water. Then, with a supreme disregard of the thirty pairs of eyes that were watching him, he began his daily toilet. A dud bomb was lying only a few steps from the pump (duds were such a common sight in Warsaw, no one paid any attention to them) and a stick with a card attached to it marked the place. The soldier hung a hand mirror on the stick and proceeded to shave. After that he stripped to the waist and with a great deal of splashing began to wash in the bucket.

How well equipped those German soldiers were: a heavy green sweater matching the tunic (I wondered whether it was real wool or ersatz), a spotless white shirt, an undershirt, everything brand new. Was he trying to impress us? Probably.

He rubbed himself dry with a turkish towel, dressed again, combed his hair neatly and put away the toilet articles into an oilcloth case. Bright and shiny, he was now ready to help everyone. So pleased with himself! He stood by the pump and put his hand on the handle. It was the turn of two little nuns, dragging an enormous heavy cauldron. He pumped the water for them. My turn now. His hand was still on the handle.

"No, thank you," I said dryly in my broken German, "I would rather do it myself."

He looked at me with pain and surprise; I was spoiling his fun. The idiot! Didn't he understand?

Mother had said, "The only proper way for civilians to act towards an army of occupation is to ignore them completely. Don't even look at them!" and Mother knew her rules of savoir faire better than anyone.

I didn't look at the soldier while I pumped the water. Then, calling George, I grabbed the bucket and the pitcher and walked away trying not to stoop. It was hard not to stoop, for the pitcher was much smaller than the pail and didn't balance it. (We had only one bucket left now, the two others had somehow disappeared during the fire.) Carrying water uphill nearly broke one's back; it proved too much for George. We hadn't walked one-third of the way home before I had to carry his pitcher too.

But I didn't mind, George was alright.

Every day while going for water I had to pass the house in which Roman's mother and Rose lived. By the end of the week I decided to go in, perhaps by now Rose was up to seeing visitors. I found her still lying on the bed but already fully dressed, although it had been only nine days since the baby was born. With her dark curls spread on the pillow she didn't look more than fourteen. The newborn lay at her side; the older, twenty-month-old Maciek, was playing on the floor by the bed. The room, with plywood replacing glass in the windows, was almost dark.

"Rulka," Rose exclaimed stretching out both her arms. And then she burst into tears. "You know...? You've heard...?" she sobbed.

Silently I nodded. Rose threw her arms around my neck and nestled against me, shaken by sobs. "How will I ever be able to live without him!"

This childish grief broke my heart. For a while neither of us spoke. I held her in my arms. We were both crying.

"Tell me about yourself," I said at last. "How was it when the baby was born? It must have been terrible!"

Instantly she was calm again.

"You bet it was," she said, almost with her old vivacity. "He was born Sunday at ten AM. Remember that horrible artillery bombardment on Sunday? Well, he was born during the hottest part of it. The doctor was furious, because they had taken me upstairs to the delivery room. As soon as the baby was born I baptized him myself. I was

From the collection of Sam Bryan, courtesy of Julien Bryan

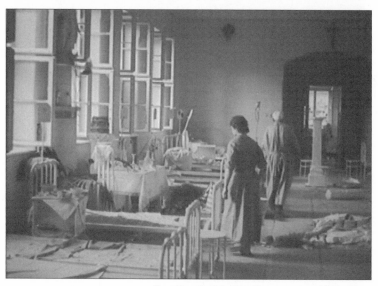

From the collection of Sam Bryan, courtesy of Julien Bryan

Hospitals throughout the city are heavily damaged by German bombers.

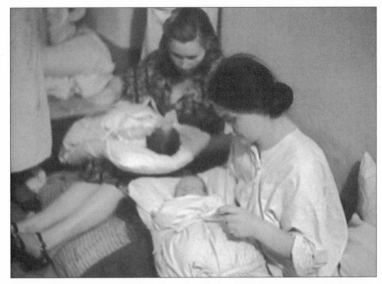

From the collection of Sam Bryan, courtesy of Julien Bryan

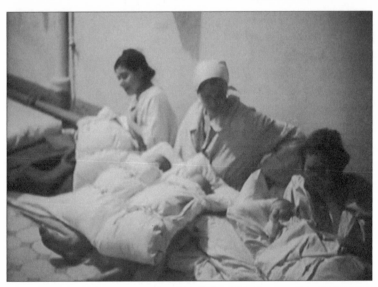

From the collection of Sam Bryan, courtesy of Julien Bryan

Mothers, with their newborns, sit on the floor of a maternity hospital's basement to shelter from German bombing.

sure, you see, we were both going to be killed instantly. No one wanted to come upstairs to carry me down, so I walked to my room all by myself."

"What? Do you mean you walked downstairs right after the baby was born?" I gasped. "How did you ever find enough strength?"

"I don't know, I did. It didn't seem very hard at the time. Roman arrived half an hour later; I had somebody telephone him that he had another son. I didn't let him know when the pains started coming, and he thanked me for this with tears in his eyes. He said he was so nervous that he simply didn't know how he would have stood the knowledge that I was in pain, when he was unable to run to my side. He remained only ten minutes with me. His companion was downstairs with the ambulance, and he wouldn't let him stay. Roman just kissed me and the baby and was gone. I never saw him again."

Her face puckered once more but she quickly controlled herself. "The next morning, Monday, the first thing I knew an incendiary bomb had fallen on the windowsill in my room, and the woodwork was burning. I leaped out of bed, grabbed the baby, grabbed my fur coat and ran into the hall. They put the incendiary out and told me to go back to my room and dress. I dressed with a nurse's help and once more returned to the hall. No sooner had I got there than the whole building was on fire. We all ran out into the courtyard, and later to the doorway of the front building. The front building wasn't burning, you see. Someone brought me a chair and told me to sit down. I sat on that chair from ten o'clock one morning till six o'clock the next..."

"How did you ever stand it?"

"I don't know. It was pretty infernal. The baby was hungry and he was crying. I didn't have any milk yet, and there was no sweetened water to feed him with. At last a woman who had a five-day-old baby offered to nurse him. We couldn't change his diapers either. But the night was the worst. A woman staggered into the doorway and proceeded to have a baby there. Another ran in screaming; she was wounded, a shrapnel splinter in the back. The doctor told her to undress, and she stood there all naked while the doctor was taking the splinter out by candlelight. It was like a scene from Dante's Inferno. But... but... it was all simply idyllic compared with the news that was awaiting me!" Her childish face puckered again.

"How did you get home?"

"I walked. At six o'clock there was a moment of quiet, so a nurse took the baby and we came here."

There were at least ten blocks from Sano to this house, but she seemed quite casual about it. I remembered how Mother had carried the big case of silver down to the cellar, how I myself had pushed the heavy wardrobe out of my way... People under stress can do anything, apparently.

For a while we were silent. Rose was crying again. Suddenly she propped herself up on the elbow.

"Tell me, Rulka," she asked with tragic earnestness, "do you believe in the hereafter?"

"Of course I do," I said with conviction.

"You mean that we will be reunited with the ones we love after we die?"

I was not so sure of that, but I nodded.

"I do believe in it," she cried. "I do, I do, I do. If I didn't I wouldn't be able to stand it. Never. Oh, God! Why couldn't we die together! I prayed and prayed all through the siege: If one of us should die, let it be both! But God would not listen to my prayers..."

"What about the children?" I asked softly.

346

"They should have died too," she said vehemently.

Again we were silent.

And then little Maciek threw the toy he was playing with on the bed and began to struggle desperately to recover it. At once Rose leaned forward and picked up the toy.

"Here, darling. Here is your block. Why didn't you ask your Mommy for it? Your Mommy would do anything for you, you precious little one. Mommy's own darling boy." She kissed his small head. Maciek stuck the block in his mouth and stared at me with big, grave blue eyes... Roman's eyes...

In the hall I met Roman's mother. She was as calm and composed as ever. Only the lines of her face had deepened.

"How are you, Rulka?" she greeted me with a smile. "I'm so glad you came. Come and see Rose often, will you? She needs company."

"Poor Janinka," Mother repeated once more as I told her about my visit.

"But Mother, Rose is far more unhappy right now. If you had only seen her, the poor child...!"

"She is young, she will forget. Perhaps even some day she will get married again. She is so pretty, has so much charm..."

"Mother, for Heaven's sake, don't be such a hateful realist!"

"But it's true. She is only twenty-one, a mere child. Children can't go on being unhappy forever. They forget. But for Janinka it's the end. Mothers never forget..."

There was a shadow on Mother's face as she said that.

"Mothers never forget..." I knew what she was thinking about. Franek.

CHAPTER 26

In Need of Candles

WE WERE down to our last candle. Dusk fell now at four, by four thirty it was completely dark. We couldn't live without some sort of light. And there were no candles to be had anywhere, they had altogether disappeared from the market.

I was racking my brain for a solution of this problem when suddenly snatches of conversation overheard sometime, somewhere, came back to my mind: "...in the wardrobe... my wife has stocked up a lot of soap, candles and chocolate... you can have it..." Who had said that? Where? When? I had it! Of course, it was Jan talking to Tomek on the day of the Bank's evacuation. I remembered it all now. The silver, the keys in the right drawer of the little antique desk... I ran to Krysia.

"Krysia, how many candles have you left?"

"Just one. I really don't know what we will do after it's gone. Go to bed at five I suppose."

"No!" I cried triumphantly. "I know where we can get candles. Lots of them!" I told her.

"Of course," she exclaimed. "Why hadn't I thought of it before? Tomek told me about it before he left; he gave me a note from Jan to the superintendent of the house with instructions to let Tomek or me in." She rummaged through the desk. "Here it is. He told me to go and rescue that silver if I could. But how could I? During the siege Jan's house was almost on the front line. Let's go now!"

"I hope the house has not been looted!"

We took some suitcases to put the silver and candles in, and started at once: Krysia, Ina, Zbyszek and I. We did

348

not enjoy Zbyszek's company for long. On Ksiazeca a barricade was being torn down. A man touched Zbyszek on the shoulder as we passed.

"Come on, young man. Take off your coat and help us with this barricade. Just twenty minutes. After that you can continue on your way." That was the way barricades were demolished. Every man passing by was stopped and told to help for twenty minutes. Simple and effective, typical of Mayor Starzynski's methods. Zbyszek, however, did not relish the idea. Perhaps if I were a man I wouldn't either.

The house where Jan used to live, a big block of apartments inhabited by the Bank's employees, had one corner torn off by a high explosive, but otherwise seemed to be in pretty good shape. Jan's apartment was in another wing. The superintendent did not seem particularly eager to let us in.

"Forty soldiers have been camping in that apartment for a week," he said slightly embarrassed. "I really don't know what state you'll find it in."

To our surprise and, let it be said, to the credit of those forty soldiers, we found the apartment in perfect order. Except for the shattered glass lying on the floor and thick layers of dust everywhere, the place looked very much as usual. We had no trouble locating the antique desk and the keys, and proceeded to open all the wardrobes, closets and drawers. Neat piles of linen, suits, underwear (it was strange to be rummaging in someone else's things) shoes... hats... but no silver. And no candles, either. Where did they put them? (In an empty drawer of the dining room cupboard I found a tiny piece of bread. It was stone-dry and dusty, but... no one looked... I slipped it in my mouth.) We searched the kitchen; no silver, no candles.

"Look," Krysia called from the bedroom. "There is another wardrobe in here. It's locked and I can't find the key. The silver and the candles must be in there."

"What shall we do?" I asked after vainly trying all the keys again.

"Let's break the door!"

It seemed a shame. The wardrobe was an antique, solid mahagony. The silver was safe in there. But the candles. . . ? That was what we came here for, wasn't it?

"Alright! Let's."

I brought a meat ax from the kitchen, and all three of us began to work on the wardrobe door. It did not give in easily, but at last there was an ominous crack, the end of a long splinter caught me on the nose and the door flew open. There on the second shelf from the bottom lay the coveted candles wrapped in blue paper.

"Hurray!"

Next to the candles, the soap, dozens and dozens of cakes. The silver was on the bottom shelf. But no chocolate anywhere.

Krysia was still rummaging through the shelves looking for it, when suddenly Ina exclaimed, "Look! What's that on the third shelf? A child's warm coat? Why, that's exactly what Christopher needs. I'll take it!"

That started it.

"A blanket," this from Krysia. "Don't we need an extra one? Let's take it along."

"Gloves! Look—warm woolen gloves. I left mine in the old apartment and they are gone."

Suddenly the lust for pillage seized us. We began to pull out things from the wardrobe and stack them in two piles, one to be taken with us, the other to be left behind. None of the treasures the wardrobe contained were of any interest to me, except, of course, the candles and the soap, but I remembered suddenly that somewhere in the kitchen a white enameled pail had caught my eye. It would come in handy for carrying water! I ran to the kitchen. A pitcher! An extra pitcher would be fine, too. I looked around, and then quickly but systematically I went through every drawer and shelf, filling the pail with all kinds of oddments that might prove useful around the house...

When half an hour later we left Jan's apartment we were all three heavily loaded with loot. For that was exactly what it was, loot! Of course we were going to return those things to Jan and his wife when and if they ever came back, but...

Since that day I have not quite been able to share the righteous indignation with which my law-abiding family and friends spoke of "those monsters" who looted houses and stores while Warsaw was being bombed. And to think that those forty soldiers had not touched a thing.

As we passed through the main entrance we saw a small crowd of people standing in front of the janitor's cubicle. Joyous shouts and laughter were coming from the inside.

"What has happened?" we asked.

"The janitor and his son have just returned. They had left at the time of the evacuation. That's his wife laughing," someone informed us.

So people were coming back already. Perhaps Franek would return soon, too! A new hope entered my heart. I must tell Mother.

Yes, the refugees of a month ago were returning now. They came singly and in flocks, dragging their sore feet or crowded on top of horse-drawn carts. They were a sad sight. Those awful, blank "refugee" faces reappeared once more in the streets of Warsaw. Those people had never lost them. What's more, when the peril of the Bolshevik invasion turned them back from their eastward flight and sent them back to Warsaw, they didn't know what fate had befallen the capital. They were not prepared for the shock.

Men came back staggering and exhausted only to find their homes burned to the ground, their wives and children buried under the ruins or in the hospitals. Even those whose homes and families had escaped destruction could not readjust themselves to what they saw. They wandered aimlessly along the streets, surveying with eyes full of horror the charred and twisted wreckage. By that time, we who had never left Warsaw paid no attention to the ruins. We were too busy, too intent on the everyday problems of living.

Yes, every day thousands of returning refugees flowed into Warsaw, but Franek was not among them.

Tomek Malachowski returned only three days after our looting expedition to Jan's apartment. Krysia and Ina were wild with joy, but Tomek was a shadow of his old self. For two days he had to stay in bed, unable to stand on his swollen and bleeding feet. His black, sunken eyes shone feverishly in his ashen face.

"You know," he told me, "I've always thought that the trouble with me was that I had led a too-protected life. Home, school, the university, the Bank, well... all that is not what people call real life. I used to crave for some real experience. I certainly have it now. If you only knew what I've seen... I can't tell you... it's too atrocious, but...," he paused for a moment then added in a whisper, "I didn't know human bodies contained so much blood..." His eyes were staring in front of him blindly.

"It's funny," he continued after a while, "but do you know what I worried most about on my way back? My future relationship to Krysia. Of course I didn't know what peril you all were in all that time so I didn't worry about that. But you see, I was fleeing with two married couples and the way those two women behaved just made me sick of the whole of womankind. One was constantly nagging her husband because they had left the cookbook behind, and the other never stopped bragging because she could find food where no one else could. We were dreadfully hungry, and she would show us her purchases and laugh. But she never shared anything with anyone. Hateful! I was so afraid some horrid streak like that might develop in Krysia. Those things do happen in wartime you know, and just think what it would feel like to see a person you adore turn into something despicable."

"You shouldn't have worried about that. You've got the bravest, most courageous little wife I've ever seen," I assured him. I told him how Krysia had run through a flaming street and under a hail of bombs to invite us to her shelter.

"Besides," I continued, "I don't think you're right. People don't develop nasty streaks in wartime. They've always been there, unsuspected. In war people show their true nature. They are exactly what they are, nothing more and nothing less. All that war does is to dispel pretense. People are put to the final test, and they either make the grade or fail."

A note of bitterness crept into my voice. I knew I had failed. The hateful memory of that half hour during which I could not bring myself to run to Mother's help still rankled in my mind and made me writhe in an agony of shame every time I thought of it...

Tomek reassured me as to Franek's fate.

"I know your brother. I saw him climbing mountains

last summer. He is a resourceful man. I am sure he didn't follow the main highways, but took some byroads, and only highways were attacked by planes."

Days passed, however, and Franek did not return.

It seemed strange now that all through the duration of the siege we (or I at least) had not given Franek a thought. Facing death every day makes one forgetful of the absent ones. Only those who share the common danger seem to matter. But now that immediate death faced us no longer appalling visions assailed me constantly: Franek lying in a ditch among heaps of other dead, Franek dying of wounds in some small provincial hospital...

Mother and I seldom spoke of him, even now, but Mother went about her daily duties with a strained expression on her face that I hadn't seen there even during the worst days of the siege.

We asked every returning refugee we knew if he had seen Franek somewhere on the roads, but none of them had. Perhaps Franek's closest friend and colleague, an assistant at the University, would know. I went to see him. The house was burned to the ground and no one could tell me where the former inhabitant lived now.

Mother spent every spare moment in church.

CHAPTER 27

Major von Kraven

ANOTHER THOUGHT that weighed heavily on my mind was that of Olgierd. Poor Olg! What agonies he must be going through! To live in safety and comfort while you know that your wife and children are being bombed day and night, that they are perhaps dying at this very minute, perhaps already dead...

The mere thought of those mental tortures made me wince. How could I let him know that we were alive and well? The post and telegraph offices were still closed and would probably remain so for months.

Iza W., a friend of mine, came to see me. Her parents were also in the United States, also in all probability frantic with worry. We decided to do something about it together.

First we tried the American Consulate. The old consular office had been completely bombed out of existence, graced as it was with seven artillery shells. But the consular staff under the only remaining vice-consul had already assembled in the chancellery on Aleje Ujazdowskie. No, we were told, the American Consulate had not so far been able to establish contact with the American Embassy in Berlin, much less so with the United States. If, however, we knew anyone in the State Department in Washington, D. C., we could try the German military Kommendantur.[1] They had already established their field post and in several cases agreed to transmit messages to Washington.

Well, we could try anyway.

---

[1] Command Headquarters.

As we set out on our way, Iza said, "My folks have one bit of bad news coming to them. Do you remember all the lovely antique furniture we used to have? Mother was crazy about antiques." I certainly remembered it—it was a beautiful collection. "Well, it's all gone. When father was transferred to his present post in the States, they left all those things in storage at Wegielek. Wegielek's storehouses burned to the ground, so there you are. I just learned about it this morning."

"Are you sure all the storehouses were burned?"

"Positive."

"In that case," I said almost casually, "all our things are gone, too. That's where I left them when Olgierd went to America and I moved to Mother's."

All the precious belongings we had accumulated in our eight years of married life! Yet, at that moment their loss didn't seem to matter. What was it compared with the horrible, wholesale destruction that surrounded me from every side? Besides, I had thought we would lose our lives, and we had only lost our property; it looked like a pretty good bargain to me.

It was not till weeks afterwards that, lying in bed at night, I would go over in my mind the things that were stored with Wegielek. The dining room set Olgierd himself had designed... his library... the beautiful antique desk (we really could not afford such expensive antiques at the time we bought it). And then there were the pictures. Olgierd had a real passion for them, for the peasant girl in particular. A watercolor she was, by a famous woman painter. That girl had the most engaging smile, half mischievous, half wistful. A Mona Lisa in sheepskins, a critic had said at the time she was exhibited. It seemed a shame such a smile should perish in flames. Oh, well...

As Iza and I walked now to the German Kommendantur

From the collection of Stefan Mucha, courtesy of Julien Bryan

The American Consulate on Jasna Street is bombed out during the siege.

The American Embassy on Aleje Ujazdowskie is also damaged.

I noticed with amazement how quickly the aspect of the streets was changing. The ruined houses still stood as dramatic and ghastly as ever. But the sidewalks had been partly cleared and were now lined with hundreds of street vendors, exhibiting all sorts of goods. Bright red and green sweaters flapped in the wind, colorful splashes against the dismal background of battered walls. Heavy cotton stockings, cheap underwear, cigarettes, tobacco, sugar at two grosze a lump... probably all stolen during the siege. The vendors in loud voices called out their wares. A weird, noisy, cheap fair among the ruins. No stores were open yet but many already showed signs of life; the sound of hammering came from the inside, plywood was fitted into windows. Life, in spite of everything, was slowly returning to Warsaw.

I noticed that many walls were spotted with tiny posters written out in hand. "Room for rent," one said. "I am going to Lublin, will take messages. Inquire... ," "Fur coat for sale," "German lessons at 1 zloty per hour."

So that was the medium Warsaw had found for what used to be classified ads in the daily papers! Newspapers... we hadn't seen any in a long time. During the week that followed the capitulation the old Warsaw dailies had issued bulletins which were posted on the walls, but after the German Army entered the town even those had disappeared. How we were craving for news...

Suddenly as we passed in front of the main post office we heard the old chant of newsboys. What was that, a newspaper?

"Let's buy it," I exclaimed.

Quickly I unfolded it, glanced at the headline and with a loud *"Psia krew!"*[2] threw it into the gutter. The headline

---

[2] "Bloody Hell!" (translated literally from Polish, "Dog's blood!").

splashed in big bold letters across the front page said "HOW THE POLISH GOVERNMENT HAS BETRAYED THE POLISH PEOPLE."

So that was the stuff we were going to be fed from now on!

As we passed through Mazowiecka a terrific explosion suddenly shook the air. Involuntarily we started.

"What's that? A belated bomb?"

No, it was not a bomb, as we later found out, it was a burned house that had suddenly collapsed, killing fourteen passersby. The empty, charred shells were already beginning to crumble down. Soon, very soon, walking in the streets of Warsaw would become extremely dangerous, even though ruins were fenced off and whole streets closed to traffic.

A vast crowd was thronging the entrance to the Kommendantur's headquarters. Two German sentries were pushing it back.

"Zurück! Zurück!"[3] they shouted.

But the crowd would not withdraw. They were people from out of town places who had been caught in Warsaw during the siege and now wanted to return to their homes. They had come here to get permits which would allow them to leave the city. They didn't speak German, however, so they could not explain to the sentry what they wanted. We pushed our way through the crowd and soon learned from the sentry that permits were not issued by the Kommendantur, but by some other department in a different building. We passed on the information to our immediate neighbors and they withdrew, but new faces and bodies began to press forward again.

---

[3] "Back! Back!"

From the collection of Stefan Mucha

One of the many street markets that sprang up among the ruins.

From the collection of Stefan Mucha

USNARA

Despite its destruction, Varsovians gather to shop at Plac Za Zelazna Brama, one of the city's largest pre-war market places. Before the war, anything from apples to armaments could be bought at such markets.

362

"Zurück! Zurück!" shouted the sentry, pushing them back.

I began to have my doubts as to that famous German ability for organization. Couldn't they put up a poster giving the necessary information instead of having their own sentries, who didn't understand Polish, wrangle constantly with a crowd that did not understand German?

The sentry was unexpectedly nice to Iza and me. Perhaps because we spoke some German, perhaps because we were the only decently dressed people in the crowd. Germans are dreadful snobs.

We told him we wanted to see Herr Major Schauman and he immediately sent an orderly to see whether the Major was in. He let us stand on the steps away from the pushing crowd. While we waited I observed that his manner towards the crowd was really quite friendly. He was pushing them alright and shouting "Zurück!" but he did it with an amused grin on his face.

"Are you an Austrian?" I asked him. This would explain it.

"Unfortunately not," he flashed his white teeth at me. "A Bavarian. Austrians are far more gemütlich." [4]

The orderly returned with the news that the Major had been called out. "The ladies will have to come back in the afternoon," the sentry told us.

We came back in the afternoon, but the Major was at a conference. For three days we returned to the Kommendantur, but without success. The Major was either busy or out.

On the third day the weather was awful. It was drizzling, a damp mist hung over the city, after half an hour of waiting among the crowd we were soaked to the skin. We

---

[4] Pleasant or friendly.

were about to give up any further attempts and go home when suddenly a German officer who was pushing his way through the crowd stopped in front of us.

"What can I do for you?" he asked in a crisp, business-like voice. He was short, slight, there was something bird-like about him.

We told him.

"Major Schauman is busy right now, I know," he said. "But come back in the afternoon. Here is my card. Ask for me and I'll take you to the Major."

He handed us his card and disappeared in the crowd.

"Major Heinrich Maria von Kraven," said the card.

Now at last we were getting somewhere. It was nice of him to offer his help, unrequested.

We came back in the afternoon and with the Major's card in hand were immediately let in. Major von Kraven was busy right now, the sentry upstairs informed us, we would have to wait for a while.

It was a strange anteroom we were waiting in. The portraits of Polish generals, Marshal Pilsudski, Marshal Smigly-Rydz, still hung on the walls. This used to be the general headquarters of the Polish army garrison. And all around us, the hateful gray-green uniforms hurried through drafty corridors. The glass in the windows had not been replaced yet, and it was damnably cold. Colder than outside.

At last Major von Kraven appeared. He saluted us stiffly and told us to follow him. Walking rapidly along the desolate corridors at the heels of our German guide we at last reached the door of Major Schauman's office. Von Kraven went in first, leaving the door open. The room was filled with people, evidently all kinds of petitioners. We had seen some of them in the crowd outside. A large, tall man sat at a desk littered with papers. Von Kraven went straight to him and spoke a few words in low tones, then beckoned to us. "Yes, I'll do it at once," Schauman said amiably, rising to his feet. "Have you your message with you?"

We handed it to him. "It will go out in today's mail," he promised.

We thanked him and turned to the door. Von Kraven had disappeared.

Outside we sighed with relief. At last it was done; our respective families would be reassured.

"I am cold," Iza shivered. "Those Kommendantur quarters are colder than a doghouse."

"Let's go into the Europejski," I suggested. "We will get warm in there. I haven't been inside a café since war started. It will be fun to see one again."

Warsaw's most famous café, once the rendezvous of the elite and the hotbed of all political gossip, was across the street from the Kommendantur. It was open.

The inside was blue with cigar smoke, but warm. Very warm. The place was swarming with German officers and, surprisingly enough, soldiers. The German army was not so democratic during the First World War, I remembered. A soldier would not dare to enter a café where an officer was seated. Only a few tables were occupied by Poles. We found a small table in a corner and ordered coffee, and we got it—at least the waiter brought us each half a glass of a brownish, slightly sweetened, tepid liquid. It had no taste at all, so it wasn't even bad.

"Look!" Iza whispered to me excitedly, pointing to the ceiling.

A bulb. An electric bulb actually burning! It was over three weeks since we had seen electric light. We watched it now with childish fascination. Then again I began to look around.

"Iza, I can tell you the exact time when a shell hit the Europejski. The hour and the minute."

"How?"

"Look at that clock. Nine fifteen. That's the precise time of the explosion."

"Right. Like a detective story. The victim's watch telling the exact time of the murder."

We were amused to notice at a neighboring table two German officers talking to two obviously Jewish women. What would the Führer say to that? Probably it wouldn't last long anyway.

But the company of so many Germans was oppressive. So was the cigar smoke.

"Let's get out of here," Iza said. "I am warm now but I am getting a headache."

We paid for our coffee and received in the change a little purple cash bond issued, according to the inscription, by the Occupation Army at Lodz. Iza decided to keep it for a souvenir.

As we went out through the swivel door in which glass had been replaced by boards, and caught a refreshing whiff of the damp, cold air, I suddenly remembered von Kraven.

"Don't you think this Major von Kraven was nice? If it were not for him we would never have been able to send that message."

"Yes," Iza agreed, "good old Major von Kraven!"

Three days later posters appeared all over Warsaw. The first execution posters. Twelve men and two women had been condemned to death for offenses against the Reich. The sentence had been executed. The announcement was signed by the president of the court-martial, Major Heinrich Maria von Kraven.

Good old Major von Kraven.

The Europejski Hotel is damaged by German bombs and artillery.

Execution posters printed on red paper begin to appear all over Warsaw.

Announcement

The following have been sentenced to death by the Temporary Police Court:

CZESŁAW BIAŁOBRZESKI
for failing to turn over concealed Polish Army equipment,

LEIB MICHEL HOCHMANN
for refusing to carry out a task and running away,

CZESŁAW WOŁOWSKI
for conspiring against the German civil police,

ADOLF KRYŚKIEWICZ
for the illegal possession of weapons and ammunition,

LUCJAN KOZŁOWSKI
for the illegal possession of hand grenades,

WACŁAW GOŁOMBIOWSKI
for the illegal possession of weapons and ammunition,

JAN KARPIŃSKI
for the attempted murder of a woman and the illegal possession of weapons and ammunition.

The sentences have been carried out.   Commandant

Warsaw 11/16/39.   Warsaw Police Regiment

CHAPTER 28

Priests and Teachers Arrested

IT WAS a bleak October morning. Rain was drizzling from gray, leaden skies, water dripped from every battered roof. Mother, as usual, had gone to church while I inspected with apprehension my pride and joy, the two cellophane panes I had fixed in the dining room windows. The rest of the windows were covered with heavy cardboard, I couldn't get more cellophane, but thanks to those two small panes the room was not entirely dark, and they did look almost like glass. But in this damp weather would they hold? I reinforced the cellophane with paper stickers on the inside, perhaps that would do the trick.

Someone was knocking at the front door; probably Mother. I went to open the door. Yes, it was Mother but— what had happened? She looked positively ghastly.

Carefully she closed the door behind her and then in a strange, choked voice said, "Priests have been arrested."

"What...?"

"Yes, all the priests in Warsaw were imprisoned this morning. When I arrived at church I was surprised to see that no Mass was being celebrated at any of the altars. You know how many Masses are celebrated around this hour, almost at every altar there is one. The church was dark, no candles lit anywhere. Nothing but the flickering little red light in front of the Holy Sacrament. I waited for twenty minutes, growing more apprehensive with every minute. People came and went. Nothing. At last I went to the vestry and there they told me that the Germans had come at half past seven and had arrested all the priests. I ran to the Church of the Savior." (The Savior's Church, although half-burnt, was still being used.) "Same story. Apparently all over town priests have been rounded up. They didn't spare a single one. Not even the vicar of St. Alexander who is over eighty years old...," Mother's voice broke, almost in a sob.

"The Gestapo must have arrived."

"Yes."

Once more I was conscious of that strange hollow feeling in the pit of my stomach. So it had started. Terror— ruthless, cold, cruel terror. All the priests in prison. What next? Who next?

That afternoon Mother went out again to find out more about the fate of the arrested priests. I stayed home, still busy with the windows. How many windows that apartment had! I had never before realized we were so rich in window space. And the heavy cardboard was hard to handle; I had nothing but a kitchen knife to cut it with. And no nails. After standing for an hour in a line at a hardware store all I got were two-inch carpenter nails. They were useless. I had to extract nails we had used when we made the children's room gas-proof. It was tedious work.

I was standing on the top of the ladder struggling desperately with a huge piece of cardboard that would not fit in, when there was another knock on the front door. Who was that? Mother? She had left only ten minutes ago. Perhaps she had forgotten her umbrella or something. I jumped to the floor and ran to open the door. And there on the threshold...

"Franek!"

"Sis!"

We both went mad with joy. Franek grabbed me in his arms, lifted me in the air, as he always did, and then, still clinging to each other, we started a wild dance round and round the dark hall.

"Come in here," I said at last, dragging him by the hand into my room. "Take a comfortable chair and tell me all about it. I wish Mother were here! She is out but will be back shortly. God, won't she be glad!"

Franek slumped heavily into an armchair. What a sight he looked! Even worse than Tomek Malachowski. Thin to the point of emaciation, his hair wild, and a three weeks' growth of red beard covering his hollow cheeks. Franek with a beard! It made him look like a disreputable tramp. His hands were trembling as he lit a cigarette. In a few words he told me his story.

He had left Warsaw on foot that night of the evacuation. But as he crossed a railway track somewhere in the suburbs, he saw a train advancing slowly in the darkness. The train was completely dark, too. He jumped on the running board. From there he managed to climb through a window into a lavatory where he securely locked himself in for the rest of the night. The train took him as far as Brzesc. From there he continued on foot, steadily advancing eastward and avoiding main tracks whenever possible. Once, lying in a ditch, he witnessed a regular battle between Polish and German troops. Another time, hidden in a potato field, he saw someone giving flashlight signals from a church steeple to German planes overhead. He ran to the village to denounce the traitor. But by the time he got there the Polish troops had already left.

Later, he fell in with a group of other refugees. Thus, walking, mostly by night, they reached the farthest point east, the Marshes of Pinsk. They felt secure there, no mechanized army could get through these treacherous plains. They had just settled in a gamekeeper's house hidden in the woods when the horrible news swept through the countryside like flame: "Bolsheviks are coming!"

Then began the mad scramble back. Franek didn't seem to remember much of it. Roads choked with people, carriages and cars... People he knew, passing by in automobiles, nodding, but never stopping to give him a lift... In the rush of the departure he had lost his companions.

Now he found new ones, an elderly man and a young boy. The three of them at last reached Minsk where for the first time they saw the German army. The patrol they met was about to arrest them when suddenly Franek remembered that Cisowa, where Hanka was staying, was only four miles away. He told the Germans they were going there, and as he spoke excellent German the soldiers, evidently impressed, let them pass. The three men arrived at Cisowa looking like dying men, and no sooner had they arrived than they collapsed from hunger and exhaustion. For a week Hanka nursed them back to health. Yesterday, feeling better, Franek decided to continue on his way to Warsaw.

At this point, all of a sudden Franek broke down. He leaned forward, hid his face in his hands and began to sob. I hadn't seen him weep since he was a little boy, and the sight gave me an awful pang. The poor thing didn't even know how to cry, he made little whimpering noises like a kitten, not like a big grown man.

"What is it? What has happened, dearest?" My heart was filled with compassion.

Franek did not lift his head, his shoulders continued to shake with sobs.

"Oh! you don't know... you can't even imagine what it was like to see Warsaw again. I hadn't an idea Warsaw had been bombed and destroyed... When I saw the ruins, the burnt houses... I was sure you were all killed... No

Mother, no sister, no home to go back to... And I've been dreaming of being home with you all these weeks... I couldn't face it. I entered the nearest church and stayed there for an hour praying... praying... Then I came here... But when I saw the burned street I turned back again. It was too much. For two hours I wandered in the streets in an agony of despair. Oh, it was hell... Then I went to church again. Only after that I braced myself to come here... "

"And we are all alive and well. Everything is O.K."

"I know it... I know it... ," he repeated but continued to sob. The memory of those agonizing hours was too much for his overwrought nerves.

He was still wiping his eyes when Mother arrived.

The moment I saw her on the doorstep I knew she was the bearer of some more bad news. Terrible anxiety was written all over her face. But I didn't let her speak.

"We have a visitor. A marvelous visitor!" I shouted. "Come and see."

They were in each other's arms now. Mother's face was flooded with tears, and beaming. I couldn't see Franek's face, it was hidden on Mother's shoulder.

"Mommy!"

"Sonny boy!"

They had gone back to pet names of childhood days. And yet, even in these moments of overwhelming joy, I could see that Mother's anxiety had not relaxed. She was not letting herself go completely. Presently she freed herself from Franek's wild embrace.

"Darling," she said, still looking at him with hungry, loving eyes, "you can't stay here. You must flee at once. You are in danger."

And then turning to me she added, "I've met Irene. They are arresting the teachers, too."

Franek was a teacher. For a moment we all remained silent.

"Where will he go? Where can he hide?" I asked at last.

"Oh, that should be easy. We have so many friends living in the country around Warsaw. He could go to Aunt Flika. She would be glad to have him. And once he is outside the city he will be safe. No one needs to know that he is a teacher. You better start at once, Franek."

"Please, Mother! Don't chase me out. I've just arrived, I've been pining for you all for so many weeks, and when at last I reached Warsaw...," once more I saw his chin quiver, "... I was sure you were all killed," he finished in a whisper.

I was afraid he was going to break down again.

"Really, Mother," I interposed, quickly coming to his rescue, "Franek can't leave right now. He walked twenty-two miles this morning, and is all in. How can you expect him to walk ten more? It's absolutely impossible!"

"But what is to be done then?" Mother asked, looking from Franek to me almost in despair. "He can't remain here. Do you remember that yesterday a policeman was asking the janitor if Professor Rayski had returned. They are looking for him!"

"Did anyone see you when you entered the house now?" I asked Franek.

"No, I didn't meet a soul."

"In that case no one knows he has returned. The servants won't tell. He can remain here till it gets dark, and then we can take him...," for a moment I racked my brain for a proper hideout. I had it! "... to Tilly's apartment. She hasn't returned yet, and the apartment is hardly damaged at all. Her maid is there. She'll be glad to take care of Franek. And when he is rested he can leave Warsaw." Tilly was a widowed relation.

374

Both Mother and Franek agreed to my plan, and Franek spent that afternoon with us. In spite of our apprehensions and fear it was a wonderful afternoon, we had so many things to tell each other!

"You should be proud of your mother," I told Franek. "I wish you had seen the way she acted under the bombs. Simply ignored them. Bombs... such little noisy gadgets, you know. But they didn't even disturb her sleep. Nothing can disturb Mother's sleep, except strong tea, of course."

"Stop making fun of me," Mother protested. "Haven't you got any respect for the older generation?"

"None," I assured her, kissing her hand, "none whatsoever."

"Besides," Mother turned to Franek, "she exaggerates. She's been as brave as I."

"Was I?"

"Well, older people should cling less to life than young ones."

"What about Aunt Madzia?"

"Yes. Poor old Madzia was so afraid to die. She was so young at heart you see... "

"So are you, Mother, darling!"

But we wouldn't dwell on painful memories, not on that day of Franek's return.

"Another thing you don't know about Mother," I told Franek, "is that she is as strong as an ox. She carried the big case of silver to the cellar alone, can you imagine?"

Yes, it was a pleasant afternoon. Franek had brought back from Cisowa in his rucksack a loaf of bread and two pounds of salt pork. These were acclaimed with cheers. What a treat! We all talked exultantly, George and Ania hung around Uncle Franek and would not be chased out of the room, Mother could not take her eyes off the son whom for many days now she had considered lost...

Of course, this arrest business still clouded our minds. Mother told us more details of it. Apparently all the school principals had been advised two days before that the German authorities intended to reopen the schools. They didn't know, however, how many teachers were available. So all teachers in town were ordered to come to the City Hall Friday at ten and register with the authorities.

The teachers, eager to take up their educational duties once more, flocked to the City Hall. And as they arrived, one by one, they were arrested and sent to the local prison.

Franek stayed with us till dusk. When it was reasonably dark we took him to Tilly's house where Kasia, the maid, received him with shouts of joy (she was immediately told to shut up) and rushed to prepare Tilly's bed for him. He tumbled into the clean sheets as dirty as he was; there still was no water in our part of the city.

As we returned home groping our way through the dark streets, and we had to hurry for the curfew would be sounded any minute now, Mother leaned heavily on my arm.

"I am tired," she said. "I don't remember being so tired in all my life." The joy of seeing Franek again had been too much for her.

The next day Franek came down with a strong attack of rheumatic fever. He lay in Tilly's bed quivering with fever, his large eyes wide and bright in a face contorted with pain. But we didn't dare to visit him in daytime.

Only after dusk, just before the curfew, we would carry to Tilly's house his daily ration of soup. There was no more talk about sending him out to the country.

A week went by. Franek was on his feet again. No new arrests of teachers had been reported, but we still didn't want him to show himself around our house and street. He was unable, however, to stand the solitude of Tilly's house any longer, so he began to take short walks and call on his friends. After the first of these outings I found him sitting idly at the table, staring at the candle with unseeing eyes.

"What's happened?" I asked.

"Halusia is dead," he whispered, not looking at me.

Halusia! His little girlfriend! The one we used to tease him so much about; she was almost a child, just out of high school.

"She was killed by a bomb in the Red Cross hospital where she had volunteered as a nurse. I went to call on them, and it was her mother who told me. Her mother is very calm. Only her little sisters cried. They don't know what's become of their father. He was an army doctor and presumably was taken prisoner by the Bolsheviks."

And they used to be such a happy family...

Franek spent most of his free time at their house.

Two weeks after their arrest the priests and the teachers were released. Most of them, not all. Those who returned never told anyone what they had been through. Not even their wives and friends. People who have been in German prisons never do.

Schools were finally reopened; then, after three weeks, all the high schools were closed again. Inferior races do not need higher education.

Franek found a post teaching grade school.

But the wave of terror and persecutions had already set in, never to abate again.

CHAPTER 29

My Brilliant New Business

"HOW MUCH money do you have left?" Mother asked me about a week after Franek's return.

Gingerly I opened the desk drawer and took out the big white envelope where I kept the money I had gotten from the Bank on the day of evacuation. I had noticed before that the envelope was growing alarmingly flat. I counted the remaining bank notes.

"Eight hundred zlotys," I announced.

"That won't last you much more than a month," Mother commented. "Don't you think you better get a job?"

"I wish I could."

Mother's confidence in my ability to land a job at one day's notice in a bombed city where practically all business had been destroyed was completely disarming. True enough, I've never had any trouble in finding jobs, and good ones at that. With a thorough knowledge of English and French and an American college diploma, I could always find a market in Warsaw for my abilities. Yes— always, but not now. My knowledge of French and English were worse than useless under the present regime, and my German was completely inadequate. Besides, who on earth would be looking for new employees? Warsaw was swarming with unemployed white-collar workers.

Nevertheless, just to please Mother, I called that morning on the managers of two firms which I knew were still in existence. One, a big manufacturing concern, was just in the process of being taken over by German management. Confiscated. Nothing doing there. The other, an old publishing firm, had been ordered to discontinue all its publications. Loyally, the management did not give its employees the sack, but of course they could not take on new ones. It was hard enough to meet even a reduced pay-roll when all bank balances were frozen, and only small weekly payments were made upon closely scrutinized applications.

I returned home, convinced more than ever that any further job hunting was useless.

Yes... but eight hundred zlotys, and myself and two children to support... Mother and I had two distinct budgets, although we shared the common household expenses. Besides, Mother's financial position was little better than mine. And Franek, if he started earning again, would certainly not be making much. Not in the teaching profession.

Well, I decided, if you can't get a job, you can always start some business of your own. That was the obvious solution. But what kind of business?

I was still asking myself this question when Wanda L. came to see me the next morning. Wanda was twenty-three, attractive, smart, and had an old mother to support.

"No job?" I asked her.

"No, our factory was bombed out of existence. What about you?"

"I am in the same spot. I think the only thing to do is to start some business of my own. There are no jobs to be gotten. But what business?"

"That's exactly what I thought. That's why I came to see you. If you hit upon a good idea, will you take me as a partner?"

"I'd love to." Wanda seemed like an ideal partner.

We agreed that each would do a bit of hard thinking and tell the other about the results.

That night, tossing in bed and smoking endless cigarettes, I did my bit of thinking.

A secondhand store was what came first to my mind. It looked like a pretty good idea. We could have it right here or else in Wanda's apartment—no need to rent expensive store space; most of it had been destroyed anyway. No trouble about finding the merchandise, we would get plenty. Very soon now, people will be running out of money and selling their belongings to pay for bread and rent. Only... who would buy them? The peasants, of course. All the money Warsaw people possessed went now to the neighboring villagers in return for victuals. I still remembered how in the years after the First World War peasants used to buy pianos, patent leather shoes and gold watches. They probably would do it again. Country folks don't trust paper money that comes too easily to their hands.

But here another problem arose in my mind. How would the farmers who came to the market every Tuesday and Friday know that here, on the second floor of our house, or even worse on the third floor of Wanda's house, there was a store where they could buy things? No window display...

For a few minutes I was stumped, and then a simple solution came to my mind. We could (if we tipped the janitor) hang on the front door a poster listing the articles for sale and their prices. Such posters, if big enough, would attract the attention of all passersby.

I liked the idea of these posters. I could almost visualize them: "Black sealskin coat in good condition 600 zlotys." "Two pairs of men's shoes size eleven only slightly used at 20 zlotys." Just like the classified ads in the old *Kurjer Warszawski*.

Suddenly I sat up in bed. Classified ads... posters... Why, this was exactly the idea I was hunting for! That was the business for Wanda and me! Why bother with a secondhand store? Warsaw was choking right now with uninserted classified ads—the small slips that dotted practically every wall in Warsaw were evidence enough. People had been deprived of their old favorite medium, the newspapers (no one so far read or advertised in the new pseudo-Polish organ of German propaganda). The ruined walls were the only solution they had found to their advertising problem. But if all those tiny notices were brought together into one huge, properly laid-out poster which would appear all over town in thousands of copies... why, it would be a boon.

And there was a fortune in classified ads too, everybody knew that. How other papers used to envy the old *Kurjer Warszawski* which for decades had practically held the monopoly in the field. Now *Kurjer Warszawski* was closed, so were other papers. The field was open again, and Wanda and Rulka were going to jump right into it!

That's how the scheme looked to me at that moment.

In the cool darkness of the night my ideas grew big and hot. Yes—we would change our posters once a week at first. Later perhaps twice a week, or even every day. And we would have every issue printed on paper of different color, so people could see at a distance that a new poster had appeared. Before I fell asleep I had it all worked out beautifully.

The next morning, even before I went to tell Wanda about my plan, I ran to a friend of mine who was a publisher. I trusted his solid business sense; would he think my idea really good, or was it just one of those screwy schemes evolved during a sleepless night? Thank goodness, my publisher friend thought the idea very good, excellent in fact.

"Only you must first get the permission of the German authorities," he warned me.

"Do I really have to?" The prospect did not appeal to me.

"Unless you are willing to take the risk of being arrested. You can't do anything nowadays without the Germans' consent."

"What department will I have to apply to?"

"The Propaganda Amt." [1]

Somehow the Propaganda Amt sounded ominous.

Wanda, whom I went to see next, accepted my plan enthusiastically.

"Of course," she said. "You will have to take the lead in this, Rulka. I don't know a thing about advertising. It's your line."

Well, in a way, advertising was my line. Besides working with the Warsaw branch of the J. Walter Thompson Advertising Agency as copywriter and production manager, I had been in charge of all advertising campaigns for my publisher friend. I had helped Olgierd, who was a *real* advertising expert, in many of his campaigns and I had enjoyed every bit of it. Advertising to me was fun, more fun than any other job I've ever had. A great game! No wonder that now that I had to start some business of my own, my mind had almost unconsciously turned to it.

I told Wanda about the necessity of obtaining the permission of the Propaganda Amt. How would we go about it?

"I know a way," Wanda said at once. "A very simple way. Do you know Bilski? Yes, of course you do. But did you hear about the mess he got himself into? Quite innocently, of course. Bilski went to school in Vienna years ago. And when the Germans came in he met an old classmate of his

---

[1] Propaganda Branch or Office.

in the street. They used to be quite close friends in the good old days, apparently, so quite naturally Bilski hailed the Austrian. Well, the two friends spent a delightful afternoon together talking about old school days, and Bilski thought no more of it. But the next day he was summoned to the Propaganda Amt and ordered to submit twice a week reports on the state of public opinion in Warsaw. It was his Austrian friend who had put him in this fix. So far Bilski has succeeded in making the best of a rotten situation. He tells the Germans exactly what he thinks of their methods, which of course isn't much, and does not implicate anyone. No names. But it's a dreadful strain on him and he is determined to flee the country if he can. I am sure, however, that he will be glad to give us an introduction to the Propaganda Amt."

We set out at once to call on Bilski. We found him home, packing a suitcase.

"You caught me just in time," he said when we had explained our errand. "I am leaving tonight for the country. Warsaw air does not seem to agree with me," he added with a wry smile, "and I'll be glad to see my family again."

We did not pursue him with questions. One did not discuss such problems. One week later he had crossed the Hungarian frontier.

He was very nice about giving us the introductory letter to the Propaganda Amt. "But," he said, "I doubt very much that the Germans will let you go ahead with your plan. You see, they have set their hearts upon that new rag they are publishing now, it's their particular pet. They won't allow anything that may look like competition to it. Of course, you can tell them that no one reads the damn thing anyway, and so no one will advertise in it. I tell them so myself. But it won't help much, I am afraid."

"We can always try," Wanda said hopefully.

"Of course."

The sentry at the door of the Propaganda Amt would not let us pass at first.

"We want to see Herr Regierungsrat[2] Hempl from the Propaganda Amt," announced Wanda haughtily in perfect German, her hand on the doorknob.

The soldier was so impressed with her manner that not only did he open the door for us but escorted us all the way upstairs.

A white card on the door of the third floor apartment read: "The apartment of the Jew X.Y. has been confiscated for the use of the Propaganda Amt." Four big Nazi seals decorated the corners of the card.

Inside there were no other callers but ourselves. A brisk German girl, evidently the secretary, took Bilski's letter and told us that Herr Regierungsrat was absent but if we wanted to we could see the man who was temporarily in charge of the office.

We were introduced into an enormous, sumptuously furnished drawing room. Heavily carved furniture, deep Turkish carpets, paintings by famous Polish artists on the walls, a black marble chimneypiece... the Jew X.Y. had certainly prepared a beautiful office for the Propaganda Amt.

A little man in a gray uniform sat behind a huge, carved desk. A typical German martinet. He ordered us to sit down (ordered, I mean, not asked), then began to fire rapid questions at us. Our names? Addresses? Polish or Jewish? Profession? Were we married? Where was my husband? What was he doing? On a pad he

---

[2] A senior government official.

jotted down all our answers. Only after this interrogation was completed did he ask us what our business was.

Wanda explained.

He pondered the matter over for a while, then said, "This has nothing to do with us. It's a matter for your mayor to decide. If he gives you the permission, we will have no objections. Only you must submit to us every poster for censorship."

This was good news. We left the Propaganda Amt in good spirits although we felt a little contrite. Why on earth had we rushed to the Germans for a permission which could be granted by our own Polish authorities? Somehow, it seemed disloyal. But how could we know?

"And now for Starzynski," I exclaimed as soon as we were in the street. We had no time to lose. My idea, even if brilliant, was not unique. Anyone in Warsaw could hit upon it. We had to be on the market (or rather on the walls) first.

One of my uncles knew the Mayor personally. He gave us a letter to him to which we attached a short outline of our plan. The next morning we took it to the City Hall.

We found the place bustling with life. The shattered windows had been already replaced, masons were filling the ugly gaps left by bombs and artillery shells. Men rushed in and out of the building: streetcar repair crews, water-pump crews, electric and gas plant employees.

The man who had done more than anyone else to make Warsaw beautiful and modern, and then in a magnificent gesture of defiance had allowed it to be destroyed, was now throwing all his fierce energy into the gigantic job of reconstruction.

My uncle's letter gained us admittance to Starzynski's private secretary, but this young man showed extreme reserve. He didn't seem to be a bit impressed with our scheme.

"Certainly, I will give the letter to the Mayor," he said, "but he is terribly busy right now. I don't know if he'll have time to give it consideration. However, please come back day after tomorrow. Perhaps by then I'll be able to give you a definite answer."

When two days later, however, we entered his office, Starzynski's secretary was all smiles. "Your idea is splendid," he told us, "and the Mayor is very enthusiastic about it. It will at the same time be an effective medium of advertising and rid the city of all those little slips which are disfiguring the walls right now. Tell me," he looked from Wanda to me, "how did you ever hit upon such an excellent scheme?"

Wanda lowered her eyes with a modest smile. "Necessity is the mother of invention, you know," she said.

I could have kicked her! Taking credit for the idea, as if it were her own.

"I see," the secretary continued. "Anyway, the Mayor has called the head of the Municipal Commerce Department for a conference on the matter tomorrow at ten. If you come at twelve I'll be able to give you a definite answer. It looks as if it is going to be a favorable one." He escorted us to the door.

I was a little dizzy with triumph as we left the City Hall.

"Let's celebrate," I told Wanda. "I've seen pastry in a window on Krakowskie Przedmiescie. Only twenty-five grosze apiece. Aren't you dying for some?" Pastry had reappeared in Warsaw, and every time I passed a pastry shop window the sight made me feel faint. But so far I had resisted temptation. I well knew I couldn't afford it.

"Isn't it a little early to celebrate?" Wanda suggested cautiously. "I haven't much money left."

"Oh, if the Mayor himself thinks our plan good and is ready to back us, we will be rich in no time."

We entered the pastry shop and ordered two big pieces each. We devoured them in almost religious silence.

When the next day at noon we returned once more to City Hall my heart was pounding with excitement and anticipation. Perhaps the Mayor himself would want to see us. I was dying to meet the hero of Warsaw.

We had to wait very long for Starzynski's secretary that day, and when at last he appeared he was not smiling. His face wore a strained expression which made him look years older.

"I am sorry," he said, "but I cannot give you the answer I promised for today. The Mayor has been taken sick. You will have to see Director Hartman about your business—he knows about it."

"Is the Mayor seriously ill?" I asked.

"No. Here is Director Hartman's address," and then he added cryptically, "I hope Mr. Hartman is not sick, too."

What a piece of bad luck! Why should the Mayor get sick on the very day we were to get permission to start our business?

"What do you think?" I asked Wanda. "Should we wait till he gets well or go and see Hartman now?"

"Let's try Hartman."

We were passing through Wierzbowa, once one of the smartest streets in Warsaw, now a double row of ruins with only two houses left, when we met Tomek.

"Did you hear," he whispered in my ear, "that Starzynski has been arrested?"

So that was the sickness that had befallen the Mayor!

I remembered now with a shudder what Cook had told me only three days before: "Do you know, Madam, what they say in the bread lines? They say that our Mayor is a crook. People say he has collected a fortune for himself out of city funds. How can you trust anyone, nowadays? We all thought he was so wonderful, and now — "

At that I flew off the handle. "See here, Cook, if I hear you once more going around repeating such infamous lies I'll kill you. Don't be an idiot! Don't you see that it's the German agents who are sowing these lies to discredit the Mayor because he is a hero? It is the Germans' game you are playing!"

Cook was evidently impressed with my wrath. She promised to defend the Mayor in the lines and to denounce any attack upon him as German propaganda. But what good would that do? How many bread lines were there in Warsaw, all fed with similar venom?

The German game was quite obvious. It was exactly four weeks since Warsaw had capitulated on the express condition that the civil authorities should not be arrested or removed from their posts. So they could not arrest Starzynski on any political basis. But the Germans did not forget his fierce denunciations during the period of siege. Germans neither forget nor forgive—they were simply biding their time. They first proceeded to undermine public opinion by clever insinuation of graft, spread in the bread lines. And now they had arrested him, probably on some dishonesty charges based on forged evidence. The beasts!

For five days after the Mayor's arrest our classified ad posters were lost in a maze of municipal red tape and indecision. We were sent from one department to another, and wherever we went it was evident that the city authorities had completely lost their nerve. No one was willing to make any decisions that were in any way outside the daily routine. At last we rebelled.

"We are simply wasting our time," Wanda told me on the fifth day. "Why do we try to start our business in a proper and legal way? No one cares about such things any more. As long as the Germans say they don't care, let's go ahead and forget about permissions."

I agreed that she was right.

"We can start at once to collect the ads," I decided.

"How does one do that?"

"That's simple enough. We will make a list of all the people we know and then call on them soliciting ads. You bet everyone will have something to advertise, and we will set very low rates for the first issue, one zloty per ad, let's say, regardless of how long it is. We have to fill the space, anyway. Of course, later the people will come to us, we will have office hours, a sign on the door and all that. But to begin with we have to go after the ads ourselves."

By the end of another five days we had forty-seven ads. And there was a story behind each of these short, matter-of-fact items. "Man's sheepskin coat, absolutely new—300 zlotys." This was a present a grandmother had prepared for her grandson's birthday. The grandson was killed on the battlefield of Warsaw. "Doctor's office for rent. Furnished." The husband of the lady who put that one in had been caught by the war somewhere near the Bolshevik frontier and she hadn't heard of him since. Not a word. True, a stranger had come to her house one day and told her that her husband had been killed in a Ukrainian peasant riot, but she didn't believe him. "Lady recommends an excellent cook." That was Rose's ad. She didn't need her old cook, she was never going back to the apartment where Roman and she had been so happy together.

Forty-seven in all. It was enough for the first poster. We found a cheap printer's shop in the back of a bombed house and had them set, classified in exactly the same way as the old *Kurjer Warszawski* used to do.

How thrilled we were when the first copy came out from the printing press! It was scarcely two weeks since the night I had hit upon the idea.

"Let's take it for German censorship and then we can post them on the walls ourselves."

Once more we went to the Propaganda Amt, but this time without any misgivings. It was only a formality, there was nothing in our ads to alarm the strictest censor.

It was Herr Regierungsrat himself who received us. An extremely civil man of about thirty-five, clean-shaven, good-looking and in civilian clothes. A German in mufti looks quite human. He shook hands with us at the door, introduced himself, placed two chairs in front of his heavy desk. We handed him our poster.

"For censorship," Wanda announced.

He gave it a glance and suddenly jumped up.

"Why," he almost shouted, "I cannot let you publish this. It's impossible, absolutely impossible!"

"Why not? Those are just classified advertisements."

"Exactly. Classified advertisements don't appear on posters, they appear in the daily papers. We have lots of them in Germany."

"But this is not Germany, and these are not normal times. No one reads the papers nowadays."

"I forbid you to do it just the same. Where did you intend to post them?"

"On the walls."

"If you do that you will be jailed. Walls are reserved for our official announcements."

"Everybody is using them right now."

"I know, but we will put an end to that soon. You can't do it, that's all."

Wanda and I exchanged a quick glance. We were not going to give in. We would remain here in these comfortable chairs till he gave us permission to go on with our business or had us thrown out of the room.

"We must do it," I insisted. "She has an old mother to support and I have two children. We have no other source of income and this is our business."

He looked from Wanda to me.

"If you need money why don't you collect advertisements for *Nowy Kurier Warszawski?*"[3] he asked slowly. (That was the new German rag.)

But we pretended not to hear.

"Besides," I said, "we have already taken money from all these people, we cannot disappoint them now. If you don't let us post those ads on the outside walls, we could hang them up inside, in stores and other places. What about that?"

He shook his head. For twenty more minutes we continued to argue back and forth. At last feminine persistency won. He rose.

"Here," he handed the poster back to me, "I've never seen this, I've never heard of it. You understand? I don't want to see it on outside walls. What you do about it otherwise, I don't care. But not on the outside walls, or you'll be jailed," he shook his finger at us as we got up to leave.

Three days later one hundred classified ad posters appeared inside the stores, cafés and on the walls of waiting rooms. One hundred posters in a city the size of Warsaw was a drop in a bucket. But it was all we could manage running from daybreak till nightfall with a roll of posters under our arms and a box of tacks rattling in our pockets. Anyway our business was launched, and we

---

[3] *The New Warsaw Courier,* like all press outlets controlled by the Germans, was referred to pejoratively by the Poles as *gadzinowka* ("reptile press").

knew we were not going to be jailed for it. This was something.

The first posters brought us more offers of partnership than advertisements. We accepted some of them on commission basis, we knew we couldn't carry on alone.

Slowly, painstakingly, our business grew. Every week a new poster appeared. Gradually the circulation increased from the initial one hundred to five hundred, fifteen hundred, till at last it reached four thousand copies.

Very soon competition appeared, too, posting itself all over the outside walls.

"Probably they will soon be jailed," Wanda and I would wink at each other. But two months passed before the ruined walls of Warsaw were cleared for the use of "official announcements exclusively."

I was soon to find out how slowly the much-proclaimed German organization and discipline are set in motion. From the very first the German authorities were completely baffled by the problem of Warsaw, this huge, war-stricken city, full of ruins and dead where life, in spite of everything, was trying to reassert itself in a freakish, abnormal sort of way. They just couldn't cope with it. As a result, in the first few months of occupation the Germans left Warsaw pretty much to its own devices.

This, of course, did not exclude terror. Terror needs no organization. Its very essence, in fact, consists in the eternal uncertainty as to where the next blow will fall.

And almost every day a new shudder of terrifying news ran through the stricken city.

CHAPTER 30

In Terror's Grip

I WILL never forget the horror in little Andrew's eyes (Hanka and the children had returned to Warsaw two days after Franek), when he came to tell me that his Uncle Edward who owned a large property near Posen[1] had been executed by the Germans.

It just couldn't enter the boy's mind how his jolly, fat Uncle Edward, with whom he and his brother used to have such fun, could have been shot like a criminal right in the middle of the village square. He had never been engaged in any anti-German activity; it was just that at the beginning of September two German spies had been caught on his property by the Polish army, shot and buried in his garden. The Germans made him pay for it.

Uncle Edward had faced the firing squad with a loud, ringing "Long live Poland!" and before he left the prison he told Aunt Eliza that no German should ever see her tears, so Aunt Eliza didn't cry. Neither at the execution, nor afterwards. She was trying to come to Warsaw if the Germans would let her.

That was the first news we had of the bloody terror in the district of Posen. Many similar ones followed in the next few days. Prominent people, people we knew and liked, men with whom we had played bridge and danced, were now daily facing the firing squad.

Every bit of news that came from Posen and Pomerania[2] sent cold shudders down our spines. It was nightmarish.

---

[1] Posen, currently known as Poznan, located in west-central Poland, is one of the largest and oldest cities in that country.

[2] The area of northwestern Poland along the Baltic Coast.

Then we learned about the mass arrests, the thousands of families that were sent to concentration camps.

For weeks our whole family followed with breathless suspense the fate of little Zosinka. Zosinka was also a cousin of Andrew and Thad. She was only three. Her parents and her three older brothers had been taken to a concentration camp. But at the time the German police came Zosinka was in bed with flu, so the Germans let her stay in the house with her old nurse. But they promised they would return for her as soon as she was well. The old nurse somehow had sent the news to Zosinka's relatives in Warsaw imploring them to come and take the child away before it was too late, and Zosinka's uncle was making desperate attempts to go to the little girl's rescue. Would he succeed? It was terribly difficult to get permission to enter German territory and the Posen district was already incorporated into the Reich.[3]

When at last we learned that Zosinka was safe on a farm in another part of the country we all sighed with relief. Thank goodness! What an escape from the hands of German police at the age of three...

Bloodcurdling news did not come from Posen and Pomerania alone. Terror was striking nearer home, right here in Warsaw.

A young Jew, exasperated by baiting and beating, had shot a German soldier, then escaped through a double-entrance house. The Germans charged that the

---

[3] With the surrender of Warsaw, Poland was partitioned between Nazi Germany and Soviet Russia under the terms of the Molotov-Ribbentrop Pact.

The German-annexed territory was divided into three administrative areas: Reichsgau Wartheland (the western part of Poland) which was directly incorporated into the German Reich, Reichsgau Danzig-West Prussia and the "General Government" which included the two major cities of Warsaw and Cracow.

The region annexed by Soviet Russia was comprised of all Polish territory east of the line of the rivers Pisa, Narew, Western Bug and San, except for the Wilno Voivodship with its capital Wilno (Vilnius), which was transferred to Lithuania, and the Suwalki region, which was annexed by Germany.

inhabitants of the house had helped him to escape. Sixty-five men who lived on the premises were taken at random and shot. Just a lesson.

A few weeks later two German soldiers were shot by bandits they were helping the regular police to round up. This happened not in Warsaw proper, but in Wawer, a small suburban community. The bandits escaped, but one hundred and twenty-five citizens of Wawer were roused from their beds at night, taken into a dark open field and shot down. The youngest was fifteen, the eldest nearly seventy. The bodies were not allowed to be moved for forty-eight hours.

After that the ghost of a dead German began to haunt Warsaw. "Did you hear, the body of a German soldier has been found in Mokotow? All the men have fled from there. Two spent the night in our house." "A dead German has been found in Czerniakow this morning. They found him lying behind a wooden fence. The Germans don't know about it yet, but... oh, God, what is going to happen when they discover him?" Men were fleeing from Czerniakow. What if a dead German were found in our own courtyard?

Other whispers went around. "Did you hear that X. was arrested last night?" Or: "Imagine, Mr. and Mrs. D. were ordered out of their apartment two days ago. They were given two hours to remove their things, but were not allowed to take a single piece of furniture. It's no longer safe to live on Koszykowa. And their apartment is only half a block away from ours." Or: "Did Dola tell you what happened at the L.'s the other night? They had some people up for bridge, two bridge tables in fact. And three drunken Germans broke in on the party and beat everybody up. Countess T. M. is still in bed with a high fever and bruises all over her."

One afternoon one of my many nephews arrived at our house all flushed and excited. "Auntie, I've seen a dead man lying in the archway on Wilcza. They say the Germans have killed him. It's just around the corner, would you like to see him?"

"No, thank you, I would not." No dead bodies for me.

Cook on her way back from the market would bring daily reports. "They are searching Hoza today," Or Piusa, or Wiejska...

We no longer dared to leave the house to the servants' care. Someone who spoke German always had to be there in case a search party arrived. On the mornings when a search was carried on somewhere in the vicinity both Mother and I stayed home. Those search parties were known to take "souvenirs" ranging from knickknacks to silverware and bedding. You had to keep an eye on them. Sometimes a word to the officer would help. Not always.

Our house was never searched, though. Perhaps because it stood in a row of burnt buildings, and the Germans did not consider it worth their while.

One Sunday morning, however, while I was still dressing, the door of my room suddenly flew wide open and two tall men in Nazi uniforms marched in. For a second my heart stood still. I knew I had been overstepping my rights with regard to the Propaganda Amt lately. My posters were no longer posted but distributed by the dozen in restaurants and cafés. Had they come for me? But also I was furious. How did they dare enter a woman's room without knocking? I was only partly dressed. They didn't even take their caps off, the brutes! I didn't get up.

"Are you a Pole or a Jew?" one of them asked me.

"A Pole."

They looked around, glanced at the battered ceiling, and went into the children's room. Quickly I finished

From the collection of Stefan Mucha

USHMM, courtesy of Instytut Pamieci Narodowej

*The Germans terrorize Poles with arrests, executions and deportations—
one of the Germans' special targets was Polish Jews.*

397

USHMM, courtesy of Instytut Pamieci Narodowej

From the collection of Stefan Mucha

It is estimated that the German occupiers ultimately killed approximately six million Polish citizens, of whom approximately half were Jewish—representing about 90 percent of the pre-war Jewish population of Poland.

dressing and followed them to the dining room. What did they come here for? I kept asking myself. Mother, who was lying on the sofa, made a gesture as if to rise.

"Don't," one of the Germans told her. The other sighted Ania and tried to pet her on the head. But Ania ran away. They seemed inoffensive enough, but...

Again they looked around; one went to the bomb-smitten door and touched it. Then they both walked back to the hall. I could hold my curiosity no longer.

"What did you come here for?" I asked. They both turned around sharply, evidently surprised, as if not used to being asked questions.

"We just wanted to take a look at the apartment," one said. They saluted this time and left.

They never came back. Apparently they found the place too damaged to suit their needs. Nevertheless, each time we heard an unexpected knock on the door everybody would give a start.

Terror, like a black cloud, hung over Warsaw.

And yet, in spite of it, spirits began to revive. The black days of bitter self-recrimination were over. People no longer said: "It's our own fault. We didn't value our liberty as we should have, we didn't work hard enough during these last twenty years to keep it." They no longer said: "It's the army's fault. It's the government's fault." They said: "The day will come..."

And all the city, all the country, lived in the hope of that day. After all, the war wasn't over. France and Great Britain were still carrying on and they were bound to win. No one doubted it.

What were they doing there at the Western front? The wildest rumors were circulated, bred of wishful thinking and a complete lack of legitimate news (no one believed a word of the German papers): a big offensive had been launched already and thousands of wounded and gas-poisoned Germans were being shipped to hospitals in Poland. Or Berlin had been bombed by the R.A.F. "My dear, I've just met a man who came back from there. Berlin looks worse than Warsaw, really."

All this amazing news originated with the so-called A. L. T. M. (A Lady Told Me) Agency. The prize one, I think, referred to the alleged war between Germany and Italy. Italy had declared war on the Nazis, it said, and the Germans had already bombed Rome. The Pope is seriously wounded.

All these rumors were of course later denied, but new ones kept cropping up every day. People were starved for news—good news—for there was plenty of bad. With hope the old spirit of defiance returned, too. That's one thing about Warsaw: you can bomb it, turn it into a heap of ruins, kill off one-fifth of the population, but you cannot make it humble. Not the old City of the Mermaid!

There was the old lady who, when asked by a Nazi official whether she was German (she spoke German like a native), told him: "I'd rather be anyone other than a German." I don't know how the Nazi official ever managed to swallow this, but he did.

There was the street urchin who jumped on the front platform of a passing streetcar. The front platform was reserved for German nationals and a soldier pushed him rudely off. The kid, insulted, turned around and shouted: "Say, don't be so high-handed, Mr. Temporary!"

There were the street bands composed of jobless musicians that in the ruined streets played patriotic songs and Polish military marches. People would stand around them listening in silence, and when the hat was passed many a coin dropped into it. But the minute a German uniform appeared the tune would be changed to a

A German propaganda poster:

"England! It's your fault!" a wounded Polish soldier exclaims to Neville Chamberlain, the Prime Minister of Great Britain.

From the collection of Zygmunt Walkowski

As an act of defiance, the word "England" was sometimes torn away or painted out, leaving the words: "It's your fault!" – meaning the Germans.

Such an act of defiance was a serious offense punishable by death—as happened in the case of two young women, Eugenia Wlodarz and Elzbieta Zahorska, who were executed by the Germans in November 1939 just for tearing down a copy of this poster.

gay popular waltz, the words of which were in Polish: "In a year, in a day, in a minute, Forever shall we part..."

People would laugh, and the German stared, not knowing what it was all about. Germans don't like to be made fun of.

Even Ania, according to Leosia's report, whenever she met a "Hitler" during her daily walks would start to sing the Polish national anthem "Jeszcze Polska nie zginela" at the top of her voice. This extremely patriotic gesture was somewhat marred by the fact that Ania could not carry a tune.

I had a hard time keeping George from tearing anti-British posters from the walls. He insisted that all the boys in his class did. But it was dangerous, very dangerous. A girl, a university student, had been condemned to death and shot for that very reason.

This poster represented a Polish battlefield full of dead and wounded. In the foreground Mr. Chamberlain turned his back with a gesture of complete indifference to a wounded Polish soldier evidently appealing for his help. Underneath there was an inscription in bold, red letters: "England! It's your fault!"

The trick consisted in tearing off the word "England," so that all that remained was "It's your fault." Everybody knew whose fault it was. The days of bitterness against England were over, and the intense anti-British propaganda conducted by the Germans had, I am sure, a lot to do with it. Strangely enough, there was not a word of anti-French propaganda... just as if France were not in the war at all.

But if the Germans hated the British so fiercely there couldn't be anything wrong with England. Whatever was black to the Germans was white to us.

Once on a busy corner I met an old woman selling the "dirty rag" *Nowy Kurier Warszawski*. She was shouting so loud that everyone up and down the block could hear her: "Come on, folks, buy this pack of lies. It costs only twenty grosze. The whole family will die laughing just to read them. Worse lies there never were, and only twenty grosze. Come on, folks."

People laughed and bought. An elderly gentleman asked her if she was not afraid to sell her paper in such manner.

"I might be poor, but still I am a Pole," she replied proudly.

CHAPTER 31

Christmas 1939

EARLY IN December I had another brainstorm, and ran to see my publisher friend about it.

"Say, I've hit upon another scheme," I announced excitedly. "Would you like to be in on it with me? I can't do it alone, and my partner Wanda has just got herself a regular job. Besides, what I really need is a publisher. The idea is grand, I tell you!"

"Dear lady," my friend smiled, evidently amused by my enthusiasm, "I'll be glad to be in on anything with you. What boundless energy. . . What's this latest stroke of genius?"

"Do you know what this place needs? A new directory! The old telephone directory is absolutely useless—the whole city has been reshuffled. Houses are burned, many old firms have gone out of business, there are lots of new ones. People have changed their addresses, hardly anyone lives in the same place where he used to before the war, it's just impossible to find anyone. And it will be ages before the new telephone directory is published. Besides, who is going to have a telephone? It's dangerous with all this wiretapping and whatnot."

My friend became suddenly serious. "Say, this is really good," he admitted.

We discussed the idea at great length, and the more we talked about it the more we liked it.

"Will you take it upon yourself to get the Propaganda Amt's permission?" my friend asked me at last. "We can't do anything without it."

"Heavens, no!" I protested. "This business of asking Germans for permission makes me sick. Besides, I think I completely exhausted their patience on the occasion of those posters. Why don't you go?"

"I'd rather not," he said.

"Can't someone else do it for us?"

"The Chamber of Commerce perhaps..."

We tried the Chamber of Commerce. A business directory would certainly be to their advantage. But although they were in favor of our plan and were supposed to have a good standing with German authorities, they wouldn't do anything about it. The fact was, everybody in Warsaw was loath to ask the Germans anything.

At last my publisher friend and I decided to go to the Propaganda Amt together. This time we found Herr Regierungsrat in a Nazi uniform and what a difference this made! All the previous geniality of his manner was gone, he had become the regular German martinet. All through the interview I had the uneasy feeling that Gestapo men were about to march into the room and arrest us. But in spite of his rude manners Herr Regierungsrat promised to send our request on to Cracow, where the General Government decided such things.[1] He would let us know the answer as soon as it came.

But weeks passed, and there was no answer.

Christmas came. Ania was very much worried about the fate of the angel. It is an angel, and not Santa Claus, that brings Christmas trees and toys to Polish children.

"Mommy, are you sure the Germans won't shoot the angel if he comes after dark?"

Ania knew that Germans shot at anyone who was out in the streets after the curfew was sounded. Every night,

---

[1] Cracow was the capital of the German Occupation's General Government.

in the two front rooms we occupied again, we could hear isolated shots, sometimes a regular cannonade. At first these sounds would give me gooseflesh, later I got used to them. Someone told me that the two first shots were always fired in the air—just a warning. Only the third was aimed at the transgressor. Perhaps, too, the German sentries got nervous in those dark, empty, ruined streets and shot just to prop up their own courage. Anyway, shooting continued all through the night.

"Oh, I don't think so, darling," I reassured Ania. "The angel has wings. He will fly and not walk about the streets. Besides, Germans don't see angels, I am sure."

We were all determined to have a real, traditional Christmas Eve celebration. Franek had ransacked the big black trunk in which the toys of our own childhood were kept and had produced a miniature zoo, a doll's tea set, a complete farm with animals and men, and some games. These would go under the Christmas tree. The tree itself bothered me a lot, for I couldn't find any till the day before Christmas Eve. Vendors were evidently afraid to put them out sooner, lest the Germans requisition their stock. At last everything was ready, and when the first evening star appeared in the sky, as tradition demands, we all gathered around the dining room table covered with a shining table cloth bulging in spots, for there was hay underneath. Hay, like in the manger.

We first broke thin white wafers (Mother still had some of the last year's supply left), wishing each other luck. We told each other many small personal wishes but we really had only one big wish, and there were tears in everybody's eyes when Mother voiced it: "For Poland to be free." Only the children were too excited over the approaching moment when they would see the tree to pay any heed. Then we broke some more wafers with wishes to the absent ones:

Olgierd in America; Wola, which we knew now had escaped war destruction; Adzio in a prisoners' camp; Adam somewhere with the Polish Army in France...

After that we proceeded with our Christmas Eve dinner. Every course of that meal had been established by century-long tradition. Some dishes varied in different parts of the country and from family to family, but on the whole they were pretty uniform. First, dried-mushroom broth; two fish courses served with sauerkraut cooked with dried mushrooms; noodles with poppyseeds; and for dessert, sweetmeats and nuts. We had painstakingly collected each item in the preceding weeks. Of course we did not have two fish courses—instead we had one can of sardines.

"It's fish anyway," Franek declared, "and if you eat each sardine in two bites you can call it two fish courses."

"Pull out the hay," I reminded him of the old fortune-telling trick, "I want to see how many wives you are going to have."

Franek plunged his hand under the tablecloth and brought out a piece with five blades.

"Five wives, good heavens! You'll have to start getting married pretty soon, or you'll never get to the last one."

"Mommy, what's that?" Ania had followed her Uncle Franek's example and was holding up just one single blade.

"Ania, you poor child, you'll remain an old maid for the rest of your life."

"I can give her mine," George offered, "I have four blades, and I really don't want to marry, ever!"

"That's what you say now," Franek assured him.

We had just finished our meal when there was a knock on the front door. It was an elderly lady who lived in the apartment across the landing from us. She had forgotten her key and the two other ladies from whom she was renting the room were out, and would not be back till curfew time. It was dreadfully cold on the landing, would we mind if she waited here?

"No, of course not. Come right in. I am just about to light the Christmas tree for the children. Would you like to see?"

But she insisted on remaining in the hall. I brought her a comfortable chair and left the door open, so she could see the tree.

I lighted the candles and called the children. They rushed in with shouts of joy and then, for a second, stopped abruptly and stood still, gasping with admiration at the scintillating brilliance of the tree. Mother, Franek, Cook and Leosia had followed the children from the dining room and now stood around the tree. I had prepared small presents for everyone. I wanted it to be exactly like last year, and all the years before. And it was. Except for those ugly patches on the ceiling, and... last year there had been small presents from and for Aunt Madzia.

After the first excitement was over Mother read the Nativity chapters in the Gospel, while we listened, our heads bent in silence. "And peace on earth to men of good will..." Then we all began to sing Christmas carols. Absorbed as we were in the joy of our little celebration we had completely forgotten the elderly lady in the hall.

Suddenly she walked into the room, her face wet with tears. She went straight to Mother, and taking Mother's hand in both of hers said in a low, shaky voice, "Thank you... Thank you so much... I have to leave now, my land-ladies are back. But you don't know what this has meant to me. I didn't know... I didn't think such beautiful things were still possible... a Christmas tree... a united family... happy children... You just can't imagine what the sight of you all has done for me... God bless you! God bless you all!"

We wanted her to remain with us but she said she couldn't; supper was awaiting her at home. She departed, still wiping her eyes and muttering under her breath, "God bless you... God bless you all."

After she left Franek and I still continued to sing Christmas carols far into the night. There were so many of them... Child Jesus lullaby, and the one that had the gay tune of a mazurka. And the sixteenth century one, to the tune of which our forefathers used to dance the Polonaise. And the oldest of them all, about the hay in the manger... Franek and I liked it best of all because of its naive refrain that came at the end of every stanza:

Oh hay, oh hay!
Hay like a lily
On which the baby
Is laid by Mary.

We sang them all. All except "Silent Night." For "Silent Night" is a German carol.

Yes, we had a lovely Christmas and we were lucky. One of my friends had a German search party burst into the dining room just as the family was about to sit down to the Christmas Eve dinner.

Of course we didn't celebrate the arrival of the New Year. I had gone early to bed that night, taking a book along with me. I knew I wouldn't be able to sleep, but perhaps with the aid of a novel I could manage to slip quietly from 1939 into 1940 without even noticing the fateful twelve strokes of the clock. I didn't want to think what that new year, about to begin, would bring us. I didn't want to remember all the lively celebrations of the previous years; the laughter, the bands, the bright lights suddenly turning dim, the droshky horses decorated with balloons...

But it was hard to concentrate on the book. These French novels with their eternal triangle and subtle, psychological entanglements seemed so pointless after all we had been through. What on earth was the matter with all those people? They had enough to eat, a roof over their heads, they were not afraid of being killed within the next few hours, nor arrested. So what did they raise such a fuss about? Tragedies, broken hearts, mental tortures? Stuff and nonsense!

Nevertheless, I read on and perhaps would have suceeded in skipping midnight if...

A terrific cannonade suddenly broke out in the streets outside. The rattle of machine guns, the clatter of heavy armored trucks driving full speed through the deserted streets. The Germans were celebrating the arrival of 1940. They kept the racket up for a whole hour, and while I listened to it, buried deep in my bed, my heart began to sink.

What could a new year started in that fashion bring?

CHAPTER 32

New Regulations, a New Business and—

THE NEW year brought many things.

In the first place, it brought a terrific cold wave. As a matter of fact, the temperature had already dropped below zero a few days before Christmas, but at first we all believed that this was just one of those cold spells that lasts for a week or so and is followed by slushy, misty days—the typical January flu weather. We were wrong.

Weeks passed and the terrific cold did not relent. For two full months the temperature never even reached the zero mark and twice fell to thirty below. And it wasn't flu that raged throughout Warsaw—it was pneumonia.

No one had much coal left and new supplies were not forthcoming—the cold wave had disorganized transportation facilities, we were told. And the Germans had requisitioned for their own use all the remaining coal stocks.

In our own house the temperature hovered around forty degrees Fahrenheit, and often in the morning fell to the freezing point. George's hands and feet were frostbitten, Ania cried bitterly every night when she was undressed to go to bed. We all had bad coughs, but no one even tried to do anything about it. What is the use of medicine when you can't get warm? And even though we kept our fur coats on all day long it didn't do much good— the woodwork of windows and doors was so shattered by bombs that it let all the drafts in. We sat around sniffling, noses red and running, hands and feet numb with cold. When the cold inside the apartment became unbearable we would go out into the streets. After an hour of walking in

From the collection of Stefan Mucha

From the collection of Stefan Mucha

The first winter of World War II is brutally cold, compounding the misery of bomb-wrecked Warsaw.

From the collection of Stefan Mucha

From the collection of Stefan Mucha

"Weeks passed and the terrific cold did not relent."

sub-zero temperature the house seemed almost warm...
for a while.

"I can't stand this cold," announced Hanka one day
as she dropped in to see how we all were. "It simply kills
me. I'd much rather be hungry than cold, I tell you."

"Well, that's because you've never been really hungry.
What we used to call hunger before the war was nothing
but appetite. Hunger is hunger when it makes you feel
mean. Isn't that so, Mother?"

Mother agreed with me. But it was beginning to look
as if we might know hunger again. Owing to transportation difficulties foodstuffs were beginning once more to
disappear from the market. No milk, no eggs, no meat, no
vegetables. Very soon our diet was reduced to black bread,
potatoes and cabbage. But we weren't really hungry,
just underfed.

This was not the end of New Year's gifts. Not by a long
shot. The Germans were at last moving to set up their new
order. Every day fresh decrees and regulations were issued
by the dozens. We had to read the dirty rag now whether we
liked it or not, for that was where all the new "musts" and
"don'ts" were published. If you missed a single issue you
might find yourself the next day engaged in an unlawful
occupation and go to jail for it.

Soap had been regimented, all the stocks of tea and
coffee confiscated. One day George came back from
school, his blue eyes black with hatred; they had been
told to turn in all their Polish textbooks. He was already
pretty mad because he was not allowed to wear his school
cap of which he was so proud. And now the textbooks...

The order was issued that all objects of art and antiques
in private hands be registered with German authorities,
presumably to be shipped for safekeeping to Germany. Art
objects from art galleries and museums were already

packed and loaded on big trucks. Then word went around that the University was also being plundered.

Franek, who had many valuable books and notes in his laboratory, grabbed an empty suitcase and ran as one runs to a fire. Two hours later he was back, a beaten look in his eyes.

"Too late," he announced. "The laboratory is already sealed, and they are loading crates onto trucks... Oh God!"

Heavily he slumped into a chair, and for a while remained silent.

"It really doesn't matter so much as far as I am concerned. My work was of no particular value, but the Professor... He is like a lost man. Thirty-five years of work, all his notes... he walks around and around the campus... sometimes he goes up to that sealed door and just stands in front of it, staring, then resumes his aimless wanderings. He told me: 'I have no home. For thirty-five years this has been my life. It's gone.'"

For three days afterwards Franek dropped in at the University, and each time he saw his professor wandering aimlessly on the campus, unable to tear himself from the ruins of his life.

One afternoon the hateful rag published an order that sent financial panic throughout the city. All hundred and five-hundred zloty bills had to be presented within a week to the Devisenstelle[1] to be registered and stamped. Unstamped bills would be considered unlawful after February 1. The short term made the registration of all bills in circulation technically impossible, and thousands of persons who still had some money left found themselves

---

[1] Currency exchange office.

ruined overnight.

Warsaw in those weeks looked like a huge, ruined anthill in which ants are desperately trying to rebuild some kind of shelter for themselves, while someone with a malicious stick systematically stabs at their efforts.

In the general upheaval caused by the new German order I was for a while sure I was going to lose my small advertising business, too. One of the decrees required that all posters should be published in German. A Polish translation set in smaller type could be placed at the bottom of the sheet. That would mean the end of any classified ads.

My heart a little heavy—for I had spent three months building the business up—I called my staff (I had five men, seven boys and three girls working for me by now) and told them the game was up. We would have to return the money already collected and cancel the next issue. No use courting arrest. But they wouldn't let me. They all insisted that I should go to the new German authorities (commercial posters were no longer under the jurisdiction of the Propaganda Amt) and investigate the matter thoroughly. I was loath to go, I did not believe in the success of any further attempt.

Besides, the longer I saw the Germans in the streets of Warsaw the more I hated them. I don't know exactly why, they sort of grew on you. At any rate any personal contact with them was becoming increasingly distasteful. However, I owed this last attempt both to the business and to my collaborators, so I went.

And a good thing I did, too, for I soon found out that the new order applied only to posters appearing on outside walls and did not affect us.

With renewed zeal we all plunged into work. The

current issue was increased to four thousand copies, we made arrangements with several secondhand stores to have ads collected by them for our bulletin. We talked of introducing a new type of advertising copy that would make interesting reading.

One morning on my way home from the printers I dropped in to see my publisher friend. I found him in his hat and coat.

"I was just on my way to your house," he told me. "There is something I wanted to show you. Here, look at that."

He handed me a letter. It was from the Propaganda Amt. The permission to publish a new city directory was granted.

"Fine!" I exclaimed. "When do we start?"

"Tomorrow morning. Better be here at eight. There will be plenty of work for both of us, believe me."

"You bet there will be!" I was positively elated.

In spite of the bitter cold there was a warm glow in my body as I returned home from my friend's office. At last things were beginning to look up for me. My advertising business was lately bringing real money, and now this directory thing... I wouldn't have to worry any longer how to make both ends meet. At first the classified ads were not much of a financial success, in fact I had to sell a diamond brooch to meet the household expenses. There still was some money left from it, but it was melting rapidly. Now, however, it no longer mattered. I had mastered the situation, and in pretty tough circumstances, too.

The only thought that bothered me now was Mother's health. She had had a bad fall several weeks before, and had never quite recovered from it. She looked very tired, spent most of the time lying on the sofa and let me do most of her errands for her. This was not a bit like Mother's old self. Mother would never let anyone do things for her. Now she didn't mind. And every day she repeated, "I don't know what I would do without you." But she was still a most wonderful companion, sharing every little joy and grief with us.

"Hurray, Mother!" I shouted as I burst into the apartment now. "We got permission to publish the directory!"

I was surprised to see that Mother's face did not light up.

"There is a letter for you," she said in an even voice, and handed me a long white envelope. It was from the American Consulate in Warsaw.

I opened it and quickly glanced at the content. When I lifted my eyes I saw that Mother was staring at me with almost tragic eyes.

"You are going to America," she whispered.

I nodded without a word. The Consulate's letter slipped to the floor. For a long while we sat in silence, looking at each other.

"Oh, Mother, how I hate to go! How I hate to leave you!" I burst out at last.

"Do you have to go then? Stay with us." But there was no conviction in Mother's voice. She knew that already weeks before I had made up my mind.

CHAPTER 33

— *The Decision to Leave Warsaw*

IT WAS really George who unwittingly decided our fate.

About two weeks before the letter from the American Consulate arrived, I had taken George with me for a walk. We were trotting as fast as we could between high snow-drifts and ruined walls, stamping hard on the pavement to keep our feet warm, when suddenly George tugged at my sleeve.

"Do you know, Mommy, what the dream of my life is?" he asked.

"No, Georgie, what is it?" Last year at this time it was a bicycle—a real, two-wheel bicycle with a bell, and possibly a taillight.

"A warm room, a glass of milk and a slice of white bread," he said now.

It gave me an awful pang in the heart. Things are pretty bad when one's own eight-year-old dreams of white bread, milk and warm rooms. Last year he got his bicycle all right. Was I going to refuse him his present dream if I had a chance to fulfill it?

I had known for months that Olgierd was doing every-thing in his power and even more to bring us over to America. One of his letters told me he had reserved passage for us from Bergen, Norway, another from Rotterdam, and the last, from Genoa. There were some difficulties in obtaining visas and he was doing his best to overcome them. I was very grateful to him for these efforts, but up to that moment I had not made up my mind whether I should go or not. It certainly would be great to see Olg again. And I liked America—I had brought back such pleasant memories from my two years at Vassar. But...

How could I desert Mother, Franek and all my friends here? How could I leave Warsaw? I loved my old City of the Mermaid now, as I had never loved it before, every charred, battered bit of it.

If you've gone through a lot in any given place you either love it or hate it afterwards, you can't remain simply indifferent. Rose told me once that she hated Warsaw so, she couldn't abide the sight of it, and I could see her point, but as far as I was concerned I'd rather be in Warsaw than anywhere else in the world. I just couldn't imagine how I could tear myself away from it now.

But George's dream tipped the scale. I was a mother; my first duty was to the children. I had no right to jeopardize their future for any sentimental reasons.

On my return home I told Mother about my decision: if the American visa arrived, I would go. Mother did not agree with me.

"Your children are in no worse position than hundreds of thousands of other Polish children," she reminded me.

"Yes, but those other children don't have the opportunity to go away. Besides it's not only the cold and hunger that worries me. It's the prospect of epidemics. You know very well, Mother, that with all those bodies still buried under the ruins we are bound to have some kind of dreadful epidemic when spring comes. If George or Ania should die, I could never forgive myself for having sacrificed their lives when I could have saved them."

"Well, of course, you should do whatever you consider your duty. You know what your presence here means to me and Franek, but it would be selfish on our part to insist," Mother agreed resignedly. She didn't say she would probably never see us again.

Once I had made up my mind I was determined to stick to my decision. And now the American Consulate had summoned me to communicate with them at once. My papers must have arrived.

Twenty minutes later I was at the Consulate. Yes, one of the vice-consuls informed me, they had instructions from the American Embassy in Berlin to issue me a visa, and as I had no valid diplomatic passport the visa would be issued on some sort of document called "affidavit in lieu of passport."

Besides the visa, I was handed two second-class railway tickets from Katowitz to Genoa, ten American dollars with the permission of the German authorities to take them out of the country, and advice from the American Export Lines that passage had been reserved for me and the two children on any of their liners sailing from Genoa.

Olgierd had certainly thought of everything! Of all the people I knew who had left Poland in the last two months, none had been so beautifully provided for. We were going to travel in state.

It seemed to me that with all these accessories I would be able to leave Warsaw within a week, and I was eager to do so. Tearing myself from this place was like having a tooth pulled; the sooner it was over the better. And I knew that those who departed in December were able to start from Warsaw two days after obtaining their visas. Apparently German authorities had no objections to letting women, children and men of non-military age leave the country.

But that was in December... I had forgotten that in the last month the German organizing machine had been turning out red tape by the mile. When I went to a travel agency to investigate the matter I found myself suddenly facing a sea of formalities to be gone through and permissions to be obtained. A statement from the Gestapo that I was not on their black lists, a permission of the Devisenstelle to take with me my personal belongings (I had to make a list of every handkerchief, every pair of stockings I was taking with me—no jewelry, no gold objects except my wedding ring), and half a dozen other technicalities.

For five days I ran wildly from one department to another collecting the necessary documents. At last I had them all, all but the permission from the Devisenstelle which had sent on my request to Cracow. How many hours of these five days I had spent standing in lines, I couldn't tell. Each document represented at least three hours of waiting, usually outside in the bitter cold. But at last I had them.

I went to the German passport office. This time I was determined not to stand in line. The Passport Office was in the same building as the Propaganda Amt, the old Polish Ministry of Foreign Affairs, and I had found a simple device for getting inside the building. A big crowd was at the gate, but I had taken with me an old copy of my classified ads and waved it now at the nose of the sentry.

"Zum Cenzur," I announced and passed on unmolested; any paper meant for censorship had to be submitted at once. As soon as I was inside the building I carefully folded my sheet and proceeded to the Passport Department. There was a line in front of the door, too, but at least I didn't have to wait in the cold.

In less than thirty minutes I was inside the office. Here, however, bad news awaited me. If I wanted to obtain my passport in Warsaw I would have to wait at least three weeks. All the papers had to be sent for approval to Cracow, and it took a letter, even an official one, ten days to travel the distance of two hundred miles that separated the two cities. If that's what Germans call their famous efficiency... Anyway, here it was: three weeks' delay unless I went to Cracow myself taking the papers along. In that case I might be able to get it in forty-eight hours.

The prospect of going to Cracow did not appeal to me. Traveling in wartime is to say the least uncomfortable, and it meant extra costs. On the other hand, however, what if the German-Italian frontier were closed before I got my passport? According to rumors Italy was going to declare war on Germany any minute now.

I decided to go to Cracow.

This meant securing one more permission—a permission to travel on a fast train (slow trains were unbearably crowded). Another hour of waiting in line at the railway administration department.

"Are you Polish or Jewish?" the German clerk who dispensed the permissions asked me, without lifting his eyes from the papers on his desk.

I was sick of being asked that question everywhere I went, and I told him so.

"Oh, pardon me," the clerk said, suddenly apologetic, "I didn't mean to offend you. It's just that we don't allow Jews to travel on fast trains."

"I know that," I said dryly. He handed me the permission without further questioning.

When I arrived at Cracow the next morning my first reaction was one of complete amazement. For four months now I had been living among ruins, and the sight of houses and streets unscarred by bombs and fire was a shock. I looked around hardly believing my eyes—it was like walking in a dream, a dream of old pre-war days.

That first illusion did not last long. It soon dawned upon me that Cracow was a much sadder sight than Warsaw. Warsaw looked ghostly, tragic, if you like, but in spite of many German uniforms it was still an unmistakably Polish city. But Cracow, this cradle of Polish history and culture, looked now like a German city. German names and inscriptions on every street corner, swastikas in store windows, portraits of Hitler in every restaurant, a loudspeaker bawling German propaganda and news in the old market square...I felt like bawling myself! On the sidewalks I encountered groups of civilians speaking German at the top of their voices. They acted as if they owned the place, as indeed they did. They were members of the staff of the new German administration.

I had to remain in Cracow for two days before my papers sent from Warsaw by the Devisenstelle arrived. I put up at a third-rate hotel, one of the two hotels still left to Poles. All others were exclusively reserved for Germans. I ate at one of the few restaurants where the sign *Nur für Volksdeutsche*[1] did not decorate the door. But even there Hitler's portrait embellished the wall. My spirits rebelled at every step I took. I went to see some members of my father's family who lived in Cracow. A printed sign *Arisches Wohnung*[2] pinned to the door made me wince. "Just to protect us from looting and all sorts of persecutions," they explained. But the indignity of it...

While talking to my Cracow friends and relatives I soon discovered that what had happened to those people's spirits was even worse than what had befallen the city itself. They were cowed, positively cowed, by German terror and persecution. Nowhere did I find the stony hatred that gleamed in the tearless eyes of Posen

---

[1] "Only for ethnic Germans."
[2] "Aryan dwelling."

refugees. Nowhere the unlimited faith and proud defiance of Warsaw. Those Cracow people no longer even believed the Allies were going to win. Stunned, horror-stricken, they just waited for whatever calamity Fate in brown Nazi uniform was going to bring them.

I suppose the arrest of the University professors was to a large extent responsible for that attitude. Cracow, even before the war, never had much stamina. An old, beautiful, dignified city, quiet, intellectual and retired, a typical university town in fact. And so proud of its six-hundred-year-old University,[3] of its Academy of Science, of its famous faculty members... And now the faculty was in a concentration camp!

This arrest, although three months old, still was on everybody's lips. The way it was carried out had a touch of grim Teutonic humor so characteristic of the Nazi regime. All the members of the faculty were sent invitations to attend a lecture on the subject of "The Attitude of National Socialism Towards Higher Education." The cards stated that attendance was compulsory. When all the old professors had gathered in the big hall, the hall was surrounded by soldiers and all those inside arrested. It was said that a few who tried to protest were beaten with gun butts. None was allowed to return home to say good-bye to his family or take a warm coat. They were shipped to a concentration camp near Berlin.

There they were neither tortured nor persecuted. Oh, no. Just subject to strict military routine. Up at five thirty, cold shower, exercises in the cold yard, no warm overcoats, no blankets, just old military coats. All that was probably quite all right from the point of view of the attitude

---

[3] The Jagiellonian University in Cracow was founded in 1364 by Casimir III the Great, and is the second-oldest university in Central Europe, after Prague.

426

adopted by National Socialism towards higher education, but it was too much for old, scholarly gentlemen used to their mufflers and galoshes and the careful avoidance of drafts. Anyway, fourteen had died, fourteen men of science, great men of whom the whole country was proud, and their ashes were duly shipped to their widows at the small price of three marks (postage only) per urn. Neat!

The atmosphere of Cracow was so oppressive that I hardly could wait for my papers to arrive. At last they came. I had no trouble in obtaining the Devisenstelle permission to take my own dresses and underwear out of the country, and now, all documents in hand, I proceeded to the Cracow Passport Office. I felt quite confident, there certainly was no reason for any hitch.

"I want a passport to go to the United States," I told the young Nazi official in charge of the department. "Here are all the required documents."

He studied them carefully, then nodded.

"Yes," he admitted, "that's all right. But will you get an American visa? We can't give you a passport unless we know you are certain to get it."

"I have it already," I said unguardedly.

"You have it?" he seemed surprised. "Show it to me."

I handed him the document. For a while he scrutinized it in silence, then suddenly he jumped to his feet.

"That's a lie," he shouted. "That's a shameless lie!" He ran into another room, where through the open door I could see him converse excitedly with another Nazi official. He waved his arms around and pointed to my "affidavit in lieu of passport" with extreme indignation. At last he returned to me.

"This document is a fraud. See here, it says, 'As Mrs. Langer is unable to obtain a valid Polish passport.' That's a lie. You can obtain a valid Polish passport from us,

427

and you will. Like this one." He picked up a passport from the stack that lay on his desk. It was a regular Polish passport, with Polish inscriptions and a Polish eagle on the cover. Only... inside all the seals were German. I suddenly remembered what someone had told me a short time ago, at the travel agency, I think: the United States did not recognize any Polish document with German seals on it. It was a matter of principle, the United States had not legally and diplomatically recognized the German occupation of Poland. I certainly was in favor of the principle but... What was going to happen now? A nice mess I'd gotten myself into!

"Come in the afternoon," the Nazi told me. "Your passport will be ready."

"Can I have my visa back now?" I asked.

"No, the visa will remain here," he barked. "I told you it's a fraud—it's useless."

Was I going to lose my precious American visa? I could tell from the tone of his voice that there was no use arguing now. Perhaps in the afternoon...

When I returned to the Passport Office at three my passport was waiting for me.

"And my American visa?" I insisted once more.

"You'll never get it back," he sneered. "We are keeping it. You tell the American Consul to give you another one. Here. Right here," he pointed to one of the pages of the passport, "and when you have it you can come back to us for a German visa. Without it you cannot leave the country. Do you understand? *You cannot leave the country!*" he almost shouted at me.

Without a word I took the passport and walked out of the room. I was humiliated, exasperated, furious, but not beaten. That Nazi pup was not going to stop me now that I had made up my mind to go to the United States.

As soon as I was back in Warsaw I went to the American Consulate.

"Can you give me another visa?" I asked the vice-consul in charge of my case. "The Germans have taken away the one you gave me." I told him my story.

"For Heaven's sake, why did you show it to them?" the vice-consul exclaimed.

"Why didn't you tell me I shouldn't?" I retorted. "How was I to know? But the point is, can I get another one?"

"I am sorry, but you can't. The next day after I gave you the visa we received a telegram from our Embassy in Berlin with instructions not to issue any more visas. Yours was the last one."

"What is to be done then?"

"Well, perhaps we will be able to get it back from the Germans. They had no right to take it away from you in the first place. I'll ask the Consul General."

When I saw him again, he was very serious.

"Look here, Mrs. Langer," he told me, "we could insist that the German authorities return the visa to you. But the position of the Consulate here is a very delicate one as it is. To make an issue of your visa may result in a showdown, and the Consulate would have to be closed."

I looked around. At least fifty Polish girls were working in the American Consulate and I knew many of them personally. Could I take it upon myself to deprive them of their jobs?

"Forget it," I told the vice-consul. "I would rather give up my trip to America than risk the existence of the Warsaw Consulate."

"Maybe we will be able to find some other solution," the vice-consul promised.

For the next three days my case, which by that time had grown to be an "issue," was debated and discussed back and forth till, I am sure, had anyone asked the American consular authorities who was the worst pain in the neck in Warsaw they would all have exclaimed in unison, "Mrs. Langer!" At last, however, a solution was found. My papers were to be sent on to Genoa from where I was supposed to sail, so that if I ever got there, a new American visa could be issued to me.

This settled it as far as the American Consulate was concerned but for me the problem still remained: how was I going to reach Genoa?

I could and did obtain the Italian visa, even without the American one, but what about the German visa? That Nazi pup in Cracow had said I couldn't get out of the country without it, and it was certainly not he who was going to give me one, if I failed to produce an American visa on the passport he had issued me. And, I was told, only Cracow issued German visas. Well, in that case I would have to manage without one.

I went to the Warsaw Passport Department and without much ado obtained a *Passierschein*[4] that would enable me to cross the frontier into the Third Reich. I had heard of people who left Warsaw without a German visa and got away with it. But I also knew of people who had been turned back at the Italian frontier and for months remained stranded in Vienna. Neither my passport nor the Passierschein gave me the right to return to Poland. One way traffic—that's what it was. Well, I would have to risk it.

At last the day of my departure arrived. There was a direct train from Warsaw to Rome but only German nationals were allowed to take it. Being a Pole I had to content myself with a train to Cracow, hoping to get some connection from there to Vienna. There were no timetables.

---

[4] "Safe Conduct Permit."

The Cracow train did not leave till midnight but we would have to start from the house at seven-thirty, before the curfew was sounded. I planned to spend those four hours in a hotel across the street from the station. I couldn't expose the children to a long wait in sub-zero temperature. The old station building had been burned to the ground, and the new one was not heated.

It was a hectic day. Relatives and friends were constantly in and out of the house to say good-bye and wish us luck. Others brought messages to friends in America. I was still packing and segregating things I was to leave behind.

I was glad Scarlett O'Hara's green plush dress had stopped me from giving my two-year-old dresses and suits to Leosia. They would all go now in a bundle for Posen exiles. The famous German "twenty-minutes-twenty marks" system had left most of those people completely destitute. They were allowed twenty minutes to gather their belongings and twenty German marks to take along, whereupon they were turned out of their houses, put on cattle trains, and shipped in sealed cars to some unknown point of destination anywhere in Polish territory. The trip lasted anywhere from one to five days, and as the cars were unheated in this bitter cold weather none of the children under a year old survived. Many of these Posen exiles had drifted to Warsaw, and certainly no one deserved more help than those gallant people who took their hard fate without flinching, never cried, never complained. With a smile on their lips and cold hatred in their hearts they lived waiting. Waiting for the day of revenge...

With one thing and another I hardly had time to exchange a word with Mother. Perhaps it was better so. Every time my eyes fell upon Mother's pale, worn face I had the shameful feeling that for the second time since war started I was deserting her. Up to now in life it had always been I who had relied upon Mother's help and moral support. But in the last few months, ever since Warsaw's surrender, in fact, it was Mother who leaned upon me. She was tired and old, she kept repeating, and not well either. "I really don't know what I would do without you," she told me practically every day. And now...Better not to think of it.

In those two last weeks our imminent departure was never mentioned in our small family circle.

"If you have to go," Mother had said on the evening of the day on which my papers had arrived, "let's not spoil these last days we are going to spend together by a constant atmosphere of farewells. Let's enjoy our family life till the last minute."

And we did. Most of the day we were busy, but when in the evening we gathered around the dining room table we laughed and discussed the latest news and gossip, as if no shadow of parting hung upon us.

But now the last day had arrived and there was no use pretending any longer. All the guests had left at seven, and for half an hour Mother and I were left alone.

Mother as usual lay on the sofa, I sat in my favorite rocking chair, smoking a cigarette. And we had nothing to tell each other.

"Will you write me as soon as you get to Italy?" Mother asked at last.

"Yes, Mother, of course. I'll write even sooner than that. From Vienna."

Silence.

"Mother, I've left some things to be sold on the middle shelf of the cupboard. I've arranged them in the order they should be sold, from right to left. Natka will help you sell them, and you keep the money of course."

"Yes."

Silence again. It was awful.

At last Franek burst into the room. "Seven twenty-five. Time to start."

I jumped to my feet, hugged Mother in a last embrace, kissed her hands and with a stifled sob ran out of the room. I didn't look back. I couldn't.

As the apartment door slammed behind us I heard the dining room clock strike half past seven. It was home's last good-bye.

CHAPTER 34

Free!

THE TRAIN was an hour late, and the platform crowded and bitterly cold. Ania's cheeks were red as an apple, and her little button of a nose had turned blue. She was pressing Stas tight to her heart. George shivered with cold.

A German soldier came up to Ania and, laughing, poked with one finger at her red cheek.

"Puppe," he exclaimed. "Eine reizende Puppe" (A doll, a lovely doll). But Ania looked at him with solemn, unsmiling eyes. She distrusted all "Hitlers."

At last the train pulled into the station wrapped in clouds of steam. When the cloud dissolved a little, I saw clusters of German soldiers hanging at every door. For a second I hesitated, a crowded train always scares me a little, and this time I had two children and seven suitcases with me.

Suddenly I saw that the German private who had talked to Ania a minute before had now grabbed her in his arms and was running to the nearest car. I ran after them. George and the two porters followed, and before I knew it I found myself in a dimly lit second-class compartment full of German uniforms.

At first I felt slightly alarmed; this was not the company I would have picked out for myself. It was too late, however, the heavy suitcases were already on the racks and the train had began to move. Through the glass door I could see people standing in the corridor—it would be hard to find room in another compartment. So I settled back in my seat and looked around. The sparse light of a small blue bulb in the middle of the ceiling made it impossible to distinguish the faces of my travel companions, but judging by their uniforms three of them were soldiers and the remaining three officers.

The private who was responsible for our presence here had seated Ania at his side and continued to talk to her in a funny mixture of German and broken Polish. He was all grins and friendliness, but in spite of it failed to get a response from the child. Ania just sat there prim and demure, watching him with cold, hostile eyes. At last he took down his knapsack and produced a big red apple. This was too much for Ania; she had not seen an apple in months. She looked at it, then at me, then at the soldier, then at me again . . .

"Little Eve," I thought, and nodded my head ever so slightly, but with a smile. She could take it. I was afraid that if I didn't give my consent she would tell the German she didn't accept anything from a "Hitler." In a compartment full of German uniforms such a declaration might have proved somewhat awkward. Ania took the apple but did not eat it at once. She turned it around and around in her little hands looking at the fruit with a mixture of rapture and suspicion.

The soldier turned to me now. He was as friendly as an overgrown puppy. He loved children, he told me; he had two nephews about Ania's age. How glad he would be to see them again! Yes, he was going home on leave. His sister had died, and he was given permission to go to the funeral. She was already sick when he went to war in September, and he hadn't been home since. His home was in German Silesia, hence his knowledge of Polish. It was very sad about his sister but . . . Well, he was glad to go home again, even for a few days.

His story was interrupted by the arrival of the conductor.

"What are you doing here?" the conductor (he was German, too) asked the three privates. "Don't you know soldiers are not allowed to travel second-class? Get out of here! The third-class carriage is two cars ahead."

"Alright, alright," the soldier who was talking with me replied in placating tones. "We will leave presently."

He gave me a wink. It was obvious he didn't have the slightest intention of moving.

"You'd better...," said the conductor meaningfully, and went out.

Unperturbed the soldier leaned back comfortably in his seat and resumed his conversation with me and Ania. The three officers pretended not to notice, which rather surprised me. That was not my idea of the iron discipline of the German Army.

After ten minutes, however, the conductor returned once more.

"Do you want me to call the military police?" he barked at the soldiers. Reluctantly they got to their feet and filed out of the compartment.

Now that they were gone there was more room for us. One of the officers lifted the back of one of the seats, thus making two comfortable berths. He lay down on the lower one, and I put George and Ania on the upper.

Almost immediately they both fell asleep. I sat on the opposite seat between the two other Germans. Silence fell on the compartment, everyone seemed to be dozing. Everyone but me. I was too excited by the departure even to close my eyes.

"Where are you going?" the German at my left suddenly asked me in a low voice.

"To the United States."

"As far as that?" he seemed surprised. "What route are you taking?"

"Vienna, Tarvisio, Genoa."

"Genoa...," he repeated dreamily. "When you are in Genoa be sure to go and see Nervi. It's a beautiful spot. Rocks and the sea. The most beautiful spot I've seen. Another place on the Mediterranean I love is Marseilles."

"I'll see Marseilles, too. My boat stops there; it's an American boat."

"That's impossible," he assured me. "No American boat stops at belligerent ports. I know it for certain."

"I think you are wrong; mine does anyway. You've traveled a lot, I see. Do you speak English? My German is very poor."

The idea of making a German officer talk English rather tickled me. And he spoke it—quite fluently in fact. Yes, he had traveled a lot. At sixteen he had run away to sea, and before he was twenty he had been everywhere: Asia, Australia, North and South America. While still working at sea he had begun to send short articles on his travels to some provincial paper. Before long he got a permanent job on a newspaper staff, and had been engaged in journalistic work ever since, till the outbreak of the war.

"I have a two-week leave now," he continued. "I am going to Zakopane for a bit of skiing." Then after a pause he added, to my amazement, "Isn't this war silly though. If it were not for the war, perhaps you wouldn't be going to America, but to Zakopane, too, and maybe I would meet you there again."

"This war *is* certainly silly," I agreed. "But it's not Poland who started it, you know."

Quickly he shifted the topic of conversation.

"Are you going to stay in America for good?" he asked.

"Heavens, no. I am coming back."

"Coming back?" he seemed surprised. "When?"

"As soon as Poland is free!" There! I said it impulsively,

without thinking of the consequences. Now, with a slight trepidation I awaited his reaction. But evidently he was determined to avoid arguments.

"Oh well," he said lightly, "Poland is going to be free of Jews anyway."

"I don't care about that," I retorted at once. "I like the Jews!"

"You like the Jews?" he was so shocked that he positively gave a start. "That's impossible. You cannot like the Jews. No one likes them."

"But I do," I insisted. "Those I know are perfectly charming people. Intelligent, cultured people."

"But then you don't know the ghetto," there was a note of triumph in his voice. "I am just coming back from the Lublin ghetto. It's dreadful, ghastly!"

"Why, I love the ghetto! Don't you go to Harlem and Chinatown when you are in New York? Well, to me the ghetto is to Warsaw what Harlem and Chinatown are to New York. An exotic, picturesque spot.[1] I take a streetcar and in ten minutes I find myself in the midst of Asia

---

[1] At this time (February 1940), although the Germans had begun imposing restrictions on Jews beyond those imposed on the Warsaw populace as a whole, the Germans had not yet established the infamous "Warsaw Ghetto."

Before World War II, Warsaw was a major center of Jewish life and culture in Poland. Warsaw's pre-war Jewish population of more than 350,000 constituted about 30 percent of the city's total population. Jews were free to live anywhere throughout the city, and the pre-war "Jewish Quarter" or ghetto was merely an ethnic neighborhood such as Rulka Langer describes.

However, eight months after the time of this scene (in October 1940), the Germans decreed the establishment of a different type of "ghetto" in Warsaw, requiring all Jewish residents of the city to move into a designated "Jewish Residential District." Approximately 140,000 Jewish residents of Warsaw were moved into the designated area, following the forcible expulsion of over 110,000 non-Jewish Poles who were living in that part of the city at the time. The German authorities sealed this area off from the rest of the city in November 1940. It is this German-created "ghetto" that is commonly known today as the "Warsaw Ghetto." The Germans also later deported thousands more Jews from other areas and a smaller number of Roma and Sinti (Gypsies), to the Warsaw Ghetto.

Minor. Dirty, noisy, colorful, and completely foreign. I used to spend hours wandering through the streets of the ghetto just for the sheer fun of it."

He had no answer to that. It had apparently never entered his Nazi head that the ghetto could be looked upon as anything else except a blemish on the surface of the earth.

I was beginning to enjoy myself immensely. Here was a German to whom I could tell things and he took them well. Very well, in fact. Ever since the fall of Warsaw I had dreamed that some day I should meet a German to whom I would tell all I thought of his country and his people. Here was my chance.

"Tell me something," I began now in an innocent tone. "I am leaving the country, and I have certainly seen plenty of Germans, but I still don't know a thing about your uniforms. You have so many of them: brown, gray, black, green. What's the Gestapo uniform? Because, you see, every time some atrocity is perpetrated by Germans in Warsaw—like beating people or looting apartments, you know—everybody always says it's the Gestapo. What is the Gestapo uniform?"

And then my German companion began to laugh. He laughed and laughed till his laugh made me feel thoroughly uncomfortable.

"You want to know what the Gestapo uniform looks like?" he said at last. "Look here." he turned around and pointed to his left sleeve. "'SD' Sicherheitsdienst. That's the Gestapo uniform."

"I see," I said weakly. I had certainly picked out the right man!

"You aren't afraid of the Gestapo men, are you?" he asked mockingly.

"Of course not," I replied with more vehemence than sincerity. I *was* a little afraid. Not much, but just a little.

After that our conversation languished for a while, then we both fell into silence. Pretty soon I heard my Gestapo acquaintance breathe rhythmically—he was asleep. But I continued my vigil, sitting very upright, tense and wide awake. Somehow I was unable to relax. Long, dark hours of night stretched ahead of me and there was nothing, absolutely nothing I could fix my thoughts upon.

I didn't want to think of what I had left behind: Warsaw, Mother, home... It was still too fresh, too painful. No use looking back, anyway. But what lay ahead of me? The trip? *That* certainly was not a pleasant prospect: two children, seven suitcases, ten American dollars, a one-way passport into Germany and no German visa to get us out of there. Better forget it. There is no sense in worrying ahead—cross your bridges as you reach them.

Of course there was the faraway prospect of a new life in the United States, but it seemed too remote, too unreal, even to think about. It would be strange to live in an unbombed city, among people to whom war meant only headlines in the papers and news over the radio, who had never known the shameful agony of mortal fear, nor the mean pangs of hunger. Strange and a little terrifying, too. Like turning the clock back. I would feel a complete stranger among people who used to be my close friends... Suddenly, I felt very small, lost and lonely. I didn't belong anywhere.

I lit a match and glanced at my watch. Five o'clock. We must be somewhere near Rudnik, Wola's railway station. In a flash the memories of that last vacation came to my mind. The volleyball games, the tennis matches, the rides in a horse carriage. Sunny, happy days, only six months ago.

"Gone-with-the-wind, gone-with-the-wind, gone-with-the-wind" rattled the carriage wheels in a rhythmic throb.

The Gestapo officer did not speak to me again till we reached Cracow. Only when we already stood on the platform waiting for the porter to take our suitcases to the waiting room did he come up to me, and saluting stiffly, wished me good luck. I thanked him, but did not return the wishes.

The train for Vienna did not leave till nine o'clock at night—we had a whole day ahead of us. George insisted that we should visit the old town. He had been promised the year before that when he was eight he would go with me to Cracow and be shown all the beautiful historic monuments, the old castle of Wawel, the tombs of Polish kings, the famous churches, all the things he had read and heard about. He reminded me of the promise now. But I was loath to show him Cracow decorated with swastikas and Hitler's portraits.

"No, Georgie, not now. You must wait till we come back. Then I'll show you Cracow in all its glory."

Instead, we spent the day with my relatives.

The train to Vienna was completely dark and almost empty. We found an unoccupied compartment and all three lay down to sleep. After the previous sleepless night, I fell into a deep slumber almost immediately. I was awakened with a start. The door was opened with a bang and a lantern glared into my eyes.

"Passierschein," someone shouted. We were entering the Reich.

I sat up and fumbled in my bag. The frontier guard grabbed my pass, glanced at it, slammed the door and was gone.

"Wait a moment," I called, running after him out in the corridor. "Give me that Passierschein back. I need it."

"I have an order to keep them," he shouted and jumped out of the carriage. I returned to my compartment with a slightly uneasy feeling—I had understood that I would need that document upon leaving Germany at the Italian frontier. Well, I tried to reassure myself, if the Germans take it away at one frontier they cannot expect anyone to produce it at the next.

I went back to sleep.

We didn't arrive in Vienna till ten o'clock the next morning, and in the meantime I discovered that in the compartment next to ours there were two Polish women, also on their way to Italy. One was the bride of an officer who was with the Polish Army in France. She intended to join him there, but officially was going only as far as Milan. The other's husband was in Rome. She was traveling with two little girls, aged five and three. We decided to gang up together. The conductor (he had a pleasant Austrian accent) informed us that our train was more than two hours late, and therefore we would miss the only train that left Vienna for Venice every day. This meant twenty-two hours of waiting. We would have to stop at a hotel.

We went to the nearest one, an unpretentious small hotel across the street from the station. We took two rooms and ordered breakfast. I was surprised when the tray was brought in: coffee, milk, fresh white rolls and butter! Germany was certainly not starving. After breakfast I took the children for a sightseeing tour. But Vienna, the charming, elegant, beautiful Vienna, proved a complete disappointment. High snowdrifts bordered the sidewalks. Not a single smartly dressed woman, not a single good-looking car. Of course there were the store windows in Kartnerstrasse, but...

My last pair of stockings had developed a run that morning. I decided to buy a new pair.

"Silk stockings? Of course, Gnädige Frau," the vendor exclaimed. "Where is your card?"

"My card?"

"Yes, your apparel card. Without it I can't sell you anything. I am sorry." So even the beautiful show windows were in reality only a fake.

We ate our lunch in a pastry shop, but for dinner we returned to the hotel. The children were tired, I wanted them to have a good long rest before tomorrow's journey.

The hotel restaurant was small and unpretentious: a big wooden bar very shiny and polished, a few small tables covered with checkered oilcloth, bentwood chairs, artificial flowers, and a very noisy radio set. The windows were carefully covered with black oilcloth. Blackout, of course, I had forgotten all about it. Warsaw had had no blackouts since October. The restaurant was practically empty, except for four elderly men playing dominoes and drinking beer in one corner, and a middle-aged woman at a table next to ours.

A young, buxom waitress came to take our order. She was all smiles and full of Viennese *Gemütlichkeit*.

I picked out a dish on the menu, pretty much at random. My German is inadequate to cope with the intricacies of a Viennese menu.

"Have you meat cards?" the waitress asked me. "This is a meat course. I cannot order it for you without meat cards."

"Well... Is there anything we can eat? We have no cards of any kind."

"Oh yes, you can have this for instance," she pointed to the menu. "It's a vegetable dish. It's very good."

As a matter of fact it was a potato dish, and it wasn't bad.

"Will you bring us some bread," I asked the waitress. "Some white bread."

"Sorry, but you said you had no cards of any kind. I can't give you bread without bread cards."

"But we had rolls for breakfast this morning without cards."

"Yes, but that was your first meal here, wasn't it? Hotel guests are allowed bread without cards at their first meal, but not afterwards."

The woman at the next table beckoned to the waitress.

"Here," she said in German, "take my cards and bring some bread to the lady and the children." Then turning to me she asked in Polish, "You are Polish, aren't you? I heard you talking to the children."

"Yes. Thank you so much for the cards. Won't you come and join us?"

She moved over to our table.

"Going abroad?" she asked.

"Yes, tomorrow morning."

"You are lucky," she sighed. "I have been here two weeks already waiting for a German visa. My husband is in an internment camp in Hungary, and I wanted to visit him. They turned me back at the frontier, because I had no visa. It's awfully hard to get one."

"Is it?" I gasped. "I have no German visa either."

"Oh, but then you must have a Passierschein. They will let you leave the country on the strength of a Passierschein."

"I had one but they took it away from me at the frontier."

"They did? How could you let them take it? Now they won't let you out. No use even trying. You will waste your railway fare and they will turn you back at the frontier anyway. I tell you what you should do. Stay here, and tomorrow morning apply for a visa. I can give you all the necessary information. It takes two to three weeks to get one, but at least you'll be certain you won't be stopped at the frontier."

It was more easily said than done. Two children and ten American dollars cash. How could I afford a two weeks' stay in Vienna?

"No," I said. "I will have to risk it. Perhaps they will let me out, after all."

"Well, I wish you good luck, but I am pretty sure I'll see you here again soon." She sounded as if she were already looking forward to it.

I hardly slept at all that night.

Slowly, laboriously, the train ascended the steep slopes of the Alps. On both sides of the tracks magnificent mountain chains bathed in the glory of sunshine and snow.

The train, although a long-distance one, stopped frequently, disgorging small groups of skiers. It seemed strange that people should go skiing in wartime, but apparently plenty of them did. Young men, and middle-aged men, some women, too. But mostly men. The train was full of them. They all carried skis, talked loudly, laughed, sang, evidently in a great holiday spirit. One felt strangely lost in this happy German crowd. Depressing. We couldn't find room in a second-class carriage, and had moved into a first-class one. The conductor had accepted our presence there with an indulgent smile. Probably he expected a tip. He would get it, if...

The children were behaving like angels, I must say, although this was the fourth day we were on our way. Ania was busy cutting out paper dolls with the two other little girls, George with his nose glued to the window was drinking in the beauty of the landscape.

445

Rulka, Ania and George, passport photo, 1940.

"Mommy, look! Look at that tiny castle on the top of the mountain. How did people ever build it there? How can anyone get there? Oh, Mommy! Look at that mountain. Isn't it beautiful?"

But I was absolutely unable to concentrate on the beauty of the landscape.

"Are we going to retrace the same route tomorrow?" I kept wondering. I stood in the corridor, smoking endless cigarettes. A strange trepidation filled my whole body. What if they don't let us out? Two children, seven suitcases, ten American dollars, no friends in Vienna, no way of going back to Poland... (Don't think about it. Wait and see. There is always a way out of everything. Wait and see.)

But all the time I was conscious that every turn of the wheels brought us nearer Villach, the fateful frontier station. Ten hours of gorgeous scenery, ten hours of almost unbearable suspense.

Five minutes to six, twenty minutes before we reached Villach, three officials boarded the train.

"Passport inspection."

My heart stood still, but my hand did not tremble as I handed them the passport. They collected all passports and departed, apparently to study them at leisure. During the half hour that followed I was completely dazed. I hardly noticed our arrival at Villach, or the custom inspection (they even didn't open my suitcases—I could have brought anything I pleased with me), my mind was still with the passport inspectors. At last they returned, calling out the names of passport owners as they went.

"Langer."

I stretched out my hand. Here was my passport. I opened it, glanced at the last page—yes, the departure stamp was there all right—we could leave Germany.

They never asked me about that visa. I put the passport back in my pocketbook and took out a cigarette. My hands shook so I could hardly light it.

The train was leaving Tarvisio. We were on Italian soil. Out of Germany. Free!

A tremendous joy—the joy of living—once more filled my whole being. I stood by the corridor window drinking in the beauty of the moonlit night. Behind me, in the compartment, George and Ania were sucking their first oranges— the refreshing smell came to my nostrils.

"What time will we be in Venice?" the mother of the two little girls asked me.

"Eleven fifty."

"What time is it now?"

I glanced at my watch. The hands pointed to six twenty. My watch had stopped. It had stopped at the precise time when the passport was handed back to me. My excitement at that moment had been too much for it. I had heard and read before of mechanisms reacting to human nerves, but this was the first time anything of the kind had happened to me.

"Silly mechanical thing," I mused, shaking the watch and putting it to my ear. "Couldn't take it, could you? Why, human beings can stand anything!"

AFTERWORD

Afterword

"BLITZ" GRADUATES

by Rulka Langer

POST-WAR PLANNING seems to be the order of the day. Statesmen, politicians, economists, even geographers (geopoliticians) are busy preparing blueprints of a new and better world. But, in the end, it will be the people themselves who will rebuild that world. And the outcome may be quite different from that which even the boldest among the draftsmen of the future can conceive today.

For most post-war planners base their calculations and programs on pre-war experience. They correct the obvious mistakes of the past. They prepare "a just and durable peace" as it should have been signed in 1918. Only few of them have had actual war experience. The vast majority do not realize what war, *this* war, does to people. The humanity which will emerge from the present struggle will be as different from the humanity of 1917, as this war is different from the previous one. It may develop trends so new and unexpected that even the most radical of today's programs will prove obsolete and inadequate.

Post-war planners are fond of calling this war a revolution—a political revolution, a social revolution, an economic revolution. They are right. But it is even more than that. It is a revolution of all human standards of values, it is a worldwide revolution of the human soul.

I am no post-war planner. But I have gone through war experience and I know what war does to one. In September 1939, I was in Warsaw during the siege. For three weeks, night and day,

---

First published in *Tomorrow* magazine, December 1942.

I lived under constant artillery and aerial bombardment, expecting to die any minute. It was then that I learned what mortal fear means. I have seen wounded and dead, I lost many of my friends and all my belongings. I have known hunger and cold. The house in which I lived was hit by a bomb. In mad panic I ran through the streets that were a sea of flames, dragging my two children, aged eight and three, by the hand while roaring bombers swept overhead . . .

Horrible? Yes. But how commonplace! How many millions of men, women and children, in Holland, England, Russia, China, all over the world, in fact, have gone through the same or worse? How many more millions will have to face similar ordeals before the cataclysm is over?

And none of us will ever be the same again.

For war is not only a chamber of horrors. It is also the greatest personal experience any human being can go through. War means facing death. In peacetime, during a serious illness or in an accident we face death. But in sickness our faculties are dimmed by pain, fever, by bodily exhaustion; and an accident usually happens so quickly that it is all over before we have time to realize what has occurred. In war, however, perfectly healthy, fully conscious people face death for hours on end.

How does it feel? It is agony! But once you have been through it, you will be forever grateful to be alive. Apparently it takes facing death to make us appreciate the true value of life. In normal times we take our right to live pretty much for granted, and very often we do not think much of it. Not till we have faced death do we realize that life, any kind of life, is a wonderful gift.

War also fundamentally changes our attitude towards death. Death, according to our peacetime concept, is the supreme injustice nature inflicts upon us; something to be glossed over, fought off or forgotten. In wartime, death becomes commonplace, and as with anything commonplace it seems natural. When you have seen hundreds of dead (and it is amazing how quickly you get used to the sight), when you, yourself, have expected to die within the next ten minutes, you not only know that you are going to die some day but the realization stays with you. I have always thought that such awareness of death would spoil the joy of living. But it does not. It only makes everyday troubles seem less important.

Thus, standards and values are shifted; life is no longer a natural right but a wonderful gift; death, no longer nature's supreme injustice, becomes a natural part of life.

There is something comforting in this acceptance of death. Death is the supreme trump life holds against us. Once we have squarely faced it, it is no longer a menace lurking in the dark. We acquire a new, truer perspective on life.

Another thing war teaches us is honesty. Honesty with ourselves. For war is a merciless debunker; it debunks great and small alike. Under ordinary circumstances most of us indulge in a lot of harmless make-believe. We have a mental picture of ourselves (often quite different from what we really are), and we do our best to live up to it. We try so hard, in fact, that finally we are convinced we have become what we have been trying to appear—strong personalities, with kind hearts full of concern for others; good sports; heroes. But no such pretense will ever stand the supreme test of mortal danger. When bombs are crashing and fires raging, people are exactly what they are— nothing more, and nothing less. How often the "strong character" turns out to be an hysterical coward, and the meek, shy girl, the real heroine. At such times you have the sensation of standing morally naked in public, and you will never be able to forget it afterwards, try as hard as you may.

War means a lot of privations and hardships. For days and weeks you go about hungry, so hungry that you feel like crying every time you get up from a meager meal, knowing that you could eat five times as much, and still not have enough. You sleep on benches, on the floor, on stairways. For days you have no chance to change your clothes nor wash yourself or them. Privations such as these make one more appreciative of the small comforts of life which in peacetime are called the "bare essentials." You also learn that these comforts, or "essentials"—whatever you choose to call them—have little to do with happiness or unhappiness. I know that I was never so gloriously happy in all my life as on that bleak October day in 1939, when answering a knock at the front door, I found my brother whom we believed lost, standing on the threshold. We both went mad with joy. Yet, we both looked dreadful. We were dirty, disheveled, half-starved, and shivering with cold in a bomb-wrecked apartment which gave us no protection against the icy wind.

Strangely enough, the war which makes you so appreciative of small comforts of life, at the same time breeds a sort of contempt for material riches. When you have witnessed the wholesale destruction of wealth and property, when you have seen beautiful buildings which have stood for centuries—the pride of a nation—turned within a few seconds into heaps of ruins, and above all when you, yourself, have lost all your dearly loved and long-accumulated belongings, all material things acquire a perishable aspect which seems to rob them of half of their attraction. Besides, if you ran the risk of losing your life, and only lost your property, it looks like a good bargain, and wealth does not seem very important after that. In fact, even the peacetime god, called Higher Standard of Living, appears futile. After all, it stands for comfort, not happiness.

Thus, war strikes at the very roots of our pre-war, materialistic conception of life. Will materialism return as soon as war is over? It did after the First World War, and with a vengeance. This war, however, is different, it is total. It teaches its lesson directly to everyone, regardless of age, sex or social position. One of the greatest tragedies of the previous war lay in the fact that, when the men returned home from the trenches after their excruciating experience, they were told to "forget it" and go back to normal life. They could not. A deep gulf developed between those who had gone through the horrors of front-line warfare and those who had not—a gulf which could not be bridged.

This resulted, in this country and in England, in personal tragedies, in a terrific waste of human material, in general disillusionment and cynicism. In Italy and Germany it led to Fascism and Nazism; for it was the embittered war veterans, eager to seize power, and to rule with an iron rod the war-spared civilians, that made the ascent of Mussolini and Hitler possible.

But when the soldier of the present war returns home—if there is still a home to return to—he will find his parents, his wife, even his children war veterans. There will be fewer misunderstandings. And there also will be no "normal" life to go back to. Everything will have to be started afresh.

What kind of a world will they rebuild, those men and women who have faced death, witnessed wholesale destruction, lost their beloved ones, whose entire standard of values was changed in the process? Will they devote the rest of their lives to re-creating what has been so easily destroyed under their very eyes? Will they return to the pre-war game in which material things are tricks, and whoever succeeds in accumulating most of them wins? Will material security become once more the supreme goal of individuals, groups and nations? Or will they be satisfied with "bare essentials" and direct surplus energy elsewhere?

If they do—and it seems likely they will—this would mean the greatest revolution in centuries. It means the collapse of not only the materialistic conception of life, but also of all the other by-products of materialism itself: rationalism, technical progress, high standard of living, individualism, capitalism, socialism, communism... All of them are different aspects of the same materialistic era, all of them will go. All the world as we knew it, and know it now, will come to an end, and an entirely new phase will begin. What will be its motivating force, its primary motive? It is difficult to imagine, but it is not improbable that the pendulum will swing back again, and that humanity, after so much suffering and hardship, will turn to some mystical goal, to a strong religious feeling which will sway the world just as it did in the Middle Ages. Is history about to repeat itself?

There are already signs of this spiritual revival on the continent of Europe. In the conquered countries half-starved people live, actually *live*, on such immaterial things as faith and hope. Those two alone seem to hold many an emaciated body and soul together. People once more have become God-conscious. Churches are full everywhere, even in Germany.

But there is also another tide rising. A tide of bitter, corroding hatred. A hatred such as no one in this country or even in Great Britain can imagine. For it is not war that breeds it—it is the occupation. As a matter of fact, the highly mechanized blitz does not breed much hatred. It is too impersonal. One can hardly connect that swift death and destruction which come from the sky with human beings. And it is not so easy to hate an abstraction. That is the reason why the English, after having gone through the horrors of the bombings of 1940, still can refer with good nature to the German plane overhead as "the Jerry." They could not do it, I am sure, if they saw the same "Jerry" swaggering down their own street, if they had, constantly, to rub shoulders with him, if, instead of killing from the sky, he came at night to their own house, to arrest a son and shoot him at dawn.

No, under the circumstances in which half of the world lives today hatred is unavoidable. But unless its cause is removed, its rising tide will drown, corrode, and kill the new spiritual revival, thus robbing humanity of the greatest benefit of the agonies and pain through which so large a part of the world is going and will go before the war ends.

That is why the victory of the United Nations is so essential to the spiritual and religious cause of the world.

EPILOGUE

CLARK·H·GETTS, Inc. • WALDORF-ASTORIA • NEW YORK CITY

Presents

RULKA LANGER

Vassar graduate and leading jour-
nalist of Poland, Rulka Langer
lived through the German siege of
Warsaw and several months of
German occupation of her country
before managing to get away to
America. Now she has written *The
Mermaid and the Messerschmitt* which
Pearl Buck calls "The Polish Mrs. Miniver" and Lewis
Gannett of the *New York Herald Tribune* describes as "one of
the best books that have come out of the maelstrom."

She comes from a family of distinguished Polish intellectu-
als—writers, university professors and statesmen—and was
born and reared in Warsaw. Fond of books from her cradle,
she was a brilliant student and at 19 was awarded
a scholarship to study in America. She graduated from
Vassar in 1928, having mastered the English language and
fallen in love with America and its democratic way of life.

Returning to Poland, she became a political and economic
writer on the leading daily newspaper and did special writing for radio and advertising purposes. Her articles were
distinguished for their thorough-going economic research
and the clarity and soundness of her opinions. Visiting
this country for a second time in 1934, she came as the
wife of an official of the Polish Embassy in Washington but
had returned to Poland for a visit when the Blitz struck.
With her two small children and her old mother, she survived the siege of Warsaw and 5 months of the Nazi "New
Order."

Young, attractive, full of vitality and enthusiasm, she
delivers stirring addresses that are bound to be remembered
for their substance and importance. She brought out of this
ordeal a strong conviction that war experience, for all its
horrors, makes for positive values which, if we take full
advantage of them, will favorably influence the post-war
world. And she has a great faith in democracy and the
future influence of this country and its ideals.

Lecture Topics: BLITZ GRADUATES FACE THE FUTURE
A FOREIGNER LOOKS AT AMERICAN DEMOCRACY
FIVE MONTHS OF THE NEW ORDER
THE FUTURE OF SMALL NATIONS
THE WAR MAKES A GREAT OPPORTUNITY

Epilogue

by

GEORGE O. LANGER

EVEN AFTER nearly seventy years, many of the events described in *The Mermaid and the Messerschmitt* are still vivid in my memory. The one really overwhelming impression remaining to this day, rekindled each time I look at this book, is one of gratitude for my mother's pluck, and for our amazing good luck in escaping the hell of war, Nazi occupation and possible extermination.

These events have had many long-lasting effects on me. The foremost is an abiding distaste of war—I am greatly exasperated with those who blithely pursue armed conflict without regard for the suffering of the societies involved.

Another personal trait I acquired is the revulsion at seeing food wasted. To this day, I feel a compulsion to eat every morsel on my plate. This too will probably never go away.

The Rest of our Journey

The narrative of the book ends at the tension-filled crossing of the border from Austria into Italy. After the terrible stress of the previous days, the remainder of the trip seemed by contrast almost a holiday.

We finally reached Genoa, and found a small but cozy hotel with a statue of Christopher Columbus right outside. We stayed just over a week, until our sailing date. In the meantime, we became tourists and took in the local sights. We rode the funicular up the hill above the city. We even followed the advice of our Gestapo railway companion and visited the rocky coast at Nervi, a short distance from the city. He was right; the view was truly spectacular.

The only reminder of the war was the sound of the Carabinieri[1] marching down the street, pausing at every block to stamp their boots and shout in unison, *"Il Duce!"*[2]

At last the departure day arrived. We boarded our ship, the American Export Lines *Excalibur*. The voyage was pleasant and uneventful. We docked first in Boston, where we were delighted to see our father boarding the ship! You can imagine the joyous reunion.

Late the following night we disembarked at Jersey City. It was too dark to see the Statue of Liberty—the only disappointment of the trip.

One wartime postscript to our journey: the *Excalibur,* subsequently pressed into war service as an American troop transport, was torpedoed and sunk by a German submarine off North Africa in November 1942. A sad end for a lovely ship.

In the United States

We stayed the next few months with friends in New Jersey and Pennsylvania, then moved to southeastern Connecticut. There was one big problem: being in the country on a diplomatic visa barred both my parents from most gainful employment. This could be remedied by getting an immigration visa. Immigration rules required, however, that such visa could only be obtained by personally applying at an American consulate in the country of origin, i.e., Poland. This was clearly impossible.

Fortunately this requirement was relaxed, so the required visa could be obtained at the American consulate

---

[1] Carabinieri are Italian military police.

[2] *Il Duce* is the name by which Benito Mussolini, the Fascist dictator of Italy at that time, was popularly known.

in any foreign country, including Canada. We therefore took a round trip by rail to Montreal, returning with our precious new visas to the immigration office on Ellis Island, following the footsteps of millions of others whose path to American citizenship began at the very same place. This time the Statue of Liberty was in plain sight.

The Mermaid and the Messerschmitt

It was about this time that my mother went on the lecture circuit to tell American audiences not only about her experiences, but also what the war was doing to Europe and what it should mean to the United States. There were other speakers with similar experiences, among them Maria von Trapp, later immortalized in *The Sound of Music,* who became a personal friend of my mother's.

Mother began writing *The Mermaid and the Messerschmitt* as part of her effort to explain to Americans the devastation of this war for the average, ordinary human beings caught in it. She changed the names of family and friends left behind in Poland because she feared Nazi reprisals against them—for example, my maternal grandmother is called "Mrs. Rayska," while her true name was Elzbieta Godlewska, and my uncle, Mother's brother, whose name was Aleksander Lech Godlewski, is called "Franek" and "Professor Rayski."

The book was originally published in 1942 by Roy Slavonic Publications in New York. The reviews were generally quite favorable. The title *The Mermaid and the Messerschmitt* was, I believe, my mother's idea.

My Sisters

In a heartbreaking turn of Fate, my little sister Ania survived the terrors of Nazi bombing and occupation, including the two-foot long shard of broken glass that somehow slipped miraculously under her while she lay on Cook's bed during the relentless bombing of Black Monday, only to die a few years later, at age nine, in the United States. For Ania, the Christmas straw, described in Chapter 31, proved eerily prophetic.

It was in 1945, while visiting a farm near Philadelphia, that Ania was infected by a relatively rare disease called Rocky Mountain Spotted Fever, which is transmitted by the bite of a tick. Today this affliction is little feared, as several antibiotics provide effective treatment. In 1945, however, there were no such antibiotics.

Facing the grief caused by this loss, my parents chose to have another child. My sister Barbara Joy was born in 1946, and now lives in California with her husband, Barry Melton, and two grown children. Followers of popular culture may recollect Barry as the lead guitarist in a famous rock band of the 1960's, Country Joe and the Fish.

After the War's End

After the war, my father accepted a post with the new Polish government as the Polish consul in Detroit. He worked tirelessly to raise relief supplies, including draft horses, from the local Polish community. But he was soon at odds with the Stalinists in the postwar government. He quit in disgust, and returned to Connecticut.

My mother started a new career. She worked for the Hooper Company, a pioneer in devising rating sampling and rating techniques for the radio broadcast industry. After we moved to New York in 1953, she became a copy-writer with the prestigious advertising firm J. Walter Thompson, for whom she had worked in Warsaw following her graduation from Vassar College; then with a smaller organization, Ellington, until her retirement in 1973.

Her literary achievements did not end with *The Mermaid*. She specialized in translations from Polish, of which the best known is Zofia Kossak's novel, *Blessed Are the Meek,* published in 1945 by Roy Publishers.

My father died in 1970, my mother in 1993 (long beyond her old hunch that she would live until age sixty-seven), both of natural causes. They both lived long enough to fulfill a dream: in 1969 they returned to Poland for the first and only time, to visit relatives and old friends. It was a tearful reunion, both happy and sad.

Those Left Behind

But what happened to the family left behind in Poland? During the long war years, with no means of communication, with stories of Nazi brutality appearing every day, we could only hope for the best, fear for the worst... and pray.

Sometimes news did arrive. My maternal grandmother's sister Celinka, who had become a nun years before, survived in the relative tranquility of an Italian convent. But from Poland came only silence, until the Russian army pushed the Germans back over their own border. As feared, some news was bad indeed.

Soon after the Nazis arrived, my paternal grandfather, who was Jewish and a cardiologist retired from a medical career in the Austrian Army, was beaten to death, by whom we never knew. Also Uncle Adam did not survive, nor did Uncle Adzio, who died at Auschwitz. Uncle Adzio is, incidentally, my one link to world literature. As a child he accompanied his parents on a vacation in Italy. While playing on the beach, he reputedly caught the attention of the novelist Thomas Mann, whose fantasies about the boy inspired *Death in Venice*.

My maternal grandmother and her sister, Aunt Nina,

died during the occupation, but at least through natural causes, without violence.

Most of the others survived. My cousin Tereska, who eventually became a nun and capped her career as the Mother Superior of a convent in Argentina, came to the United States with her parents. Best of all, my mother's brother, Lech, not only survived, but resumed his academic career, becoming a distinguished professor of anthropology at the University of Wroclaw. I have one of his books but, alas, I am unable to read it as I no longer remember my Polish.

As for me, I will be brief. I obtained my Bachelor of Science degree in physics from MIT in 1952, and followed an electrical engineering career until failing eyesight forced me into retirement a few years ago. I had a long and happy marriage to my first wife Jane; our two sons are now grown with children of their own. Since losing Jane to a stroke, my life has been blessed with another special woman, my new bride Ingrid Asmus.

I never returned to Poland. My only memento of Poland, which I brought with me to the United States as a nine-year-old, is a small album of good wishes from my schoolfriends. My awareness that the places I knew as a boy have been wrecked by war and the passage of time, as well as my having forgotten most of the language, have made me reluctant to make the journey back.

But sometimes I wish I had.

G.L.

January 2009
BOULDER, COLORADO

*"My only memento of Poland, which I
brought with me to the United States
as a nine-year-old, is a small album of
good wishes from my schoolfriends."*

Page from album

*"I will set you three conditions, all of them modest:
Love God and your country, don't forget me."*

Romus Krupiczka—February 9, 1940.

During the pre-war months of 1939, Polish school children were
encouraged to save their pocket money to help purchase submarines. ORP
Rys, drawn by the young shcoolboy Romus Krupiczka, was a Polish mine-
laying submarine belonging to the Wilk class. Her name *Rys* means
"Lynx" in English. The suspenseful escape of the battle-damaged *Rys*
from the German Navy to neutral Swedish waters during the September
1939 campaign captured the imagination of schoolboys throughout
Poland.

"A souvenir to my friend."
Jurek Nasiorowski—Warsaw, February 9, 1940.

"A souvenir to my dear school friend."
Tadeusz Jakubiak—Warsaw, February 9, 1940.

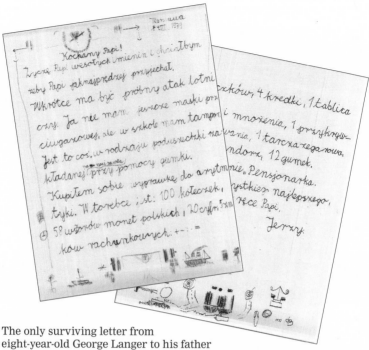

The only surviving letter from
eight-year-old George Langer to his father
Olgierd, who had been working in the United States for
the Polish Ministry of Foreign Affairs since the spring of 1938.
Having forgotten most of his Polish, the adult George could no
longer read his own letter.

Warsaw, March 4, 1939

Dear Papi!

I wish Papi a happy name day and I would like Papi to come as quickly as possible.

We are soon going to have a mock air raid. I don't yet have my gas mask, but I do have something at school like a little cushion which you put over your nose and mouth with the help of an elastic band.

I have bought myself an arithmetic set. In the bag there are 100 rings, 58 patterns of Polish coins, 20 numbers, 5 arithmetical signs: + - : - =, 100 little sticks, 4 chalk crayons, 1 addition and multiplication table, 1 adding cover, 1 clock face, 1 measuring tape, 1 calendar, 12 erasers.

I went to see the film The Boarding School Girl.

I wish Papi all the best, I hug you and and I kiss Papi's hands.

George

467

"This logo identifies paper that meets the standards of the Forest Stewardship Council. FSC is widely regarded as the best practice in forest management, ensuring the highest protections for forests and indigenous peoples."